WHAT REALLY HAPPENED: THE LINCOLN ASSASSINATION

WHAT REALLY HAPPENED

THE LINCOLN ASSASSINATION

ROBERT J. HUTCHINSON

REGNERY
HISTORY

Regnery History™ is a trademark of Salem Communications Holding Corporation
Regnery® is a registered trademark of Salem Communications Holding Corporation

ISBN 978-1-62157-886-4
ebook ISBN 978-1-62157-887-1

LCCN 2019955224

Published in the United States by
Regnery History, an imprint of
Regnery Publishing
A Division of Salem Media Group
300 New Jersey Ave NW
Washington, DC 20001
www.Regnery.com

Manufactured in the United States of America

10 9 8 7 6 5 4 3 2 1

Books are available in quantity for promotional or premium use. For information on discounts and terms, please visit our website: www.Regnery.com.

For Teddy, Ella, and Miles

We here highly resolve that these dead shall not have died in vain—that this nation, under God, shall have a new birth of freedom—and that government of the people, by the people, for the people, shall not perish from the earth.

—*Abraham Lincoln*

CONTENTS

INTRODUCTION

Since the dawn of the third millennium, it has become fashionable in the United States to speak of unprecedented levels of political polarization in American public life, even of a "second civil war." The vitriol, partisan name-calling, and outright hatred strike many as unprecedented.

This is, of course, an illusion.

One of the salutary benefits of studying the U.S. Civil War is that you learn just how divided Americans have been in the past—and how, in many circumstances, they have been forced to live together even when their moral and political beliefs are opposed, as in the case of slavery.

People today often don't realize just how porous the border was between the United States and the Confederacy during the war. It was not uncommon for former Confederate civilians to move north for jobs and be forced to work side by side with enthusiasts for a war that was literally killing many of their relatives and friends back home. Union soldiers patrolled occupied New Orleans throughout most of the war. People on both sides often had to bite their tongues to avoid needless confrontation.

In addition, thousands of loyal Unionists opposed the Civil War on practical grounds.

Abraham Lincoln is lionized today as one of the greatest presidents in American history. Yet during his own lifetime, he was reviled by millions on both sides of the Mason-Dixon line as a tyrant who ignored the rule of law. When the war began, the Lincoln administration arrested thousands who criticized the government, including editors, judges, and legislators. Lincoln himself suspended the ancient writ of habeas corpus. Many believed he could never be reelected.

As a result, now is a good time to take a second look at the events that led up to Lincoln's assassination—and at the unhinged political passions that drove a maniacal but beloved actor to take matters into his own hands in an act of vicious terrorism.

Finally, this book is the first in the What Really Happened series.

It, like the series itself, aims to discover what really happened at one of the key events in history. It seeks to separate the myths and urban legends from the bare facts established by historians.

That is not always an easy task to accomplish. In the case of the Lincoln assassination, the story definitely grew in the telling. There are often marked discrepancies between the accounts of eyewitnesses, written in the weeks and months immediately following the assassination, and the lengthy memoirs and theories written twenty, thirty, even forty years later.

We aim to present in this book and others, as clearly as possible and as far as the evidence permits, what really happened without embellishment. History doesn't need any help from Hollywood. As is said, the truth is usually far more interesting than fiction. In the case of the Lincoln assassination, this is especially true.

I would like to thank a few people who made this book possible. First, I would like to thank the editors at Regnery History, especially Alex Novak, for backing the idea of the What Really Happened series. I would also like to thank my agent, Alex Hoyt, for being my advocate for the past decade. And as always, I would like to thank my wife Glenn and our five children for their patience as I read mountains of books, took trips far from home, and locked myself away in my office for hours on end. I am thankful for their support and encouragement over the years.

Robert J. Hutchinson
Washington, D.C., July 2019

1 | SUMMER SUNSHINE

The White House, 7:00 a.m.

At seven o'clock in the morning on Friday, April 14, 1865, Abraham Lincoln swung his long, spindly legs out of the special nine-foot walnut bed where he slept in the second-floor bedroom at the White House.

A light sleeper who often suffered nightmares, he slept in a separate bedroom from Mrs. Lincoln. However, on this day Lincoln could hardly wait to get up. The severe headache he had suffered the night before, which had led him to miss the Grand Illumination celebrations, had vanished.[1]

It was Good Friday, part of the normally somber Lenten season. Yet the city was in a raucous, jubilant mood. Tens of thousands of revelers had flooded into the capital over the past few days, to celebrate the coming end of the war and to join in parties and special exhibitions throughout the city.

Just five days earlier, on April 9, Confederate general Robert E. Lee had surrendered the Army of Northern Virginia to Union general Ulysses

1

One of the last formal portraits of Abraham Lincoln (1809–1865), taken in February 1865, two months before his death at the age of fifty-six, shows how the burden of his office aged him. *Wikimedia Commons*

S. Grant following the last major battle of the war, at Appomattox Court House, in Virginia. Although Confederate president Jefferson Davis was still at large, and as many as ninety thousand Confederate troops were still in the field, the war, everyone knew, was effectively over.

The president's own son, twenty-two-year-old Robert Lincoln, then serving as a military aide in General Grant's personal entourage, had been an eyewitness to the surrender. He had just returned home the evening before, on Thursday night, and Lincoln eagerly awaited Robert's report at breakfast.

At fifty-six, Lincoln looked much older than his years. The war had aged him noticeably, and he knew it. He was once a virtual giant of a man, standing six feet four inches and weighing 180 pounds, with large hands and a grip of steel. Now he was stooped and walked slowly. Lincoln had lost nearly 30 pounds in the past few months. Friends said he looked like a walking skeleton.

Yet this morning, the tall, thin president slipped into his old bathrobe, pulled on his tattered slippers, and shuffled down the hallway to the library with a light heart. This day would be one of the happiest days the president had enjoyed in many years.

As was his habit—and Lincoln was a man of disciplined habits—the president sat down in his favorite chair in the library, and began the day reading a short passage from the Bible. Although never a conventional Christian, Lincoln did believe in God and was a lifelong Bible reader.

Just a few days earlier, he had mentioned to his wife a secret desire to visit Palestine and see Jerusalem.

The Bible he read, a small King James edition bound in burgundy red velvet with gilt edges, was given to him at his first inauguration by the clerk of the U.S. Supreme Court, William Thomas Carroll. Later, both Barack Obama and Donald Trump would place their hands upon this Bible when swearing their oaths of office.[2]

After his morning meditations were completed, Lincoln stood up and walked a few more feet to his office (an area that is now called the Lincoln Bedroom). The president liked to get a little work done before breakfast.

The office was a medium-sized rectangular room with a low ceiling, plush green and gold carpet, and walls covered with purple wallpaper. On one side was a modest fireplace, covered with soot. Next to it stood a small, second-hand desk with a stool where Lincoln worked. A window to the left of the desk overlooked the half-finished Washington Monument, the Potomac River, and encampments of Union soldiers on the Mall. In the center of the office was a large conference table, piled high with books and maps, with chairs encircling it, where Lincoln's cabinet and two male secretaries spent much of their time.

As Lincoln entered his office, a stack of mail was already waiting for him on his desk. It included a mysterious check made out to him personally in the amount of five hundred dollars from a Philadelphia lawyer named Eli K. Price. Also on his desk was a copy of the *New York Tribune* with an editorial celebrating the end of the war, declaring, "the road before us smiles with summer sunshine."[3]

Lincoln proceeded to write four quick notes. One was to his secretary of state, William Seward, who was recuperating at his nearby home, just off Lafayette Square, having suffered a carriage accident two weeks earlier. As a courtesy, Lincoln informed him that a cabinet meeting would be held that day at eleven o'clock.

He also wrote to General Grant, just arrived in Washington the day before, who had graciously driven Lincoln's wife, Mary, around the city in his place. Lincoln asked Grant if he would come to the White House

LINCOLN IN THE MEDIA

"Lincoln is a worse tyrant and more inhuman butcher than has existed since the days of Nero.... The man who votes for Lincoln now is a traitor and murderer...And if he is elected to misgovern for another four years, we trust some bold hand will pierce his heart with dagger point for the public good."

—*Wisconsin newspaper editor Marcus M. Pomeroy*[4]

at eleven and not at nine o'clock as they had previously agreed upon. The third note was to the commissioner of Indian Affairs about an appointment he wished to delay. These first three notes would be delivered by the White House messengers who worked round the clock.

The final note was to an old friend, General James Van Alen, who had written to Lincoln warning him to be mindful of assassination attempts. The general had been horrified to discover that Lincoln had personally visited the captured Confederate capital of Richmond the week before, where a hidden rebel sniper could have easily picked him off.

In fact, an unidentified rifleman had taken a shot at Lincoln the year before when he was out riding his horse late at night. The bullet took the famous stovepipe hat off Lincoln's head.

"My dear Sir," Lincoln wrote back to the general. "I intend to adopt the advice of my friends and use due precaution"—advice that the president did not always follow.

He may have glanced at one of the cubbyholes in his desk, the one that held the more than eighty letters with assassination threats he had received. Lincoln wrote two more brief comments and instructions on letters he had

received from congressmen, and then stood up. It was now almost eight
o'clock and time to get dressed and have breakfast.

*   *   🎩   *   *

Abraham Lincoln may not have been the poorest man ever elected
president—he was a successful attorney at the time of his election—but
he was probably the one with the poorest childhood.

Lincoln was born, just as schoolchildren learn, in a one-room log
cabin in Hardin County, Kentucky, on February 12, 1809, the second
child and first son of an illiterate, hardworking farmer named Thomas
Lincoln and his wife, Nancy Hanks. Lincoln's elder sister, Sarah, whom
he loved deeply, would later die in childbirth. His other sibling, Thomas,
died in infancy.

When Lincoln was seven years old, the family moved across the Ohio
River to Indiana, where they staked a claim in a vast, wild forest and
survived primarily by hunting. It was there that occurred the first in a
series of tragedies that were to mark the future president's life.

Soon after moving to Indiana, Lincoln's biological mother, Nancy,
succumbed to a disease called milk sickness, caused by drinking milk
from cows that had eaten a poisonous local plant. Thomas Lincoln realized he could not raise his two small children alone, so he returned to
Kentucky and found a widow with three young children of her own,
Sarah Bush Johnston, who was willing to be his second wife.

Sarah Johnston arrived in Lincoln's wild, impoverished life like an
angel of mercy, bringing to the forest outpost furniture, clothes, plates,
knives, and an immeasurable quantity of motherly kindness and love.
She raised Lincoln and he called her "Mamma."

Because of Sarah, who made Thomas install a wood floor, windows,
and other improvements in the primitive cabin he had built, Lincoln
remembered his childhood in the Indiana forest as a "joyous, happy
boyhood" in which there was "nothing of want."[5]

The Indiana farmstead where Abraham Lincoln grew up. He lived here from age seven to twenty-one. *Wikimedia Commons*[6]

Both of Lincoln's parents were illiterate, but his stepmother Sarah insisted that Lincoln and her own children go to school. Unfortunately, in the woods of Indiana there were neither many teachers nor schools. As Lincoln put it in his first autobiography, "No qualification was ever required of a teacher beyond 'readin, writin, and cipherin' to the Rule of Three.'"

Lincoln spent three months attending a log cabin school about a mile from his own cabin; then went intermittently to another small school four miles from his home; then, for six more months, attended the first school again when another teacher took over.

Altogether, the time Lincoln attended school amounted to no more than a single year. "I have not been to school since," Lincoln wrote in 1858. "The little advance I now have upon this store of education, I have picked up from time to time under the pressure of necessity."

What the young backwoodsman lacked in formal education he more than made up for by his voracious love of reading. Once Lincoln learned how to read and write, he never looked back, reading every book he could lay his hands on, often more than once.

The tall, gangly boy would memorize long passages, copying out entire pages on wooden planks because his family had no writing paper. Lincoln's reputation as a booklover was firmly established in his neck of the woods. In fact, Lincoln read so much that eventually he was accused of laziness—although his later work record would disprove such a claim.

Lincoln also quickly mastered the basics of "ciphering," such as multiplication and division, and he worked his way through a geometry textbook on his own. These rudimentary math skills proved useful when eventually he ran a small dry goods store and worked as a surveyor, which required a knowledge of basic trigonometry.

In later political campaigns, Lincoln would make much of his time as a backwoodsman, but in reality he had always longed for something better. The future president had little respect for his father's choices in life. A decent man who bequeathed to his son a love of tall tales, Thomas Lincoln did not see beyond the boundaries of his own subsistence farm—and young Abe certainly did.

Lincoln also differed from his parents with respect to religion. Thomas and his wife were members of a Baptist church (strongly opposed to slavery), while Lincoln was a natural freethinker, respectful of Christianity and a lifelong Bible reader, but never a conventional or orthodox believer.

Lincoln's alienation from wilderness life was made complete when his elder sister Sarah died in childbirth. Abe, who was seventeen at the time, blamed his sisters-in-law for not calling for a doctor sooner.

While Lincoln owed his father all the wages he earned until he turned eighteen, he began to take jobs that took him away from home. He worked as a farmer's helper, split rails from logs, and killed hogs. Young Abe built a small rowboat to ferry passengers across the Ohio River, marveling that he could sometimes earn "a dollar in less than a day."[7]

Eventually the lanky teenager accepted assignments to take local goods on a flatboat all the way down the river to the bustling metropolis of New Orleans, the first city Lincoln had ever seen. These riverboat trips introduced the young Lincoln to the realities of the local economy

IN LINCOLN'S OWN WORDS

"I was raised to farm work, which I continued till I was twenty-two. At twenty-one, I came to Illinois, and passed the first year in Macon County. Then I got to New-Salem [at that time in Sangamon, now in Menard County], where I remained a year as a sort of Clerk in a store. Then came the Black-Hawk War; and I was elected a Captain of Volunteers—a success which gave me more pleasure than any I have had since."[8]

(knowledge he would later use as a state legislator) and introduced him to the grocery business.

*   *   ∎   *   *

President Lincoln's family was waiting for him at the small breakfast area downstairs on the first floor of the White House when he arrived. His wife of twenty-three years, Mary Todd Lincoln, now forty-seven years old, was plump and round-faced and had her dark brown hair pulled back in a bun.

The deaths of two of their four children had put considerable strain on the Lincolns' marriage over the years. Most recently, the death of their much-loved eleven-year-old son Willie, who had succumbed to typhoid fever in 1862 shortly after they had moved into the White House, had almost destroyed them both. The stoic Lincoln had sat in Willie's bedroom for hours at a time, sobbing openly and uncontrollably. Mary was so devastated she couldn't get out of her bed for weeks.

The Lincolns were doting, permissive parents who lavished time and money on their children. The two youngest boys, Willie and Tad,

often interrupted cabinet meetings and turned the White House
into their personal play area. The
children were widely considered
to be holy terrors.

The daughter of affluent Kentucky slave owners, Mary was
smart, well educated, and spoke
her mind freely and often. Yet she
and Lincoln had many dark periods over the years. On this day,
however, Mary was in a jubilant
mood, as were most people in
Washington, and she greeted her
husband warmly.

Lincoln ate his customary
single egg with a cup of coffee. The
first order of business concerned
the evening's entertainment.

Mary Ann Todd Lincoln (1818–1882),
photographed in her late twenties, in the
mid-1840s. *Wikimedia Commons*

The Lincoln family would
receive two invitations to the theatre for that evening. One had come
the day before from Grover's Theatre, also known as the National
Theatre, located just three blocks from the White House on Pennsylvania Avenue, where the company was presenting *Aladdin! Or, The
Wonderful Lamp.*

The other invitation, which arrived during breakfast, was for Ford's
Theatre, located a few blocks further east on Tenth Street between F and
E Streets, where the famous actress Laura Keene was starring in the
celebrated British comedy *Our American Cousin.*

The Lincolns' young son Tad, then just twelve, instantly voted for
Grover's and *Aladdin.* He was good friends with Bobby Grover, the
theatre owner's son, and he could instantly see that *Aladdin* would be
much more fun than a stuffy British comedy.

Thomas Lincoln III (1853–1817), known as "Tad," Lincoln's fourth son, photographed in 1864 at the age of eleven. *Wikimedia Commons*

However, Mary wanted to see *Our American Cousin*. It was one of those plays that everyone had seen except for her. This was to be the final performance of the play at Ford's.

After a brief discussion, the family decided that Tad could go separately to Grover's to see *Aladdin* and Lincoln and his wife would attend Ford's. Once that was agreed upon, Mary had the White House staff send messengers over to the theatres, requesting the usual box seats at Ford's and informing Grover's that only Tad would be attending that evening.

Just then the Lincolns' eldest son Robert joined them, beaming and eager to tell what he had seen as a member of General Grant's entourage.

Robert Lincoln had graduated from Harvard College the previous year and intended to follow his father into the law. Yet like most young men his age, Robert was anxious to do his part in the war effort—a desire his mother, who had already lost two beloved sons, could not bear even to contemplate.

Mary begged her husband to stop Robert from volunteering for the Army. This was delicate, however. The Lincoln family had been widely denounced for hypocrisy because of Robert's college deferment. As commander in chief, Lincoln was sending young men off to die by the tens of thousands in an unpopular war, yet his own son was safe at Harvard, reading books.

With his talent for compromise, Lincoln figured out a solution. He wrote to his top general, Grant, asking if he could perhaps find a spot on his staff for Robert if he, Lincoln, would pay the boy's expenses. Lincoln figured that this would allow his son to see the war effort up close without putting him in serious danger. Referring to Robert, Lincoln wrote Grant a letter.

"Could he, without embarrassment to you, or detriment to the service, go into your military family with some nominal rank, I, not the public, furnishing his necessary means?" Lincoln asked. "If no, say so without the least hesitation, because I am as anxious, and as deeply interested, that you shall not be encumbered as you can be yourself."[9]

Robert joined Grant's staff with the rank of captain on February 11 and served until June 10, 1865, a total four months.[10] He received regular military pay.

"Well, my son, you have returned safely from the front," said Lincoln, beaming as Robert sat down. "The war is now closed, and we soon will live in peace with the brave men that have been fighting against us. I trust that the era of good feeling has returned...and that henceforth we shall live in peace."

Lincoln asked what Lee's surrender had been like.

"Oh, it was great!" the young man exclaimed.

He described the meeting of the two great generals and the enormous contrast between them.

Lee, he said, "with his white head and spotless uniform, his jeweled sword and gold spurs," was dramatically unlike Grant, Robert's commander, whom he described as a "small, stooping, shabby, shy man in the muddy blue uniform, with no sword and no spurs—only the frayed and dingy shoulder straps of a Lieutenant General on the rumpled blouse of a private soldier."

Robert had brought with him a portrait of the great Confederate general. He presented it to his father to illustrate the contrast.

Robert Todd Lincoln (1843–1926), Lincoln's eldest, served four months as a captain on General Ulysses Grant's personal staff and witnessed the surrender of Confederate general Robert E. Lee on April 9, 1865, after the Battle of Appomattox Court House. *Wikimedia Commons*

Lincoln studied the portrait of Lee closely. "It is a good face," Lincoln concluded after some moments. "It is the face of a noble, noble, brave man. I am glad the war is over at last."

A White House aide interrupted the family's breakfast. The Speaker of the House, Schuyler Colfax, a congressman from Indiana who would soon be the seventeenth vice president of the United States, was waiting to see the president.

"Now, listen to me, Robert," the president said, as he rose from his chair. "You must lay aside your uniform and return to college. I wish you to read law for three years, and at the end of that time I hope that we will be able to tell whether you will make a lawyer or not."[11]

★   ★   🎩   ★   ★

In 1830, when Abe Lincoln was just twenty-one, he helped his father and stepmother move from rural Indiana northwest to a tract of land on the Sangamon River, just west of Decatur, Illinois. It was a dangerous, difficult journey with a wagon and oxen, but the family made it safely. Lincoln helped his father clear fifteen acres of land that

CRITICAL MINUTES

Lincoln's fate was likely sealed at breakfast on the morning of April 14 when the family decided to split up the evening's entertainment, with young Tad going to Grover's Theatre and Lincoln and his wife Mary to Ford's Theatre.

summer but then struck out on his own, supporting himself with odd jobs and work as a riverboat captain. He first settled in the small village of New Salem, Illinois, population one hundred, where he would spend the next few years trying out a number of different professions to put food in his mouth.

A virtual giant, although quite thin, Lincoln attracted attention immediately. By this time, Lincoln stood six feet four inches tall and weighed about 160 pounds. This was during an era when the average height of a grown man was only five feet six inches. Lincoln's life in the forest, splitting rails with his trusty axe, had made him into a strong, confident man who would not back down from a fight.

Yet in addition to his stature, Lincoln also had an amiable, free-wheeling personality, attracting crowds with the same tall tales and ribald jokes his father told. The women in the village quickly noticed his natural kindness to children and small animals. Despite his poverty, Lincoln thrived in the small village of New Salem because he was willing to accept all kinds of jobs and temporary assignments—working as the village postmaster, grocery store owner, blacksmith, and surveyor.

Although shy, Lincoln made friends easily, even winning over the local roughnecks by his willingness to wrestle their leader. Most important, Lincoln, who could now read and write well, became known as

? WHAT WE STILL DON'T KNOW

Where did John Wilkes Booth spend the night on April 13, 1865? Historians have not been able to find out. Early in the morning on April 14, friends asked the concierge at the National Hotel to check his room, but his bed had not been slept in. Some suspect he spent the evening with his favorite Washington call girl, but there is no evidence that this is true.

the village intellectual, helping friends write their letters and then, after watching court proceedings a few times, draft simple legal documents, such as deeds and bills of sale.

The final ripening experience of Lincoln's young adulthood came when he enlisted in the local Illinois militia (he needed the job), and, as was the custom then, was elected captain of his unit. Despite his many later accomplishments, Lincoln was very proud of his time as a militia captain. The militia was formed in response to an armed insurrection by Native Americans, known as the Black Hawk War, in which a number of tribes attempted to reclaim lands in Illinois that they believed they had been tricked into ceding to the U.S. government.

Beyond training exercises, Lincoln saw no combat action at all and later would poke fun at his military service. Referring to a political rival, an alleged military hero in the War of 1812, Lincoln said that if the other man saw real combat it was more than he had done, but, Lincoln added, he had "a good many bloody struggles with the musquetoes."[12]

By his own admission, Lincoln got into politics out of financial necessity. He frankly needed the money, and ran for the Illinois State Legislature twice. The first time, in 1832, at the age of twenty-three, he lost. But the second time, in 1834, he won handily, largely due to a tireless campaign of handshaking and speechmaking.

At this time, Lincoln had few concrete plans and no firm political agenda. However, he did support the pro-development policies of the Kentucky senator and U.S. statesman Henry Clay (1777–1852) and the group that eventually became known as the Whigs.

The forerunners of the Republican Party, the Whigs believed in economic development, protective tariffs, and the development of infrastructure projects such as railroads and canals. They were opposed by the Democrats, who were then the champions of small farmers and rural America. It was around this time that Lincoln started reading law in earnest.

At that time, many if not most lawyers were self-taught. They won the right to practice law by passing an exam or being authorized to do so by a state supreme court. Lincoln used his earnings as a part-time mailman and surveyor to buy law books, such as Blackstone's classic *Commentaries*. He also borrowed two hundred dollars from New Salem's richest man—a sizable sum for that time and place—and used a quarter of the amount to buy his first suit.

However, just as young Lincoln's life was coming together, tragedy struck once again.

Lincoln had gradually fallen in love with one of New Salem's most beautiful women, a young lady named Ann Rutledge. She was the daughter of the man who owned the tavern where Lincoln boarded. By all accounts, the entire village cherished Rutledge as a gentle, kindhearted young woman. At this time, she happened to be engaged to another man. That meant Lincoln, always shy around single women, felt free to joke around with her and be more himself.

Rutledge's fiancé, a man named John McNamar, left the village suddenly under mysterious circumstances (allegedly to bring his family out West) and soon his letters stopped coming—a fact that Lincoln, as village postmaster, knew very well.

Eventually, Lincoln and Ann Rutledge reached an understanding. However, before their marriage plans could be announced, in the summer of 1835, she contracted a mysterious fever and died. It was another heavy blow that contributed to Lincoln's lifelong melancholy and fatalism.

★ ★ ▮ ★ ★

With breakfast over and the evening's entertainment decided upon, President Lincoln went back upstairs to his office. There Schuyler Colfax, the Speaker of the House, was waiting for him along with another congressman, Cornelius Cole of Santa Cruz, California.

The forty-two-year-old Colfax recognized immediately the change in Lincoln's appearance. Gone were the sad, weary eyes. The president was positively buoyant. He would later write that on that day Lincoln was the happiest he had ever seen him.

"You are going to California, I hear!" the president said to Colfax, with a wide smile.

"I am, if there is no extra session of Congress impending."

"How I would rejoice to make that trip, but public duties chain me down here," Lincoln replied. "I can only envy you its pleasures!"

The two men then discussed the vast mineral wealth lying out West. Lincoln knew the staggering costs and debts of the war had undermined the nation's fiscal health, and he couldn't help but hope that the vast deposits of gold and silver discovered in California might help to pay that down somewhat. At the cabinet meeting two hours later, the secretary of the treasury, Hugh McCulloch, would report that the national debt after the war now stood at a staggering $2.3 billion.[13]

After Colfax and Cole left, Lincoln spent the next two hours meeting with a stream of dignitaries and supplicants of all kinds. These included William Howard of Michigan and Senator John Creswell of Maryland.

"Hello, Creswell, the war is over!" Lincoln almost shouted when meeting the senator. "But it has been an awful war, Creswell, it has been an awful war! But it's over!"

The senator was smiling, happy to see the president in such an ebullient mood.

WHAT WERE THEY THINKING?

YOUNG WASHINGTON SOCIALITE Lucy Lambert Hale dated some of Washington's most eligible bachelors, including the president's son, Robert Lincoln, future Supreme Court justice Oliver Wendell Holmes Jr.—and the famous actor John Wilkes Booth.

"But what are you here for?" Lincoln asked. "You fellows don't come to see me unless you want something. It must be something big, or you wouldn't be so early."

Creswell admitted he was there on a personal errand. A college friend had received a letter from a cousin, a Confederate soldier, who was being held at a military prison in Maryland. Creswell's college buddy had asked him if there was anything he could do to spring the poor fellow's release.

"That's not so hard!" Lincoln said. He took the letter from the senator's hand, turned it over, and wrote, "Let it be done. A. Lincoln. April 14, 1865."

Another meeting that morning that would raise eyebrows later was with John Hale, the New Hampshire senator and abolitionist whom Lincoln had recently appointed minister to Spain. Hale had been one of Lincoln's strongest supporters.

Unbeknownst to Lincoln, Hale's oldest daughter Lucy, then twenty-four, was the secret mistress and fiancée of the famous actor John Wilkes Booth.

Lincoln might have been concerned, had he known the truth.

That's because Lincoln's son Robert had also carried a torch for Lucy for years, ever since they had spent time together in Boston while he attended Harvard.

Although not a conventional beauty, Lucy Hale's keen intelligence and flirtatious personality had bewitched many male admirers, including the future Supreme Court justice Oliver Wendell Holmes Jr.

Lucy Lambert Hale (1841–1915), the daughter of U.S. senator John Parker Hale of New Hampshire, carried on an affair with John Wilkes Booth. Her photograph was later found on Booth's body. *Wikimedia Commons*

When in Washington, the Hales lived at the enormous National Hotel, which occupied an entire city block at the corner of Pennsylvania Avenue and Sixth Street—later the site of a museum dedicated to journalism and the First Amendment.[14]

Booth, too, usually stayed at the National when he was in Washington—and he had many opportunities to encounter Lucy Hale both in the hotel itself and around Washington.

Although Booth had more than his fair share of female admirers, he and Hale had had an intense on-again, off-again relationship for the past three years. They had even, on occasion, checked into hotels together, with Booth signing the hotel register Mr. J. W. Booth & Lady.[15] Booth's intimate, secret relationship with Hale remains one of the many little-known subplots of this day's dramatic events.

It was Lucy Hale who arranged to get a ticket for Booth to Lincoln's second inauguration the month before. This was a ticket given to Lucy's father, then a U.S. senator, giving the bearer the right to enter the U.S. Capitol Building during the swearing-in ceremony.

Booth attended the ceremony and later bragged to a fellow actor friend in New York, a few weeks later, that he was so close to Lincoln that day he could have easily shot him.

? ## WHAT WE STILL DON'T KNOW
Was John Wilkes Booth really engaged to Lucy Hale? Booth told his mother, his brother Junius, and his sister Asia of his intentions. He certainly was romantically involved with her. However, after the events of April 14, Lucy Hale did everything she could to avoid discussing her relationship with the infamous actor, including leaving the country with her family. Nevertheless, the scandal would eventually catch up to her when tabloid newspapers revived the story in the late 1870s. Lucy, then a married woman, remained silent. She died in 1915 without ever commenting on her past relationship with John Wilkes Booth.

In fact, unbeknownst to Lucy, on Inauguration Day Booth actually lunged at Lincoln when the president passed by on his way out of the Capitol to give his speech outside.

Booth was promptly accosted by security officials. The burly security officers didn't recognize him. One said he thought Booth was "a lunatic or out of his right mind—he looked so wild and seemed so unnecessarily excited."[16]

Reluctantly, the security personnel let Booth go. He would go outside and listen to Lincoln's second inaugural address, seething with quiet fury.

2 "A NAME KNOWN IN HISTORY FOREVER"

Downtown Washington, 9:00 to 11:00 a.m.

Just as Abraham Lincoln was preparing to meet with Senator Hale, a man named David Herold, a twenty-three-year-old former druggist assistant, strolled into the lobby of the National Hotel. He would play a key role in this day's historic events.

Herold was looking for the actor John Wilkes Booth.

He asked for Booth at the front desk, and the night clerk, Walter Burton, who was just getting off duty, agreed to take Herold up to Booth's room—room 228 on the fourth floor. After knocking and receiving no answer, Burton unlocked the door. Booth was nowhere to be seen. It appeared his bed had not been slept in.

Booth would later be seen downstairs in the hotel's restaurant having breakfast with his secret fiancée, Senator Hale's daughter Lucy, and a woman named Claire Bean, the daughter of a local merchant. Witnesses told the accomplished Washington journalist George Townsend, who knew Booth personally, that the couple seemed to be getting along famously.[1]

Booth and Lucy likely discussed Senator Hale's upcoming meeting that morning with President Lincoln and his nomination to be minister to Spain.

John Wilkes Booth (1838–1865) was one of the most famous and celebrated actors in America when he decided, at the age of twenty-six, to help the Confederacy's desperate war effort by kidnapping Abraham Lincoln and holding him hostage. *Wikimedia Commons*

Apparently, Lucy planned to go with her father and then return to marry Booth.

Many people in the restaurant likely recognized Booth. Although he was only twenty-six years old, he was one of the most famous actors in America. Ruggedly handsome with a receding hairline and a thick mustache, Booth cut an impressive figure. He dazzled female fans. Booth stood five feet eight inches tall and weighed 160 pounds, an athletic, well-dressed man who carried himself with poise and confidence. He was wearing a long, light-colored, stylish overcoat.[2] On his left hand, Booth had two tattoos of his initials in indigo blue ink, JWB: one on his left wrist; and one, from childhood, between his left thumb and forefinger.[3]

Booth competed with his older brothers Edwin and Junius Jr. for the honor of succeeding their late father, the British-born Shakespearean actor Junius Booth, as the most celebrated male actor on the American stage.

Throughout the war, Booth had performed in theatres across the East and Midwest, even in occupied cities of the South. Until recently, Booth had been earning as much as $600 a week from his acting. That is roughly equivalent to $10,000 today.

In truth, Booth's acting was amateurish and his pronunciation laughable. Yet audiences everywhere admired him for his athletic, robust performances. He stomped about with a wild-eyed intensity, sometimes leaping down onto stages from great heights for dramatic effect.

The previous November, President Lincoln and his wife had seen Booth perform in Charles Selby's *The Marble Heart*, at Ford's Theatre in Washington. The president even invited Booth to meet with him between acts, an honor that the actor surprisingly declined.

Unlike most citizens of Washington, Booth was not happy with recent events on the battlefield. In fact, he was downright miserable. It was an open secret that Booth was a Confederate sympathizer who despised Lincoln. On more than one occasion, the hot-tempered actor had said things that could have gotten him arrested for suspected treason.

IN BOOTH'S OWN WORDS

"I love peace more than life. Have loved the Union beyond expression. For four years have I waited, hoped and prayed, for the dark clouds to break, and for a restoration of our former sunshine. To wait longer would be a crime."[4]

As a result, his loving family—his mother, two sisters, and three brothers—had long ago forbade him from talking about politics. Booth's friends in the theatre world, even those who shared his political opinions, openly mocked his increasingly unhinged rants. Some hoped that the end of the war would finally calm Booth down.

Historians have long puzzled over what could have been going through Booth's mind on this warm spring morning. He had confided different plans to different people—to his siblings and mother, his actor friends, Lucy Hale, and to Ella Starr, his favorite Washington prostitute, with whom he may have spent the previous night.

On the one hand, Booth spoke to Lucy Hale of their future life together—and even wrote to his mother of his intention to marry the young woman. On the other hand, for more than six months Booth had

CRITICAL MINUTES

Many historians now believe that Booth made the fateful decision to assassinate, rather than try to kidnap, Abraham Lincoln when he heard Lincoln's remarks on voting rights for recently freed slaves. Booth's co-conspirator David Herold told his attorney, Frederick Stone, that it was this speech on April 11 that convinced Booth that he now had no choice but to kill Lincoln. However, Booth hinted at more ominous intentions at a meeting with his fellow conspirators March 15 at Gautier's restaurant on Pennsylvania Avenue. The conspirators involved in the kidnapping plot were horrified at what Booth hinted at and made it clear that they would have no part in murder, forcing Booth to tone down his comments to mollify his hapless followers.

been involved in a madcap plot to kidnap President Lincoln and spirit him away to the South, where he would be held hostage and ransomed to free captured Confederate prisoners of war.

Booth must have realized that, had he succeeded in his crazy plot to kidnap Lincoln, there was no way he could ever marry Hale or resume his acting career in the North, as he had told other friends he wanted to do.

What's more, it appears Booth's plans had recently taken a far more sinister turn. Three days earlier, on Tuesday evening, April 11, Booth and two of his fellow conspirators, Herold and a former Confederate soldier named Lewis Powell, had stood with a large crowd in the pouring rain in front of the White House. The crowd listened as Lincoln announced his plans to grant citizenship to some recently freed slaves—especially those who had served in the military.

"It is unsatisfactory to some that the elective franchise is not given to the colored man," the president said, reading from a prepared speech. "I would myself prefer that it were now conferred on the very intelligent, and on those who served our cause as soldiers."[5]

Apparently, this was the last straw for Booth.

"That means nigger citizenship," he blurted out in disgust. "Now, by God, I'll run him through!"

As they walked from the White House toward Lafayette Square, Booth vowed to Powell and Herold, "That's the last speech he will ever make."[7]

LINCOLN IN THE MEDIA

"People now marvel how it came to pass that Mr. Lincoln should have been selected as the representative man of any party. His weak, wishy-washy, namby-pamby efforts, imbecile in matter, disgusting in manner, have made us the laughingstock of the whole world."
—Salem Advocate, 1861[6]

★　★　🎩　★　★

Around eight thirty, Booth finished breakfast and said goodbye to Lucy and her friend, Claire. He told them he was going to get a haircut and said he would see Lucy later that day.

Outside the National Hotel, on Pennsylvania Avenue, Herold finally caught sight of Booth. The two men headed up the broad avenue towards the White House and, as they walked, were joined by two others looking for Booth.

At nine o'clock,[8] Booth and the three men strolled into Booker and Stewart's barbershop on E Street, near Grover's Theatre and next to the old Union building. Booth greeted the barber, Charles Wood, with a

The upscale National Hotel (shown here in the early 1900s), occupying a full block at the corner of Pennsylvania Avenue and Sixth Street in Washington, D.C., was the home of politicians and celebrities. Booth's room during mid-April 1865 was number 228 on the fourth floor. Originally built in 1826, the hotel was finally demolished in 1942. *Wikimedia Commons*

hearty hello. Booth had known Wood for most of his life. The barber had cut Booth's hair when he was a boy and Wood lived in Baltimore.

Coincidentally, Wood had just returned from the home of Secretary of State Seward off of Lafayette Square, where he had given the badly injured official a shave.

After draping Booth with a barber gown, Wood gave the actor a close shave. Then he trimmed Booth's drooping mustache, cut his curly black hair, and dressed it with tonic and pomade.

While Booth was getting his hair trimmed, his friends made joking comments, seemingly without a care in the world. One of the friends, whom Wood later identified as the Confederate courier John Surratt Jr., a twenty-year-old former Catholic seminarian, joked about something that looked like a boil on the left side of Booth's neck.[9]

"They say it was a boil but it is not a boil," the man told the barber. "It was a pistol shot."[10]

In reality, two years earlier Booth had had a fibrous tumor removed from his neck by a Washington physician, Dr. John Frederick May. The wound did not heal properly and left Booth with a burn-like scar. He asked the doctor to say he had removed a bullet from Booth's neck, a memento left by one of his many jealous lovers. The story stuck. It soon became part of Booth's own public relations efforts.[11]

Besides Booth's joking friend was another man, Michael O'Laughlen,

IN THEIR OWN WORDS

"In the early train next morning, Tuesday, April 4, 1865, I left for New York, and that was the last time I was ever in Washington until brought there by the U.S. Government a captive in irons, all reports to the contrary notwithstanding."

—*John Surratt Jr., in a speech delivered in 1870*

perhaps Booth's oldest and dearest friend, whom Booth had known since he was only seven years old in Baltimore. O'Laughlen had traveled from Baltimore to see Booth the evening before but had only just caught up with him that morning. He, too, had been at the National Hotel earlier in the morning, looking for Booth.

O'Laughlen had been actively involved with Booth's crazy plot to kidnap the president, hatched six months earlier, which was intended to force the resumption of prisoner exchanges between North and South.

At the time, the South was desperate for soldiers. Yet General Grant, tired of fighting soldiers on the battlefield who had just been released from Union prisons the week before, had recently put an end to all prisoner exchanges.

? WHAT WE STILL DON'T KNOW

Was John Surratt Jr., the son of boardinghouse owner Mary Surratt and a key conspirator in the plot to kidnap Lincoln, in Washington, D.C., on April 14— or, as he later claimed, far away on a spying mission in Elmira, New York? At his later trial, a handful of witnesses swore John Surratt was seen in Elmira, but the prosecution produced a dozen other witnesses who claimed to have seen him that day in Washington, D.C., including the man who cut John Wilkes Booth's hair on the morning of the assassination.

Booth, Surratt, O'Laughlen, and about a dozen fellow Confederate sympathizers had hoped to waylay Lincoln as he rode alone at night on a dark Washington street (something he had, on occasion, been known to do), bundle him into a carriage, ferry him across the Potomac, and then whisk him south to the Confederate capital of Richmond, Virginia. Once there, Booth thought that Lincoln could be traded for Confederate soldiers now rotting away in Union prisons.

The plot to kidnap Lincoln was thus a desperate attempt to give the Confederacy a fighting chance to survive. And while the plot may have sounded good in theory, it would prove utterly impracticable. The group was short on trained personnel and plagued by a comical lack of reliable information. The plotters often had no idea where Lincoln was at any given time.

Both O'Laughlen and Surratt, along with most of the other co-conspirators, had recently backed out of the plot. With the war now virtually over, they had begun to suspect that Booth had given up on kidnapping Lincoln and had something more sinister in mind.

And they were right.

Realizing he would be implicated by his lifelong friendship with Booth, O'Laughlen desperately wanted to talk Booth out of whatever he was planning.

Charles Wood finished rubbing the hair pomade into Booth's curly brown locks. He then snapped off the barber's gown with a flourish.

Booth stood up. He admired himself in the long mirror next to Wood's barber chair, impeccable as always.

"Your turn, Mac," he said to his friend.

As the others took their turn in Wood's chair, Booth announced that he was going to run across the street to Grover's Theatre.

Located on Pennsylvania Avenue between Thirteenth and Fourteenth Streets, just a few blocks from the White House, Grover's Theatre, also known as the National Theatre, was built in 1835 as a showcase for the new nation's talent. It still exists today, albeit in vastly expanded form.

At this time, there was a fierce rivalry between Grover's (then owned by a man named Leonard Grover) and Ford's Theatre (owned by the young entrepreneur John T. Ford). Both theatres were substantial establishments, massive stone buildings two-stories high. Booth had acted at both theatres. The president and his wife had attended both theatres often in the past— even though Ford's was known to have "succesh" sympathies.

Booth knew that Grover's Theatre had extended an invitation to President Lincoln to attend that night. The day before, Booth had burst into the offices of the theatre's manager, C. Dwight Hess, uncharacteristically interrupting a script reading, and demanded to know what Hess had planned for that night, Thursday.

Hess had told Booth that Grover's was going to participate in the "Grand Illumination" scheduled for Thursday evening but that he was saving the best for the next day, Friday. He wanted to do something special in honor of the U.S. flag being hoisted once again above Fort Sumter, four years to the day after the fort had surrendered.

"Are you going to invite the president?" Booth demanded to know. Hess replied that he most certainly was.[12]

As a result of this, Booth had gone upstairs to the billiard parlor above the theatre and asked the owner, John Deery, a friend of his, if he would purchase a ticket for Booth for Friday's performance. He specifically asked that Deery get a ticket for the box next to the presidential box.

Deery asked Booth why he didn't just buy a ticket himself. Booth replied, plausibly enough, that he feared the theatre would just give him a complimentary ticket and he wanted to pay himself.[13] Deery agreed and would later purchase the ticket.

Booth was covering all his bases.

By this point, Booth had plainly made up his mind to kill Lincoln. Yet even at this late date, he had not figured out precisely how or where he would do it. Like the experienced actor he was, Booth planned on improvising as events developed.

Outside the theatre, Booth ran into Hess's wife Julia and another woman, Helen Moss. They were on their way to the White House to meet with President Lincoln.

Booth shook both of the women's hands. They told him that they were distraught. A messenger had just arrived moments earlier from the White House informing the theatre that the Lincolns would *not* be attending this evening, as they had thought.[14]

Although he likely didn't show it, Booth must have been severely disappointed.

Lincoln's penchant for changing his plans at the last minute had thwarted Booth's kidnapping plans in the past—and today the pattern looked to be continuing.

★   ★   🎩   ★   ★

John Wilkes Booth is one of the enduring mysteries of history.

A warm, playful man with an abundant sense of humor, he was beloved by hundreds of friends and coworkers who continued to sing his praises even after he became the most hated man in America. An old actor friend described Booth as "impulsive, fiery, big-hearted, generous, captivating, and magnetic."[15]

Women adored him. Men wanted to be like him.

Even after the events that tarred the Booth name forever, friends remained unwaveringly steadfast; many claimed that Booth was one of the kindest, most generous men they had ever met.

Yet Booth was also hot-tempered and stubborn, a reckless fanatic who often let politics crowd out common sense. This was true even though he had friends and family members who did not share his political outlook.

Booth was born in a four-room log cabin near Bel Air, Maryland, on May 10, 1838, but he spent much of his childhood in the bustling streets of urban Baltimore. He was born illegitimate, the ninth of ten children (only six survived childhood) born to the British stage actor Junius Brutus Booth and his British mistress, Mary Ann Holmes.

The elder Booth was famous in London as a Shakespearean actor. But in 1821, he abandoned his first wife and young son, eventually emigrating to America with a pregnant Holmes when he was twenty-five and she was nineteen. For years, the young couple claimed to be legally married but weren't.[16]

The couple purchased and settled on a 150-acre farmstead about twenty-seven miles northeast of Baltimore.[17] Shortly after, Junius Booth began a successful thirty-year career as a stage actor in America. In a time when the theatre was the primary form of

Junius Brutus Booth (1796–1852) was a British Shakespearean actor who abandoned his wife and child and emigrated to the United States in 1821 with his mistress, Mary Ann Holmes. They would have ten children together, six of whom survived into adulthood. *Wikimedia Commons*

entertainment, Junius performed on stages across North America, from New York, Washington, and Baltimore, all the way to California.

Throughout his early years in America, Junius Booth sent money back to his legal wife in England, Adelaide Delannoy, not revealing that he had an entirely new family in America. He even brought his new family back to England on extended theatrical tours, somehow keeping the two families apart.

However, eventually Junius's son from his first wife, Richard, then twenty-five, came to visit his father in America. The boy soon discovered the truth that his father had another family, and wrote to his mother back in England. In 1847, Adelaide decamped to America. She confronted the large Booth clan in public, creating humiliating, often drunken scenes in which she called the mother of the Booth children a whore.

Adelaide legally divorced Junius in 1851, after the required three-year waiting period. Soon after, likely on May 10, 1851, John Wilkes's thirteenth birthday, the famous actor finally married the mother of his children, Mary Ann Holmes, with most of their children in attendance.

By all accounts, the Booth children had an unusual, bohemian upbringing, surrounded by a love of literature and the arts but with little stability in their lives. They spent part of their childhood in a rural area of Maryland, near a forest, but also a considerable amount of time in a small town house that Junius purchased in 1845, in the thriving, bustling city of Baltimore, then the second-largest city in the country after New York.

Junius was an educated man who claimed to speak four or five languages. As a result, the older Booth children were exposed to the Greek and Latin classics, Shakespeare, poetry, and the life of the stage. Despite this, their educations were somewhat spotty. The older children appear to have had more systematic schooling, John Booth much less so.

John's education began in a one-room schoolhouse across the road from the family farm in Bel Air, but eventually he attended a bigger school, Bel Air Academy—which still stands today—where both he and his teachers discovered that he hated book learning.[18] John was smart but not a good student. His poor spelling and pronunciation skills would be a source of embarrassment to him his entire life.

There was also little religious upbringing in the Booth family, with Mary Ann being a nominal Episcopalian and Junius more of a free-thinker. However, John Wilkes was eventually baptized in the local Episcopalian church when he was fourteen years old—and attended Catholic Mass at least once or twice as an adult.

Four of Junius's surviving six children followed his path into the arts. Junius's sons John, Edwin, and Junius Jr. all became actors in their own right, and his daughter, Asia Booth Clarke, became a noted poet. Her writings serve as the chief source of knowledge about the entire Booth family. Edwin Booth, John's older brother and founder of a successful theatre in New York City, was widely acclaimed the foremost American actor in the nineteenth century. John Wilkes would eventually compete with his elder brother for the title.

Despite their successes, however, the Booth family was troubled. Junius Sr. was an erratic alcoholic who was absent for long periods. With age, he became increasingly unreliable and then violent. Many considered the elder Booth brilliant but slightly mad, capable of impulsive acts of violence. He once shot a man in the face. He attempted suicide more than once. And in an 1835 letter, the elder Booth even threatened to kill the president of the United States, Andrew Jackson, whom he knew personally. (Jackson laughed off the threat.)

Neighbors would later claim that Junius was a sullen, morose man and that his long-suffering wife, Mary Ann, was the real guiding force of the family. Yet Junius could also be compassionate: He was a committed abolitionist who was sincerely kind to servants, and he forbade his children from killing even rabbits and deer on the farm (a prohibition that John, a crack shot, ignored as soon as the elder Booth was away).

Junius felt little class snobbery, cheerfully eating with farmhands and servants of all colors—a practice his more class-conscious and openly racist son John would later forbid. Junius was a political radical who hated pretense and upper-class condescension.

Junius Booth built a lavish home for his family on his rural property in Bel Air, Maryland, which he grandly named Tudor Hall. After his father died unexpectedly in 1852, John Wilkes Booth lived there for four years with his mother and sisters. The house still stands and looks much the same. *Wikimedia Commons*

The British actor somehow managed to keep his schedule full and made enough money to begin building the family a substantial home, which he called Tudor Hall, on his property in Bel Air. The house, somewhat expanded, still exists on a heavily wooded lane just off East Churchill Road in Bel Air.

★　★　　★　★

After his haircut and the brief visit to Grover's Theatre, Booth decided to head back to his base at the National Hotel to regroup. It was a twenty-minute walk down Pennsylvania Avenue.

After four years of bloody warfare, Washington in 1865 more resembled a western town in old Hollywood movies than the gleaming modern metropolis of today. Pennsylvania Avenue, a bustling street with trees planted along the sidewalks, was often a wide river of mud and horse manure. Horses and buggies were everywhere. Men wore spurs and carried guns, although usually hidden. Saloons abounded.

There were also an estimated four hundred brothels in the city. The military provost marshal kept meticulous records, still extant, which list the number of "inmates" and the "class" (numbered from one to four) of each establishment. One of Booth's girlfriends, Ella Starr, worked at her sister's bordello at 62 Ohio Avenue in the area now known as the Federal Triangle, just a few blocks southwest of Ford's Theatre.[19]

This morning, virtually all of the places Booth wished to visit were located in a relatively small area—roughly two square miles, from the White House in the west to the National Hotel on the corner of Pennsylvania Avenue and Sixth Street.

Yet during a time when the only means of travel on city streets was either walking or renting, saddling, and caring for horses, even short distances required a certain amount of time. For example, to walk from the location of the National Hotel to the Willard Hotel, two blocks from the White House, takes about twenty minutes.

As Booth walked down Pennsylvania Avenue, he passed the Kirkwood House hotel on the corner of Twelfth Street. He decided to dart in to see if the vice president was at home.

Booth's new plan, conceived only the day before, was to kill all the top leaders of the government in a simultaneous strike—Lincoln, Vice President Andrew Johnson, and Secretary of State Seward. Throwing the government into chaos might buy Confederate president Jefferson Davis and the Confederate government in exile enough time to regroup and rally their forces.

The plan was both daring and foolhardy.

The problem was that Booth now had only the dregs of his original conspiracy team—three dirt-poor men in rags who were loyal, but not very bright.

One of these men, the alcoholic German immigrant George Atzerodt, Booth had instructed to check into the Kirkwood House hotel that very morning. He was to assassinate the vice president. Atzerodt was following Booth's instructions. He had just checked into the hotel at seven thirty that morning and had been given room 126 on the second floor.[20]

But Booth had another reason to visit the Kirkwood House: he wanted to get some travel passes from Andrew Johnson before Atzerodt killed him. Booth knew Johnson personally. Once they had dated a pair of sisters simultaneously. Booth assumed that Johnson could give him travel passes that would get him and his team through whatever guards and sentry posts might lie along their planned escape route south.

With this purpose in mind, he walked into the lobby of the hotel, strolled up to the front desk, and left the vice president a note. It read:

Washington, D.C., 14 April 1865
Don't wish to disturb you; are you at home?
J. Wilkes, Booth

One interpretation of this note was that Booth was simply trying to determine if the vice president was home. Later, during Johnson's impeachment proceedings in 1867, some of Johnson's critics pointed to the note as evidence that the vice president was actually involved somehow in the assassination plot or, at the very least, knew about it. However, the official government inquiry into the plot found no evidence of Johnson's involvement.

Johnson never received the note anyway. The hotel clerk put it in the box of Johnson's aide, a man who also knew Booth personally. The aide assumed the note was for himself and never passed it on.

His errand completed, Booth continued walking down Pennsylvania Avenue toward the National Hotel. He needed to regroup and pick up some field glasses that he wanted to give to a fellow Confederate sympathizer named Mary Surratt, John Surratt's mother.

Booth walked into the hotel's opulent lobby around eleven in the morning.[21] The desk clerk, Henry Merrick, noticed that he looked deathly pale and very nervous. Booth would return to the hotel at least twice more, once in the late afternoon and again that evening, around six thirty, before he checked out.

★   ★   🎩   ★   ★

John Booth was different from the other members of his family.

The Booth children were by and large gentle folk who inherited their parents' dislike for slavery. With the sole exception of John Wilkes, they sided with the Union during the Civil War.

John was wild and reckless even as a young boy. His mother feared for his safety all of his life, certain that something horrible would happen to her favorite child.

After the ignominy of his parents' belated marriage on his thirteenth birthday, and the implications of his childhood illegitimacy, John became obsessed with his status as a Booth, the son of the famous actor. It was around this time when he began carving his initials into everything he could—trees, desks in school, even his own hand. He was determined to make his mark both literally and metaphorically.

In the fall of 1851, John was sent to a Quaker school in nearby Sparks, Maryland, known as the Milton School for Boys. It was the first of two boarding schools he attended. John continued to underperform in his studies at the Milton School but was athletic and very popular.

By modern standards, John Wilkes Booth was well-read. He was just not very good at writing, mathematics, and other formal subjects. Yet he was devoted to poetry, the classics, Shakespeare, and the thick adventure novels popular at the time. What's more, John began acting in plays. He found that his sharp memory was a considerable asset.

Yet there was a dark side to John Booth. Shortly after he started at the school, John had his fortune told by an old Gypsy woman living in the woods near the school. Reading his palm, she told the impressionable

IN BOOTH'S OWN WORDS

"[W]hen I was a school boy, my bosom friend was a boy three years my senior named Gorruge [Thomas Gorsuch]. He was as noble a youth as any living. He had two brothers grown to be men. And an old father who loved and was beloved by them. He was all that a man of honour should be."[22]

young man that he was destined to die young. "You'll have a fast life," the old woman told John, "short, but a grand one."

Shortly thereafter, an incident occurred that impacted John profoundly and came to change his views of black Americans. One of John's fellow students was a boy named Thomas Gorsuch. His father, Edward Gorsuch, was a respected local farmer who owned property near the Milton School. In September 1851, the farmer was involved in an incident that was a precursor to the struggles that would dominate the country for the next decade and a half.

The year before, in 1850, the U.S. Congress had passed the Fugitive Slave Act that required the citizens of non-slave-owning states to cooperate in the return of escaped slaves to their Southern masters.

The compromise legislation was widely viewed as an abomination in the North, an assault on personal conscience, since it made it a criminal offense to provide food and water to escaped slaves.

The abolitionist William H. Seward, the former governor of New York whose own home was one of the stops on the "underground railroad," denounced the fugitive slave laws and any compromises with slavery in a famous speech he delivered as a new U.S. senator.

Conceding that slavery was technically legal under the U.S. Constitution, Seward argued that there is a "higher law than the Constitution," a moral law that demanded that slavery be resisted and fought wherever it be found. Seward would eventually become Abraham Lincoln's secretary of state.

The Fugitive Slave Act passed Congress on September 18, 1850. Almost one year later, the law would be put to the test in a dramatic way that touched John Booth personally. Edward Gorsuch, the father of John's classmate, was a slave owner. Yet he thought he treated his slaves very well. He had promised to free all of his slaves when they reached the age of twenty-eight. Not surprisingly, the slaves did not think this as generous of an arrangement as Gorsuch did.

In November 1849, four of them, all men, had escaped from his farm. Almost two years later, on September 11, 1851, Gorsuch received word that the escaped slaves were living on a farm near Christiana, Pennsylvania. Emboldened by the new Fugitive Slave Act, Gorsuch obtained legal warrants for the arrest of the escaped slaves, gathered up some men, and, along with his son Dickinson and a deputy marshal, rode west from Philadelphia towards Christiana.

Unfortunately for Gorsuch, the approach of the posse was widely known. A large group of free blacks and white abolitionists were waiting for them as they advanced on the farm of William Parker, where the slaves were living. Words were exchanged. Gorsuch refused to leave without his "property." Eventually gunfire erupted and Gorsuch and his son Dickinson were both shot. Gorsuch died at the scene but Dickinson recovered.

The incident, which became known as the Christiana Riot, enflamed the country—and John Wilkes Booth. The Parker family and Gorsuch's former slaves escaped to Canada, beyond the reach of U.S. justice.

The local courts refused to indict anyone over the death of Edward Gorsuch. Northerners thought Gorsuch got what he deserved, while Southerners were outraged. The entire incident revealed that "compromises" such as the Fugitive Slave Act would satisfy no one. These were just the sorts of situations that inspired Harriet Beecher Stowe to write *Uncle Tom's Cabin* a year later. The novel dramatically illustrated the cruelty of chattel slavery in the South—and helped ignite Northern animosity towards any spread of slavery out West.

For John Wilkes Booth, who knew the Gorsuch family personally, the Christiana incident hardened his view of black slaves. He would adopt the attitude of some Southerners that slavery was actually a benefit to black Americans.

"Witness their elevation in happiness and enlightenment above their race elsewhere," Booth would later write. "I have lived among it [slavery] most of my life and have seen *less* harsh treatment from Master to Man than I have beheld in the north from father to son."[23] Moreover, Booth added, "This country was formed for the *white* not for the black man."

Although Booth could be friendly to individual black men and their children, he gradually developed increasingly racist views over the years—even ranting to Confederates about it. Eventually, Booth would see Lincoln's determination to offer citizenship to some free slaves and black Union veterans as the final straw.

Not long after the Christiana incident, in the fall of 1851, John and his younger brother Joe were shipped off to a military academy, St. Timothy's Hall, in nearby Catonsville, Maryland. The contrast with the Quaker school couldn't have been greater. Discipline was strict. The 130 boys in the school wore military uniforms, bathed in ice-cold water, and followed a rigid code of conduct that banned most of the things John loved (including firearms and drinking).

It was at St. Timothy's that John met Samuel Arnold, one of the two old friends he would later talk into joining a plot to kidnap President Lincoln. The students at the school noticed two things about John Booth that help to explain his future actions. The first was that he had a pathological hatred of kings and "tyrants," which he likely inherited from his anarchist father. The second was that he wanted to be famous.

The students liked John. He was widely considered a kind and generous boy. Yet they would later remark on how much he wanted to make a name for himself.

"He would do something that would hand his name down to posterity," wrote one classmate years later, describing John's ambition. "His name, known in history, to live forever."[24]

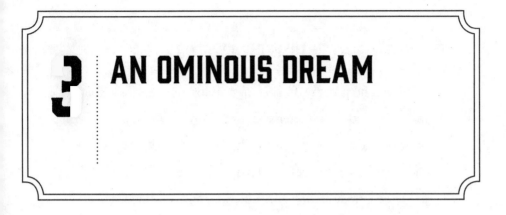

AN OMINOUS DREAM

The White House, 11:00 a.m. to 2:00 p.m.

After meeting with Senator Hale and another man, Lincoln tried to slip away to the War Department before the start of his eleven o'clock cabinet meeting.

However, two women briefly detained Lincoln in the hallway, Mrs. Hess and her sister-in-law Helen Moss. The two women had just walked over from Grover's Theatre, where they had chatted with and shook the hand of the famous actor John Wilkes Booth.

Lincoln told the women that he and Mrs. Lincoln wouldn't be attending their theatre that evening but that they would be sending their son Tad as their representative.

The women replied that they knew this already, that a messenger had arrived at Grover's before they walked over. Tactfully, the women quickly changed the subject. They asked Lincoln if he wasn't feeling happy with all the good news about the war.

"Yes, madam, for the first time since this cruel war began, I can see my way clearly," Lincoln replied with a smile.

IN THEIR OWN WORDS

"There is no great difference of opinion now, in the public mind, as to the characteristics of the President. With Mr. Stanton the case is different. They were the very opposite of each other in almost every particular, except that each possessed great ability. Mr. Lincoln gained influence over men by making them feel that it was a pleasure to serve him. He preferred yielding his own wish to gratify others, rather than to insist upon having his own way. It distressed him to disappoint others. In matters of public duty, however, he had what he wished, but in the least offensive way. Mr. Stanton never questioned his own authority to command, unless resisted. He cared nothing for the feeling of others. In fact it seemed to be pleasanter to him to disappoint than to gratify."

—*Ulysses S. Grant, Memoirs*[1]

Lincoln shook both of the women's hands. The two would later marvel that they had shaken the hands of both the president and John Wilkes Booth on the very same day.

Lincoln then made his apologies. He was determined to dash over to the War Department, located on the White House grounds.

This government department was housed in a large, three-story building with pillars outside its main entrance, located where the old Executive Office Building now stands and a short walk directly behind the White House on Seventeenth Street. Lincoln spent a lot of time in this massive building, reading the encrypted telegraphic cables sent from generals all across the front.

On this bright Friday morning, Lincoln wanted to hear what was going on with the remaining Confederate troops who had not yet surrendered, estimated to be at least ninety thousand men.

After finding out there was no news from General Tecumseh Sherman, Lincoln left the telegraph office and walked to the office of his secretary of war, the formidable Edwin M. Stanton.

Fifty-one years old, Stanton was an experienced and tough lawyer, who was born in Steubenville, Ohio. He had once tangled with Lincoln in a law case and had foolishly dismissed the Illinois lawyer as a hayseed. Now, Stanton was one of Lincoln's most trusted advisers, the man, next to

Edwin McMasters Stanton (1814–1869) was an attorney who served as secretary of war during Lincoln's administration. Like many others, Stanton declined Lincoln's invitation to join him at Ford's Theatre on April 14. *Wikimedia Commons*

Lincoln, most responsible for the day-to-day conduct of the war.

Lincoln explained to Stanton that on the previous afternoon he had invited General Grant and his wife to accompany Mary and himself to the theatre that evening. He added that Mary and he had decided on Ford's Theatre. The Grants had provisionally agreed to come, but Grant had said that if he finished his work early, he and his wife would prefer to skip the theatre altogether and return by train to Burlington, New Jersey, where their three young children were in school.

What Lincoln didn't know was that Stanton had earlier told Grant there were reports that an assassination plot against Lincoln was afoot. He asked the general to do what he could to dissuade Lincoln from attending the theatre at all.

CRITICAL MINUTES

Ulysses S. Grant, the commanding general of the United States Army, was scheduled to join Abraham Lincoln at Ford's Theatre. A battle-hardened combat veteran who was usually armed, Grant may have provided additional protection to the president—especially if he was accompanied by his military bodyguards. But at the last minute, Grant asked Lincoln if the president could do without his company that evening. His wife wanted to return home to New Jersey to see their young children over Easter weekend. Lincoln had no choice but to reluctantly agree.

Now Stanton made the same appeal directly. If the president insisted on going, the secretary added, he should have adequate security and armed guards.

"Stanton, do you know that Eckert can break a poker over his arm?" Lincoln replied with a chuckle, referring to Thomas Eckert, the superintendent of the military telegraph.

"No," Stanton said, a bit confused. "Why do you ask such a question?"

"I have seen Eckert break five pokers, one after the other, over his arm, and I am thinking he would be the kind of man to go with me this evening. May I take him?"

The secretary of war was in an awkward position.

With rumors of an assassination attempt now in the air, he wanted to do whatever it would take to keep the president in the White House. Stanton told Lincoln that he had important work for Eckert to do.

Yet Lincoln was nothing if not stubborn. He wouldn't take no for an answer. He marched back into the telegraph office and asked the iron-limbed Eckert, a tough Army officer with a thick mustache, if he would accompany him and Mrs. Lincoln to Ford's.

"Now, Major, come along," Lincoln cajoled. "Stanton insists upon having someone to protect me, but I would rather have you, Major, since I know you can break a poker over your arm."

Eckert winced. Now he was in a delicate position. The major replied haltingly that, while he was flattered by the president's kind offer, he could not accept. He had important work that simply had to be done that night.

Lincoln shook his head in disappointment. He likely surmised what was going on. Saying he would have to find a guard somewhere else, the president collected his belongings. He returned to the White House, where his eleven o'clock cabinet meeting was about to begin in his second-story office.

★   ★   🎩   ★   ★

When Lincoln strolled into his office, only three members of his cabinet were waiting for him: Gideon Welles of Connecticut, the secretary of the Navy; Hugh McCulloch of Indiana, the secretary of the treasury; and young Frederick Seward, filling in for his father, William Seward, the secretary of state, who was still at home recuperating from his serious injuries.

Stanton, whom Lincoln had just seen over at the War Department, was collecting papers that Lincoln had asked him to bring to the meeting.

After a few minutes of chitchat, the other cabinet members slowly drifted in, including the postmaster general, William Dennison of Ohio; the attorney general, James Speed of Kentucky; and the secretary of the interior, John Usher of Indiana, who had just resigned.

The mood was joyous, even giddy.

In a few minutes, at noon, the Stars and Stripes would be raised again above the battlements at Ft. Sumter in Charleston Harbor, four years to the day after they had been lowered and the Civil War begun.

Lincoln sat by the window. Through the glass he could see the still half-finished Washington Monument looming in the distance. As he had been all day, Lincoln was in a buoyant mood, overjoyed that his long ordeal was finally coming to an end.

Years later, Attorney General Speed would recall Lincoln's "cleanly-shaved face, well-brushed clothing and neatly-combed hair and whiskers"—a notable difference from his usual disheveled appearance.[2]

After a few minutes, the hero of the hour, Union general Ulysses S. Grant, strolled into the meeting to a thunderous welcome and congratulations for his decisive victory.

Grant had himself just come from the War Department. He was awaiting word that the last remaining Confederate force of any significance, General Joseph E. Johnston's army, had surrendered in North Carolina. But no news had arrived.

Grant and his wife Julia had only arrived the evening before, checking into the city's most luxurious hotel, the Willard, located just a few blocks from the White House on Pennsylvania Avenue.

When he met with Grant a few hours after his arrival, Lincoln had asked the general if he might consider joining his wife Mary on a tour of the "Grand Illumination" planned for that evening. Lincoln had a splitting headache, he explained apologetically, and Mary had been looking forward to the spectacular celebration for days. Grant agreed to accompany the First Lady in a carriage tour—yet another favor to the president for which Lincoln was grateful.

The main topic of discussion at the cabinet meeting concerned the status of the defeated Confederate political leaders. Lincoln had already made up his mind to grant broad and generous amnesty to all Confederate soldiers who put down their weapons and promised to cease hostilities. It was a policy that Grant had already put into practice.

Ulysses S. Grant (1822–1885) was the supreme commander of Union forces during the last year of the Civil War and was eventually elected eighteenth president of the United States. He was scheduled to join Lincoln at Ford's Theatre but backed out at the last minute at the urging of his wife. *Wikimedia Commons*

What was less clear was what should be done with the political leaders of the rebellion, men such as Jefferson Davis. Should they be tried for treason, as Lincoln's vice president, the Democrat Andrew Johnson, recommended?

"What terms did you make for the common soldiers?" Lincoln asked Grant.

"I told them to go back to their homes and families, and they would not be molested, if they did nothing more."

The president nodded approvingly.

"I had this strange dream again last night," Lincoln said quietly.

Lincoln had many dreams, good and bad, and he always paid attention to them.

"I seemed to be in some indescribable vessel, moving with great rapidity toward an indefinite shore. I had this dream preceding Sumter,

> **?**
>
> ## WHAT WE STILL DON'T KNOW
>
> Did Abraham Lincoln have a dream about his own
> death? U.S. marshal Ward Hill Lamon, a friend of
> Lincoln, would claim in the late 1890s that Lincoln
> told him about a dream in which he came downstairs
> in the White House and saw his own body lying in
> state. Repeated in hundreds of books, this story has
> never been confirmed by other sources and was never
> mentioned by Lincoln's wife or any of his contempo-
> raries in their later memoirs.

Bull Run, Antietam, Stone's River, Gettysburg, Vicksburg, Wilmington,
and others."

General Grant pointed out that Stone's River had actually been a
military disaster, not a victory.

Lincoln replied that the dream signaled a battle was about to be
fought, not that it would necessarily be a victory.

"Perhaps at each of these periods," young Seward ventured, "there
were possibilities of great change or disaster, and the vague feeling of
uncertainty may have led to the dim vision in sleep."

Lincoln looked at the young man, smiled, and nodded. "Perhaps that
is the explanation," he said.

Decades later, Lincoln's self-appointed bodyguard, U.S. marshal
Ward Hill Lamon, would claim that the president had described to
him a far more ominous and detailed dream. In this dream, Lincoln
had awoken in the middle of the night and walked downstairs in the
White House, only to see himself lying in state in an open casket.

Dozens of books about Lincoln over the years have repeated this
chilling story. However, no account of this dream exists among records
from 1865, including Lamon's own writings, and Mary Todd Lincoln
never mentioned such a dream.[3] Lamon's recollection of the prophetic

dream was only reported thirty years later. As a result, historians today doubt Lincoln actually reported such a dream.

The cabinet spent the next hour discussing the reopening of trade with the South and continued to debate the delicate problem of what to do about Confederate politicians who had led the rebellion.

"I hope there will be no persecution, no bloody work, after the war is over," Lincoln concluded. "No one need expect me to take part in hanging or killing those men, even the worst of them. Frighten them out of the country, open the gates, let down the bars, scare them off. Enough lives have been sacrificed."

Around this time, and unbeknownst to General Grant, his wife Julia answered the door of their room at the Willard Hotel. As she later described the encounter, a disheveled looking man had a message he said was from President Lincoln.

According to the messenger, the Lincolns would pick up the Grants at precisely eight o'clock that evening and take them to the theatre. There was a hint of command in the way the messenger delivered the message, and Julia immediately bristled.

Later, they would discover that Lincoln had sent no such message.

Julia then went downstairs to the Willard dining room to have lunch with Emma Rawlins, the wife of General John Rawlins, Grant's aide-de-camp. She saw four unpleasant, slightly menacing men sitting at a table near where the two women would have lunch. One was the same man who had delivered the message earlier—and with him, she said, was a man who looked a lot like the actor John Wilkes Booth.

★　　★　　🎩　　★　　★

The cabinet meeting broke up just after 1:30 p.m. As the other cabinet members left, General Grant lingered behind to have a private word with Lincoln.

More than anyone else, Grant was responsible for the Union victory— and Lincoln knew it. Now forty-three, Grant was famously humble for a general. This was true even though he now held the rank of lieutenant general, a rank previously reserved solely for George Washington.

Grant's everyman humility may have stemmed, at least in part, from his many business failures before the war. Grant also had a reputation for being a serious drinker—which led the teetotaler Lincoln to ask which brand of whiskey the general preferred. "If it made fighting generals like Grant," Lincoln quipped, "I should like to get some of it for distribution."[4]

The commander in chief of the Union Army was reluctant to tell Lincoln that he could not attend the theatre with him that evening. Yet it was not merely Secretary of War Stanton's fears about a possible assassination attempt that prompted this reluctance. His wife Julia desperately wanted to get back to her young children in Burlington, a small town about an hour's carriage ride from Philadelphia. She hoped to spend Easter weekend with them.

What's more, Julia disliked Mary Todd Lincoln. She found the president's wife to be haughty and imperious, occasionally downright untethered. They had had many unpleasant encounters over the years.

In fact, just the night before, when Grant left the White House with Mary Lincoln on his arm, the crowds in the street began chanting the general's name—and not that of the president. Predictably, Mary Lincoln was so offended she almost went back inside.[5] Eventually, Grant went along with Mary to see the lights around the city.

Now, as Grant walked with Lincoln down the hallway outside the president's office, he struggled to escape another evening of planned togetherness with the Lincolns.

Just then, however, a messenger arrived. The messenger handed Grant a note from Julia in which she begged once again that they leave Washington.

Julia's encounter with the strange messenger had unnerved her even more. As General Grant glanced down discreetly at the note, he abruptly explained to the president that he had promised Julia that they would leave that afternoon on the train north.

Lincoln was disappointed. He realized that the public wanted to see Grant more than they wanted to see him. Yet, as a father and husband himself, Lincoln knew he had to bow to the wishes of Grant's wife. He wished the general a good trip north.

For the rest of his life, General Grant obsessed about what would have happened had he accompanied Lincoln to the theatre as originally planned. Would he, a combat veteran, have been able to prevent what happened? Or would he have merely become a second victim?

★   ★   🎩   ★   ★

After the final cabinet meeting of Lincoln's presidency adjourned, the president returned to his office with an apple in his hand. He skipped lunch, as he often did.

The president still had a busy hour ahead of him. First he had a meeting with his vice president, Andrew Johnson, who advocated taking a hard-line stance against the defeated South. He also had a room full of official visitors waiting, including the governor and a senator from Maryland, and an old friend from Illinois, a "peace activist" named James Singleton. Although he had often criticized Lincoln's policies, Singleton was still someone Lincoln trusted. He was willing to listen to Singleton's advice and criticism.

Lincoln's vice president, Andrew Johnson, was a Southerner, a so-called War Democrat from North Carolina, who had served two terms as governor

LINCOLN IN THE MEDIA

"Had we any respect for Mr. Lincoln, official or personal, as a man, or as President elect of the United States...the final escapade by which he reached the capital would have utterly demolished it.... We do not believe the Presidency can ever be more degraded by any of his successors than it has by him, even before his inauguration."

—*Baltimore Sun*[6]

Andrew Johnson (1808–1875) was a tailor who went into politics and eventually became Lincoln's vice president, despite being a Southern Democrat, during Lincoln's second term. He succeeded Lincoln as president and became the first president to be impeached, escaping conviction by a single vote. *Wikimedia Commons*

of Tennessee. He had only become vice president a month earlier at Lincoln's second inauguration.

During the presidential campaign of 1864, Johnson had replaced Lincoln's original vice president, Hannibal Hamlin of Maine, as part of a "unity" ticket (Lincoln actually ran as the nominee of the National Union Party, not the Republican Party, for his second term).

Like Lincoln, Johnson had been born dirt-poor and had almost no formal education, working as a tailor before going into politics. Unlike Lincoln, Johnson lacked the compassion to forgive the rebels or to harbor much sympathy for newly freed black slaves. Johnson believed that the top political leaders of the Confederacy, such as Jefferson Davis, should be tried for treason and executed.

Lincoln disagreed. Lincoln's top priority was the restoration and preservation of the United States, and if that meant foregoing vengeance upon the vanquished South, so be it. Lincoln had repeatedly insisted that in this regard Johnson follow his policy and not his natural inclinations.

Yet within twenty hours, Johnson would be the seventeenth president of the United States. As president, Johnson would do everything in his power to block passage of the Fourteenth Amendment, which would grant citizenship to former slaves, and he battled with the Republican Congress over the implementation of Lincoln's plans for Reconstruction.

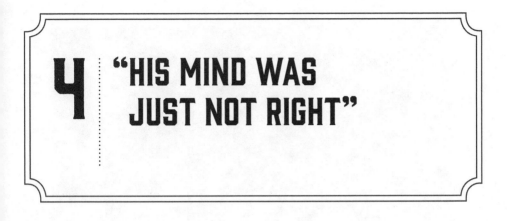

4 "HIS MIND WAS JUST NOT RIGHT"

Ford's Theatre & Environs, 12:00 p.m. to 3:30 p.m.

Booth left the National Hotel around 11:45 a.m. He headed for James Pumphrey's stable, located at 224 C Street across the street from the National Hotel, where Booth kept and rented horses.[1]

Booth announced to Pumphrey that he needed a good horse for that evening.[2] The sorrel horse he usually rented was out, but Pumphrey showed him a copper-colored bay mare, fourteen hands high, with a jet-black tail and mane and a distinctive white star on her forehead.

Booth asked for a tie rope for the horse, but Pumphrey said she didn't do well tied up and recommended that he leave the horse with a stable boy. Booth replied that would be fine.

"I am going to Grover's Theatre to write a letter," Booth said. "There is no necessity of tying her there, for there is a stable in the back part of the alley."[3] Booth asked that the horse be ready at around four or four thirty.

Booth then walked up to Ford's Theatre, likely by walking a block up Pennsylvania Avenue to Tenth Street, turning right, and then strolling two blocks north to the theatre.

Ford's Theatre was originally a Baptist church. In front is the platform from which patrons alighted from carriages, and to the immediate right of the theatre is Peter Taltavull's Star Saloon, where John Wilkes Booth had a final drink. *Wikimedia Commons*

The three-story red-brick building, built in 1833, was originally the First Baptist Church of Washington. But in 1861, the congregation moved to another location and the building, with its elaborate stage, was purchased by a shrewd, entrepreneurial theatrical producer named John Ford and eventually converted into a regular theatre. Locals called the alley behind the theatre Baptist Alley. The theatre was good-sized. It would hold 1,700 patrons that evening, who would pay between twenty-five cents and one dollar for a ticket.

Booth was going to Ford's Theatre this morning to get his mail. The theatre management allowed traveling actors to have their mail sent there.

As Booth strolled through the theatre's main entrance around noon,[4] Harry Ford, the twenty-one-year-old younger brother of the owner, couldn't resist teasing him.

"Here is a man that don't like General Lee," the young Ford called out in a loud voice to another man, Tom Raybold.

Booth's Southern political sympathies were known to all. What Ford meant was that Booth was unhappy that Lee had just surrendered.

"General Lee is a good general and I guess he knowed what he ought to do and what he wants to do," Ford said.

Booth replied that he was just as brave a man as Lee.

"Well, you have not got three stars yet to show it."[5]

As Raybold handed Booth a packet of letters, Ford announced that things were looking up at the theatre. Because of Good Friday, they had assumed they would not have much of an audience this evening. However, Ford said, a messenger had just arrived around ten thirty that morning from the White House, requesting that they reserve the box seats for the president and his guests, General and Mrs. Grant.

Booth couldn't believe what he was hearing. He had been devastated to discover that Lincoln wouldn't be at Grover's that evening. Yet now he was learning that Lincoln would attend Ford's. What's more, the president would be bringing with him none other than General Grant himself, the Union hero widely credited with winning the war. Things were suddenly looking up!

Booth picked up the plan of the house for that evening and examined it. Sure enough, boxes seven and eight, which were put together when used as the official state box for the president, were marked as taken.[6] There was a note that they were reserved for Lincoln and his guests.

Yet if Booth was excited by the news, he didn't show it.[7] His face was a blank.

Ford couldn't resist another dig.

"They've got General Lee here as a prisoner," he needled Booth. "We're going to put him in the opposite box!"

"Never!" the actor sneered back, playing along and still masking his inner excitement. "Lee would not let himself be used as the Romans used their captives, and be paraded."

Laura Keene (1826–1873) was a British actress and theatrical entrepreneur who staged the long-running play *Our American Cousin* that Lincoln attended on the last night of his life. She previously had had an affair with John Wilkes Booth's brother Edwin. Keene held the dying president's head in her lap before he was moved across the street to a boarding-house. *Wikimedia Commons*

Booth put back the plan of the house.

Ignoring Ford and Raybold, he sat down on the gallery steps and read a long letter he had been given, chuckling as he did so.[8] A woman appeared to have written it, judging from the handwriting. It may have been from Lucy Hale but could have been from any number of different women.

★   ★   ♟   ★   ★

Although he was outwardly calm, Booth's mind was certainly racing. Lincoln and Grant would both be in the presidential box at Ford's that evening. Booth's original thought had been to strike at the president, vice president, and secretary of state simultaneously. Was it possible he could also take out the Union's top general as well?

The evening's entertainment was the final performance of Laura Keene's wildly successful production of *Our American Cousin*, a popular three-act comedy by English playwright Tom Taylor which had been running on stages across the United States for more than five years.

Then thirty-nine years old, Keene, who was born in England, had had a very successful career in the United States. She is widely credited with being the country's first female stage manager and producer. Five years earlier, Keene had purchased all rights to *Our American Cousin* and had spent the intervening years performing the play at theatres all across the country, with herself as one of the stars.

Keene knew the Booth family well—too well, in fact. In 1855, Keene had toured Australia with Booth's older brother, the actor Edwin Booth, with whom she had a brief affair. The tour, though well received, was a financial disaster. In addition, Keene had never forgiven Edwin Booth for revealing to the world that Keene's supposed husband on the tour, her manager John Lutz, was merely her boyfriend and not her legal husband at all. Her real husband, Henry Wellington Taylor, from whom she was hoping to obtain a legal divorce, was a criminal who had fled to Australia.[9]

Like many male lead actors at the time, Booth knew *Our American Cousin* well. It was just the type of lowbrow farce that President Lincoln and American audiences enjoyed. The play follows the exploits of an honest but "rustic" American Yankee named Asa Trenchard, played that evening by Harry Hawk, as he travels to England to claim the family estate, Trenchard Manor, after the estate's owner disinherits his English children.

What follows is a series of improbable plot twists involving an attempt to steal the estate from the family. In the end, however, the vulgar American Asa, with his Yankee common sense and innate decency, puts everything to rights. He heroically gives up his inheritance and arranges for it to go to his dirt-poor English cousin, Mary, whom he loves and to whom he eventually proposes marriage.

★　　★　　🎩　　★　　★

As Booth finished reading his mail, the actor Harry Hawk walked by around 1:00 p.m.[10] Rehearsals for the play were still going on. Then twenty-eight years old, Hawk had just joined Laura Keene's touring company that year. Raised in Chicago, he had been acting regularly throughout the war.

"How do you do, Mr. Booth?" Hawk asked Booth politely.

"How are you, Hawk?"

Booth and Hawk got along well, although there had recently been some friction between the two male stars. Despite Booth's alleged engagement to Lucy Hale, both had recently been seeing the same call girl, nineteen-year-old Ellen "Ella" Starr, and Booth had warned Hawk to back off.[11]

Yet as he was chatting with Hawk, Booth was thinking.

Booth knew that, in the middle of the third act, following the second intermission, the character of Asa Trenchard, played by Hawk, is all alone on the stage. A moment earlier, a character called Mrs. Mountchessington urges her daughter, Augusta, played by the Southern belle Helen Truman, to use her charms to captivate the soon-to-be-rich Asa.

But then Asa/Hawk announces that he will not be the lord of Trenchard Manor after all.

"I am aware, Mr. Trenchard," Mrs. Mountchessington says haughtily, "you are not used to the manners of good society, and that, alone, will excuse the impertinence of which you have been guilty." She and daughter Augusta then storm offstage.

It's at this point that Hawk delivers what was then considered one of the funniest lines of the play. Calling to Mrs. Mountchessington offstage, Asa replies, "Don't know the manners of good society, eh? Well, I guess I know enough to turn you inside out, old gal—you sockdologizing old man-trap."

Booth knew that the line inevitably evoked explosions of wild laughter from audiences—and it was at precisely this moment that Booth could make a move. Only Hawk would be on stage at that point. The audience would be distracted, laughing at the sockdologizing line.

Assuming the play started on time at eight o'clock, Booth quickly calculated that Hawk would likely deliver the big laugh line right around 10:15 p.m. If all went well, that would be the perfect moment for a simultaneous strike. If they all moved at once, Booth and his fellow conspirators could decapitate the leadership of the U.S. government in one fell swoop.

Booth smiled. It just might work.

Despite the tension between the two men, Booth suddenly asked Hawk to join him for a drink at the Star Saloon next door.[12] His mood was improving.

Eight hours later, Booth would encounter Hawk again on the stage…only this time Booth would be holding a ten-inch double-edged dagger in his right hand.

★   ★   🎩   ★   ★

About a year after Booth began his studies at St. Timothy's, when he was only fourteen, disaster struck the Booth family.

In 1852, Junius, then fifty-six years old, went on an extended theatrical tour in California. His two older sons, Edwin and Junius Jr., had already done their best to follow in their famous father's footsteps. Edwin had had some small parts but had been forced to take a job as his father's dresser. Junius Jr., had, like his father, abandoned his wife for another woman and then moved to San Francisco, where he ran a theatre.[13] June, as he was called, wrote to his father about the opportunities in California and the old man decided to check them out in person.

By all accounts, the tour was a disaster, plagued by horrible weather and runaway inflation. Nevertheless, his two older sons wanted to remain in California. Two years later, in San Francisco, Edwin would star opposite Laura Keene and begin an affair with her—the same Laura Keene who would be on stage tonight. Edwin would go on to become the most celebrated American actor of the nineteenth century, achieving what John Wilkes wanted to achieve but never did.

As a result of his two older sons' determination to remain in California, the elder Booth decided to return back East alone. While traveling up the Mississippi River on a steamboat from New Orleans, Junius Sr.

John Wilkes Booth's mother, Mary Ann Holmes Booth (1802–1887), in an early daguerreotype likely taken in the 1850s. *Maryland Historical Society*

developed a fever from a serious abdominal infection. He died on board the boat on November 30, 1852, near Louisville, Kentucky.

Devastated, Mary Ann had to travel west, alone, to bring her husband's body back to Baltimore. It was placed in a sealed iron casket with a small window in the top so his children could see his face one last time. He was buried on December 11 in the Baltimore Cemetery.

John Wilkes Booth was only fourteen years old when his father died, leaving the family with an unfinished house in the country, considerable debts, zero income, and a famous name.

One of the first things that Mary Ann did after her husband's death was to march John down to the local Episcopal church and have him baptized a Christian.

Overnight, John Booth became the eldest Booth male in the household—a considerable burden to place on a fourteen-year-old boy. His older brothers—Junius Jr., then thirty-one, and Edwin, nineteen—were off becoming actors. Still at home were John's younger brother Joe, age twelve; Asia, seventeen; and Rosalie Ann, twenty-seven.

Their mother decided the only way the family could survive was to rent out their town house on Exeter Street in Baltimore and try their hands at being small farmers on their land in Bel Air. Unfortunately, they had neither the capital nor the practical knowledge to really succeed, although they struggled for years. The man who built their home on the farm, a rough building contractor named James J. Gifford, claimed in court that the family still owed him money for the unfinished house and tried to remove the metal tin roof as partial repayment.

However, Gifford eventually lost his lawsuit against the family and then his own home due to an inability to pay his creditors. For the rest of his life, Gifford bore a grudge against the entire Booth family. More than a decade after his dispute over the Booth family home, Gifford became the chief contractor for the rebuilding of Ford's Theatre in Washington, D.C.

Young Booth did his best to be the man of the house. He also soon demonstrated a willingness to fight for what he deemed important. Unlike his father, Booth didn't think the hired help, whether white or "colored," should eat with the family. This high-handed attitude did not go unnoticed.

When a hired farm supervisor decades his senior ignored his mother's pleas that he not work their horses so hard, and viciously insulted both her and Booth's two sisters, Booth, then just fifteen, grabbed a stick and gave the man a thorough beating. It was an act of chivalry that resulted in a court appearance and a small fine.

The result of this sudden need to defend and run the family farm meant that Booth's education, not stellar to begin with, would be far less thorough than that of his older brothers and sisters. This would

IN BOOTH'S OWN WORDS

"We had a client on the place with whom we could not agree. We had several sprees with him [and] in one he called my sister a liar. I knocked him down, which made him bleed like a butcher. We got the sheriff to put him off the place. He then warrented me and, in a couple of weeks, I have to stand trial for assault and battery, as you call it."

—*Letter to T. William O'Laughlen, August 8, 1854*[14]

haunt him for the rest of his life. To his credit, however, Booth did not really try to hide it.

Booth's spelling was atrocious. His older brothers complained that Booth, when writing love letters to various girlfriends, treated them as "living dictionaries." It was also around this time Booth took an active interest in nativist politics represented by the semi-secretive American Party movement, also known as the Know-Nothings.

The name came not from professed ignorance but because, when asked about their secret party, members would say they "knew nothing" about it. The Know-Nothings were opposed to mass immigration, especially to the flood of Irish and Catholic immigrants then pouring into America.

Booth would later have many Irish immigrant and Catholic friends, and even frequented Catholic churches enough that some historians still ask whether he was a secret convert. Yet Booth was attracted to the populist message of the American Party.

Just as he developed a prejudiced attitude toward African Americans that his parents didn't share, Booth also came to denounce "bastard subjects of other countries" whom he called "unloyal foreigners who would glory in the downfall of the Republic."[15] He said these things even though both of his parents, whom he loved dearly, were themselves foreign immigrants.

Ultimately, the attempt to run a family farm with just Booth, young Joe, and Booth's two sisters was doomed to fail. They did their best for four long years but couldn't make the farm pay.

When Booth's older brother Edwin, then twenty-two, returned from California in 1856, he took charge. He had traveled widely, run a theatre in Honolulu, and gone on tour in Australia. But now Edwin was determined to make something of himself and help his family at the same time. Edwin proposed the family rent the farm, sell what remained of their livestock, and return to their home in Baltimore where he, Edwin, would take up the family business of acting.

Booth realized that he, too, would do better in the city than out on their poverty-stricken property. Booth's childhood friends were already breaking into the acting business. Booth decided that he could do so as well.

Within six months of putting this family plan into operation, Booth managed to land a job as a working actor with the Arch Street Theatre in Philadelphia. His boyhood acquaintance, the comedian John Sleeper Clarke, arranged the job. Booth was nineteen years old, the son of America's most famous male actor, but rustic and untrained. As a result, he spent the next three years using the stage name of J. B. Wilkes so he wouldn't disgrace the Booth family name in public.

Both Edwin and his younger brother Joe also landed jobs as fledgling actors, although only Edwin stuck with it. Joe would eventually become a doctor. Soon Booth's sister Asia, who would marry John Sleeper Clarke, moved to Philadelphia along with her mother Mary Ann and sister Rose.

John Wilkes Booth worked hard at learning the acting craft. Although he lacked the education needed to pronounce many of the words he was forced to memorize, he worked at it, and very slowly the rough edges of his personality were sanded down by the nightly performances on stage.

Booth also had an abundance of physical grace and energy, and this helped tremendously. His fellow actors liked him. Booth spent the coming years traveling from one theatre company to another, learning and earning as he went, picking up instruction on the fly from veteran actors.

A big break came when he landed a job at the Marshall Theatre in Richmond, Virginia, which would soon become the capital of the new Confederacy. One of the owners of the Marshall was a young, smart, principled entrepreneur named John T. Ford. A few years later, he would launch a theatre with his own name in Washington, D.C.

Southern audiences liked John Booth's style. The feeling was mutual. Contemporary observers pointed out that Southern audiences lacked the Puritan moralism of New England cities and felt freer to indulge in the bawdy comedies then popular. They also genuinely liked actors and actresses and did not treat them as riffraff, as people did in the North.

BOOTH IN THE MEDIA

"Mr. J. Wilkes Booth is a head and shoulders above those who ordinarily attempt *Richard III,* in intellectual breadth and power of concentration. If he would husband his voice a little more in the raving parts, we think the average would be improved. But at all events he is terribly in earnest as Richard. His death scene was positively lion-hearted. All the old traditions regarding it—of fighting, standing or prostrate, returning to the charge, dealing swashing blows and dying game—he exhibits with vast force. He was called before the curtain by the general applause of the whole house."

—New York Tribune, *1862*

As a result, Booth immediately felt at home in the South. He quickly made friends. Booth spent two years at the Marshall Theatre, gradually working his way up from bit parts to more substantial roles. The newspapers began to take notice. Soon, the open secret of Booth's parentage was widely discussed.

It was around this time that Booth would appear for the first time in a production of *Our American Cousin,* the British comedy that would, five years later, attract Abraham Lincoln and his wife to the Ford Theatre.

Booth ended his first year at the Marshall Theatre in May 1859 with a "benefit" (a performance in which an actor keeps the lion's share of the proceeds from ticket sales that night) using his own name, J. Wilkes Booth. His apprenticeship was over. His career, and the bloodiest war in America's history, were about to begin at the same time.

*   *   ▐   *   *

After finishing his quick drink with Hawk, Booth walked out of the Star Saloon's main entrance, turned left onto Tenth Street, and headed south towards Pennsylvania Avenue. A plan was beginning to take shape in his mind.

On Tenth Street, Booth spotted another Ford brother, Dick Ford, who was rounding up new decorations for the night's performance. With Dick Ford were two other men, Major Thomas Donoho and John F. Coyle, editor of the *National Intelligencer* newspaper, who knew Booth well.

The *National Intelligencer* had been Washington's main newspaper since it was founded in 1813. Long considered a Whig (that is, conservative) newspaper, it supported the Union throughout the war.

But that year, Coyle, one of the paper's employees, somehow managed to buy the paper along with some investors and became the editor. Some in Washington suspected him of Confederate sympathies.[16]

After saying hello and expressing his dismay over the sudden surrender of Lee's army, Booth asked both men what they thought would happen if the top levels of the U.S. government—Lincoln and the members of his cabinet—were suddenly swept away in one fell swoop.

No doubt shocked, the major replied that it would be nothing short of an earthquake.

Coyle, however, just laughed.

"They don't make Brutuses nowadays," he said, referring to the Roman assassin who killed Julius Caesar.[17]

*   *   ▐   *   *

It was already half past one.[18] Booth said goodbye to Dick Ford and the newspaperman Coyle. He continued walking down Tenth Street past E Street and then turned left again on Pennsylvania Avenue, walking away from the White House and towards the U.S. Capitol Building.

Booth was headed to Mary Surratt's boardinghouse, located at 541 (now 604) H Street NW. It was a frequent meeting place for Booth and the dozen odd conspirators who, until just recently, had plotted to kidnap President Lincoln.

A three-story gray brick town house, built in 1843, the building still stands and looks eerily as it did in 1865. Today, the ground floor of the building houses a Chinese restaurant.

Mary Surratt was a hardworking woman of about forty-five, a devout Catholic and Confederate sympathizer, who took over her husband's tavern in the small town of Surratsville, south of Washington, when he died suddenly of a stroke in 1862. Eventually, Mary rented out the tavern to a man named John Lloyd for five hundred dollars per year

and decided to live in and run the boardinghouse in Washington, where she was involved with various underground Confederate groups. These included, at least tangentially, Booth's circle of friends. She had two sons and one daughter.

Mary's twenty-year-old son, John Surratt Jr., briefly studied to be a Catholic priest. But he quit the seminary, took on the dangerous job of working as a Confederate courier, and eventually joined Booth in his madcap plan to kidnap Lincoln.

The meeting with Mary Surratt was brief.

Booth handed her a small package containing binoculars. She agreed to deliver the package to her

Mary Surratt's boardinghouse, the three-story building on the left shown here in the 1890s, is located at 541 H Street (now 604 H St.) NW in Washington, D.C. Now a popular Chinese restaurant, it's one of the few sites from the Lincoln assassination still standing. *Wikimedia Commons* tavern in rural Maryland later that afternoon. Weeks earlier, some of Booth's co-conspirators had also stashed two carbine rifles in an upstairs cubbyhole at the tavern.

Mary Surratt delivered the package to Lloyd, the man who rented the tavern from her. According to his later testimony, she told him at the time to get the "shooting irons" ready for someone to pick up later, referring to the carbines.

A young War Department clerk who lived at the boardinghouse, Louis J. Weichmann, twenty-three and also a former Catholic seminarian, had the

Mary Elizabeth Jenkins Surratt (1823–1865) was a boardinghouse owner and Confederate sympathizer whose son, John Surratt Jr., joined John Wilkes Booth in a plot to kidnap Lincoln. *Wikimedia Commons*

afternoon off to attend Good Friday services. He had volunteered to drive Surratt down to her tavern in a buggy, a two-hour drive south.

Weichmann later testified that he saw the package Booth had left because Surratt had almost forgotten it. It was a small package about six inches square, wrapped in brown paper and tied with a string. Booth left Surratt's boardinghouse around 2:30 p.m.[19]

★　　★　　🎩　　★　　★

By his early twenties, Booth was spending most of his time in the imaginary world of the stage, pretending to be an Italian duke or an ancient Roman, while the real world of politics was becoming much more ominous. The slavery issue was tearing the country apart. Violent outbursts on both sides were becoming common. Both pro- and anti-slavery militias were taking the law into their own hands, particularly in the border territories of Kansas and Missouri.

WHAT WE STILL DON'T KNOW

Did Mary Surratt know what John Wilkes Booth's actual plans were on April 14? That afternoon, she would travel two hours south of Washington to a saloon she owned, carrying a pair of binoculars given to her earlier that day by Booth. At the saloon, Surratt allegedly told her tenant to "get the shooting irons ready" because someone would come for them later that night. Did this mean that Surratt knew what Booth had planned? Or was she merely conveying a message from Booth that he planned to retrieve his property, placed there months earlier? Surratt denied ever knowing what was in Booth's mind on the fateful day.

In July 1859, as John Booth was beginning his second year at the Marshall Theatre in Richmond, the radical white abolitionist John Brown, a granite-faced man in his late fifties with the fiery eyes of a prophet, began plotting an armed attack on slave owners. Brown's dream was to ignite a massive slave revolt across the South that would free millions of suffering black slaves from cruel bondage. Despite his violent actions and rhetoric, Brown was supported by many wealthy patrons and prominent abolitionists in the North, although few were willing, as he was, to take up arms for the cause.

Brown rented a house in rural Maryland where he planned to organize a small army of free slaves and abolitionist whites to attack the armory at Harpers Ferry, Virginia.

Despite months of organizing and lecturing, the great slave revolt that Brown envisioned never materialized. Frederick Douglass, the former slave who became an abolitionist author and speaker, was opposed to Brown's plans for both practical and moral reasons.

Brown's plan was to steal the more than 100,000 rifles housed in the armory, arm the black slaves in the area with them, and start the conflagration that slave owners had long feared—a massive slave revolt that would spread throughout the South. Brown estimated he needed about 4,500 men for the operation. He ended up with twenty-one— five blacks and sixteen whites, including three of his own sons.

The raid on the Harpers Ferry armory, which began early on the morning of October 17, 1859, went off without a hitch. The entire complex was defended by a single guard. He offered no resistance whatsoever. Brown and his men promptly cut the town's telegraph wires and rounded up a few hostages. They then seized the weap-

John Brown (1800–1859) was a radical abolitionist who advocated armed insurrection to end slavery and launched, in October 1859, an ill-fated attack on a Federal armory in Harpers Ferry, Virginia. In his sole term of military service, John Wilkes Booth volunteered to join a Virginia militia that provided security for Brown's execution two months later. *Wikimedia Commons*

ons inside the armory, sending word to local slaves that the day of liberation had come. A train that passed through town was fired upon, ironically killing a free black porter.

Unfortunately for John Brown, the local slaves did not rise up. They wanted no part of his rebellion. Within hours, small bands of local farmers were able to keep Brown and his followers pinned down in the armory until a detachment of U.S. Marines arrived the next day. The marines told Brown that their lives would be spared if they surrendered, but Brown refused to accept the offer.

"I prefer to die here," he said simply.

WHAT WERE THEY THINKING?

ALONG WITH twenty-one followers, the abolitionist John Brown led an armed attack on the lightly guarded Federal armory at Harpers Ferry, Virginia, hoping to ignite a slave uprising throughout the South. His group eventually killed four people but did not free a single slave. Even black abolitionists such as Frederick Douglass opposed Brown's violent tactics, although he was later lauded as a martyr and visionary.

Within minutes, the marines smashed down the doors of the armory. Five of Brown's men escaped, but ten were killed, including his sons Watson and Oliver. Brown and seven of his men were captured alive. Altogether, Brown's one-day assault killed four people, wounded nine, and did not free a single slave.

Although he had not personally killed anyone, John Brown was found guilty of murder, "conspiring with negroes to produce insurrection," and "treason" against the Commonwealth of Virginia. He was promptly sentenced to death by hanging. The entire world followed the case closely. The French author Victor Hugo urged that Brown be pardoned. The American writer Ralph Waldo Emerson said that Brown "will make the gallows glorious like the Cross."

The execution was set for December 2 in Charlestown, Virginia. There was widespread fear, or hope, that an army of Brown's followers would descend upon the town to rescue him. The drama transfixed the country.

Meanwhile, John Booth's second season at the Marshall Theatre had begun a month before John Brown's raid, on September 3, 1859, with the comedy *The Heir-at-Law*. The theatre kept Booth extremely busy. Yet he did have time to socialize. The young actor was warmly welcomed into the homes of Richmond's most prominent families. There he made friends with members of Richmond's many militia groups. This would lead, in turn, to perhaps the most significant event of Booth's life until his final weeks.

Militias at that time did not have the ominous associations they do today. They were primarily social clubs in which handsome young men learned military drills while also having fun at balls, campouts, target practice, dances, and similar diversions.

It was a world utterly unknown to Booth until he moved to Richmond. He was soon fascinated by Southern militia culture. He had friends who were in a unit officially known as Company A, 1st Regiment of Virginia Volunteers, but universally called simply the Richmond Grays after their sporty gray uniforms. Booth had no time to officially sign up, but he attended many of their excursions around Richmond. He was well known by members of the unit and welcome at their parties.

By November, Virginia authorities were getting nervous about John Brown's upcoming execution. Letters, many laced with death threats, poured into the governor's office. There were calls for the assassination of Virginia's leaders, threats of new raids, even warnings about possible revenge kidnappings or killings.

As a result, the governor, Henry Wise, ordered various militia units, including the Grays, to come to Charlestown to provide security. On Sunday, November 19, the Grays lined up outside the railroad station on

IN BOOTH'S OWN WORDS

"You may not agree with me. Yet thousands do. The whole South does. For John Brown was executed (yes, and justly) by his country's laws for attempting in another way, merely what these abolitionists are doing now. I saw John Brown hung. And I blessed the justice of my country's laws."[20]

CRITICAL MINUTES

On a whim, John Wilkes Booth abandoned his acting contract at the Marshall Theatre in Richmond, Virginia, and, on November 19, 1859, jumped aboard a train carrying members of the 1st Regiment of Virginia Volunteers off to guard the execution of the abolitionist John Brown. Historians believe that the two weeks Booth spent with the Virginia militia and his participation in the execution of John Brown transformed Booth, turning him into a fanatic champion of the South. Had Booth not decided to join that troop transport, he might have remained merely a well-paid celebrity actor and not become one of the most notorious assassins in history.

Broad Street in downtown Richmond, across from the Marshall Theatre. Seeing his friends lining up to do their duty, to protect their beloved Virginia from what they thought might be an imminent attack by crazed Yankee abolitionists, Booth made a sudden, impetuous decision.

"I'm off to the wars!" Booth yelled to a friend. Then, without asking permission of the theatre management, he made straight for the waiting train. When told that the train was reserved solely for men in uniform, the enthusiastic Booth offered to buy one on the spot. With his friends' encouragement and help, Booth somehow cobbled together a uniform and managed to win permission from the regiment's commanding officers.

After two train rides and a brief voyage on a steamer, the regiment arrived in Charlestown the next day, where they were treated to a hero's welcome, wined and dined by the local citizenry. Dozens of other militia units would soon flood into the small town, more than 1,200 armed men. No one was going to rescue John Brown.

Booth spent the next fourteen days living out whatever military fantasies he may have had, bunking down in an old warehouse with another militia. By all accounts, Booth made an excellent soldier, performing his assigned duties with remarkable conscientiousness. He guarded the jail where Brown was being held, stood night sentry detail, and went on patrol on the roads leading into the town.

The Commonwealth would eventually pay John Booth $64.58 for his service.[21] The fortnight Booth spent with these soldiers, participating in the execution of John Brown, would forever change him. It made him an honorary son of the South and a fervent defender of her interests.

John Brown's raid had a similar galvanizing effect on Southerners. For the first time, they understood that millions of their fellow citizens were actively hostile toward them and the "peculiar institution" of slavery. It gave them a sense of shared destiny.

Despite his involvement in John Brown's execution, Booth had a strange admiration for the fierce abolitionist—as did many of the men who put him to death. Brown was seen by many as a wild-eyed fanatic, but clearly he had the courage of his convictions. He faced death bravely, without fear.

Booth asked for permission from the sheriff to speak briefly to the prisoner and, because of his past sentry duties, received it, although no record exists of what was said between them, if anything. In Booth's eyes, Brown was a "lion," as his biographer describes it, "no coward hiding behind a New England pulpit."

On the day of John Brown's execution, December 2, 1859, John Booth's unit marched into the field where the gallows had been erected. There were dozens of units lined up that morning, and the Grays, with their smart uniforms, were given a good spot just thirty feet in front of the gallows.

Nearly a thousand men stood at attention in the cold morning air. Around eleven, a lone horse-drawn wagon brought the prisoner from the town jail. Dressed in his old black suit, unshaven, his arms tied tightly behind his back, Brown mounted the steps without a trace of hesitation or hurry.

At the top of the gallows, Brown looked out at the sea of faces, all of whom were against him. He thanked his executioner, the sheriff, for the courtesy and kindness he had extended to him during his imprisonment. It was so silent you could hear the slightest cough. The sheriff's men tied Brown's feet together, put a white hood on his head, and moved him into position on the trap door.

"I am ready," Brown told the sheriff.

But nothing happened.

The sheriff waited for the signal from the military authorities, who were still fussing about on the field. Ten minutes passed. Brown grew impatient.

"Be quick," he pleaded. Finally, at 11:15, the sheriff got the nod. He raised a hatchet and cut the rope holding the trapdoor up. John Brown dropped three feet, and then the rope jerked him upwards. He kicked and thrashed for a few seconds, then was still.

Booth's friends noticed how the young actor had suddenly grown very pale. Booth admitted he felt faint.

"I would like a good, stiff drink of whiskey," he conceded, without any false bravado. Booth would never forget John Brown.

In fact, Booth would even bring home a sliver of the old abolitionist's coffin (actually the box that contained the coffin) as a grim memento. Later, Booth would speak often of how he had "helped to hang John Brown" and made sure there was one less "trator" in the land.

When Booth got back to the Marshall Theatre on December 4, he was promptly fired by the manager. The manager was furious that one of his key repertory actors had just taken off without so much as a goodbye.

Booth's friends in the Grays, however, would not let stand such an insult to one of their own. The entire unit, the cream of Richmond's upper-class society, marched down to the theatre and demanded that Booth be given his job back. He was.

Booth finished out the rest of the season. His last night, a benefit in his honor, was on May 31, 1860, and his performances were widely praised. His two years in Richmond had taught John Booth a profession and given him a homeland, but it was time to move on to bigger things.

5 | "WE MUST BOTH BE MORE CHEERFUL IN THE FUTURE"

U.S. Navy Yard, 3:00 to 5:00 p.m.

Normally on Fridays, Lincoln opened his office to the general public. He called this the "Beggar's Opera." It was a time when ordinary citizens could state their complaints and ask for presidential pardons and favors.

The waiting rooms this afternoon were, as usual, full of supplicants. Ironically, one was a congressman from John Booth's hometown of Bel Air, Maryland, a man named Edwin Webster.

Webster was there to receive an appointment as a customs collector. But he also wanted to present Lincoln with a petition to release a captured soldier from Maryland, George S. Herron, who had served in the Confederate army. The young man was apparently afflicted with dysentery and languishing in a Union prison in Ohio. Lincoln signed an endorsement ordering Herron's release, and he was freed six days later, on April 20.

Lincoln's compassion was justly famous. He almost always pardoned those, especially young soldiers, whom others in the army or his administration had condemned to death.

"They say that I destroy discipline and am cruel to the Army when I will not let them shoot a soldier now and then," Lincoln complained one day. "But I cannot see it. If God wanted me to see it, he would let me know it, and until he does, I shall go on pardoning."[1]

Today, however, Lincoln had no time left to hear the personal appeals of those waiting to see him. He had promised his wife Mary a drive around town in their carriage, starting at three o'clock.

As a result, Lincoln spent the remaining time before the drive signing written requests for presidential pardons waiting on his desk. Many were for wounded or severely ill Confederate soldiers now suffering in filthy Union prisons.

He knew these prisoners faced a much better chance with him than with the military tribunals handling their cases. One case before him this afternoon concerned a young soldier sentenced to be shot for desertion. Lincoln scrawled on the death warrant, "Well, I think this boy can do more good above ground than under ground."[2]

After about thirty minutes, Lincoln stopped. He got up from his desk and walked over to a closet that served as his washroom. It was time to get ready for his carriage ride with Mary.

As he was washing his hands in a basin, Charles Dana, the assistant secretary of war, interrupted him.

"What's up?" Lincoln asked, drying his hands on a towel.

Dana held out a telegram from the provost marshal in Portland, Maine. Apparently, Jacob Thompson of Mississippi, a Confederate agent working in Canada, was about to board a ship to England.

Dana added that Stanton, his boss, wanted to arrest Thompson, but that given Stanton's conversation earlier in the day with the president, he wanted to see what Lincoln thought.

"I think not," Lincoln said. "When you have got an elephant by the hind leg, and he's trying to run away, it's best to let him run."

The day's business concluded, Lincoln finished getting dressed and then hurried downstairs to the doors leading outside the White House. His wife was already waiting for him in the new, shiny carriage.

★   ★   🎩   ★   ★

Lincoln's political career started slowly but gradually accelerated. He won reelection to the state legislature easily. Despite his relative youth, Lincoln had more experience than most legislators and he quickly became a leader.

It was during his time as an Illinois state legislator that Lincoln first tangled with Stephen A. Douglas, the Illinois Democratic Party leader with whom Lincoln would later engage in spirited debates over slavery.

When the legislature voted to move the state capital to the bustling town of Springfield, a town of 1,500 inhabitants, Lincoln was invited to move there and become a partner with the prominent lawyer and Whig legislator John Stuart, who had ambitions to run for higher office.

Lincoln arrived in Springfield on a borrowed horse on April 15, 1837—twenty-eight years earlier—with all of his worldly possessions in two saddlebags. He found a friend who agreed to share his room and double bed with him (a not uncommon practice on the frontier), and quickly began work as a lawyer in Stuart's law office, located at No. 4 Hoffman's Row in Springfield.

While most beginning lawyers had to struggle to find clients, Lincoln, now twenty-eight years old, had no such problem. Stuart was occupied with running for Congress, and he simply dumped his considerable caseload into Lincoln's lap.

Overnight the newly minted lawyer was busy drafting deeds and handling all sorts of complex litigation. His law practice, which typically charged about five dollars per case, required extensive travel to the various circuit courts throughout the state. This provided Lincoln ample opportunities both to learn more about his adopted state and to become better known among prospective voters. The first ten years Lincoln spent in Springfield were eventful ones, as his law practice expanded and he became more involved in Whig Party politics.

After a few false starts, Lincoln eventually found a wife when he met Mary Todd, a tempestuous, intelligent young woman from a wealthy

The first and only home that Abraham Lincoln owned is located in Springfield, Illinois, purchased by Lincoln in 1844 when he was a successful attorney. All of Lincoln's four children were born here. *Wikimedia Commons*[3]

family of slave owners in Lexington, Kentucky. From the very beginning, Lincoln's relationship with Mary Todd was difficult. She had dated Lincoln's archnemesis Stephen Douglas for a time, and Lincoln had himself called off their engagement at least once.

However, on November 4, 1842, Lincoln married Mary Todd at her married sister's home in Springfield. Later Mary Lincoln would be portrayed as a pampered aristocrat who put on airs, but in fact she worked hard and never complained about her reduced financial circumstances.

At first, the young couple lived in the upstairs of a tavern, but they soon moved to a small rented house. Two years after their wedding, Lincoln was able to buy his first and only house, a one-and-a-half story cottage with six rooms on the corner of Eighth and Jackson Streets, just a few blocks from his law office.

The handsome home, eventually surrounded by a brick-and-wood fence, was by far the fanciest home Lincoln had ever lived in. He would live there for the next twenty-three years, eventually enlarging the home to two stories with twelve rooms. Lincoln and Mary's four sons were all born in this house—Robert Todd in 1843, Edward Baker in 1846, William Wallace ("Willie") in 1850, and Thomas ("Tad") in 1853.

One son, Edward, died at age four, probably of tuberculosis. Willie later contracted a fever, probably typhoid, while Lincoln was president, and died in the White House at age eleven. The death of their two sons overwhelmed both Lincoln and his wife and most certainly contributed to Lincoln's clinical depression.

★   ★   🎩   ★   ★

As Lincoln headed downstairs from his office, he could see it was a beautiful spring afternoon. The sun was shining but it was not too hot, around seventy degrees, with a gentle wind blowing from the southwest. Mary had been looking forward to this little escape ever since Lincoln had proposed it two days earlier in a secret note he had slipped her. She had even suggested that they invite some friends along, but Lincoln demurred.

"I prefer to ride by ourselves today," he said, smiling.

"Dear husband, you startle me by your great cheerfulness. I have not seen you so happy since before Willie's death."

"And well I may feel so, Mary. I consider this day the war has come to a close."

Lincoln paused for a moment, looking at his wife thoughtfully.

"We must both be more cheerful in the future. Between the war and the loss of our darling Willie, we have both been very miserable."[4]

Lincoln's personal carriage was a dark-green open barouche model, built by Wood Brothers in 1864, with gold and white detailing and Lincoln's monogram, AL, emblazoned on both doors.[5] A group of New

Abraham Lincoln's barouche carriage was built by Wood Brothers in 1864 and presented to Lincoln as a second inauguration gift by New York businessmen. It is normally on display at the Studebaker Museum in South Bend, Indiana. *Wikimedia Commons*

York businessmen had presented it to Lincoln as a gift shortly before his second inauguration.

There were four large wheels attached to a metal chassis with a separate seat up front for the coachman. Two double seats faced each other, one in front and one in the back. A leather hood which could be pushed back for full exposure on a sunny day partially covered the back seat. One of the White House coachmen, who were always ready to carry the president wherever he wished, drove the carriage.

On this day, as on many others, an armed cavalry escort of two soldiers accompanied Lincoln on his trip. The detail was present both to guard the president from possible attack as well as to keep away his more boisterous admirers who lined the streets when he passed.

The practice of a regular military escort arose when Lincoln decided to spend his summers from June until November at Soldiers' Home, a

Lincoln spent his summers at this cottage at Soldiers' Home, a retirement home for veterans four miles northeast of the White House. Lincoln would ride his horse to and from the White House, and one night in 1864 a sniper took a shot at him near there. *Wikimedia Commons*[6]

military asylum of 225 acres built on the northern boundary of the District of Columbia. Lincoln would often ride on horseback the four miles back and forth between the cottage and the White House, often alone. The poet Walt Whitman, who lived in Washington during the war, would occasionally "exchange bows" with Lincoln as the president rode his horse about the city. Secretary of War Stanton soon decided that this was a foolhardy practice.

At one point, Soldiers' Home was only four miles from the Confederate lines.[7] Many speculated that an ambitious Confederate cavalry unit might be tempted to kidnap the president as he rode alone down lonely country roads. As a result, Stanton ordered soldiers from Company K of the 150th Pennsylvania Volunteers to be stationed at the Soldiers' Home and to accompany Lincoln on his commutes to and from the capital.

CRITICAL MINUTES

The shot that a would-be assassin leveled at Lincoln in 1864, when the president was riding back to Soldiers' Home at night from the White House, was the reason why Lincoln came to have regular bodyguards when he was out riding. The presence of these armed escorts was enough to convince Confederate spies that any attempt to kidnap Lincoln would likely fail. It may have also convinced John Wilkes Booth that the only way he could make a significant contribution to the Confederacy's survival was to kill Lincoln rather than to kidnap him, as he had originally planned.

Nevertheless, in August the year before, around eleven o'clock at night, a would-be assassin had shot Lincoln's hat off his head as he was approaching Soldiers' Home.[8] A soldier on duty at the asylum guardhouse, Private John W. Nichols, heard the shot and reported seeing a "bareheaded" Lincoln race on his horse towards the safety of the cottage. It was after this incident that Lincoln finally yielded to demands that he have bodyguards around the clock.[9]

★　★　🎩　★　★

Yet on this cool April afternoon, all was serene. The Lincoln carriage rolled silently down the now-dry streets of Washington. The coachman did his best to avoid the hundreds of bumps and potholes that lined the dirt roadways. They likely traveled east along the Mall—some witnesses thought they might have been headed toward Soldiers' Home[10]—and then drove south towards the Potomac.

"Mary, we have had a hard time of it since we came to Washington," Lincoln continued. "But the war is over, and with God's blessing we may hope for four years of peace and happiness, and then we will go back to Illinois and pass the rest of our lives in quiet."

Lincoln added that he thought they were in pretty good shape financially. One author reports that Lincoln, always careful with money and a scrupulous accountant, had managed to save $90,000 by banking most of his presidential salary,[11] which was $25,000 a year. Nevertheless, Lincoln, although fifty-six years old, assumed he would still have to work well into his sixties.

"We have laid by some money," he explained to his wife, "and during this term we will try and save up more, but I shall not have enough to support us. We will go back to Illinois, and I will open a law office at Springfield or Chicago and practice law and at least do enough to help give us a livelihood."

Lincoln was plainly thinking of his life after the presidency. He had done what he had set out to do. He had kept the country together despite the worst war in America's history. Now, he permitted himself to dream of a personal future. According to Mary, Lincoln had spoken of a desire to travel to Palestine, of all places. He also wanted to go out West, and perhaps even move to California, where so much was happening.

The Lincolns were heading out to the Navy Yard in southeast Washington, located about five miles southeast of the White House and one of the president's favorite spots. Lincoln had a keen interest in machinery and gadgets of all kinds, as well as boats and ships, and this was a place that had plenty of both. He often visited the shipyard to take cruises out on the Potomac, to inspect new weapons, and to chat with the naval officers.

It was a substantial military installation, about twenty acres in area and enclosed by a massive brick wall, with many ships at anchor or tied up at dock, including the formidable single-turret monitor USS

Montauk.[12] The yard was built along the Anacostia River just above the point where it flows into the much bigger Potomac.

We know what the Navy Yard looked like in the 1860s thanks to the arrival of the first Japanese diplomatic delegation in 1860. Members of the delegation staff took numerous photographs of the Navy Yard and its surroundings.[13] Just east of the yard, there was a long wooden bridge across the Anacostia River into Maryland that, during the Civil War, was always guarded by soldiers. It would play a small but crucial role in the events of later this evening.

The presidential carriage approached the main Navy Yard entrance at the foot of Eighth Street East. Outside a large arched gateway, two sentries in blue uniforms stood at attention. It's likely that the cavalry escort remained outside. A witness, a soldier named Thomas Hopkins, described seeing the Lincoln carriage pass through the Navy Yard entrance that afternoon and found the lack of a guard remarkable.

"The usual mounted body-guard was not in attendance," Hopkins wrote. "It was because of the absence of any guard, perhaps, that my companion and I stopped and watched them pass. The lines in the President's face had deepened and lengthened. Otherwise it was little changed. It had not hardened. Rather it had softened and mellowed as does the face of one who has come through great tribulation with faith undimmed. I turned to my companion and said: 'There is no other country in the civilized world where one may see the ruler of a great people riding on the streets with no guard or escort.'"[14]

Lincoln's coachman stopped briefly, spoke to one of the guards, and then the carriage passed under the gateway into the yard. Once the carriage stopped, the president got out.

He immediately sent for a young ensign named William Flood, the executive officer of the USS *Primrose*, which was docked waiting for repairs. Lincoln had served in the Illinois legislature with Flood's grandfather, also named William, and the president remembered the naval officer when he was just a boy.

Flood dutifully followed the president's order and soon appeared. Lincoln introduced Flood to Mary. He then asked the young man which ship he should see, which had the most "history."

"Well, Mr. President, they all got histories, more or less," the flustered midshipman replied. "But I guess you mean the *Montauk* over there. She's got the hardest hittin', and has been in the tightest spots."

"That's the one, Flood! Take me over to her."

Rattled by the sudden presidential attention and the crush of naval personnel eager to meet Lincoln, Flood escorted the president and his wife over to the battle-scarred ironside but then made his excuses and slipped away.

A Passaic-class monitor commissioned in late 1862, the *Montauk* was a small, relatively slow warship that lay low in the water but carried two large guns, 15- and 11-inch smoothbore cannons. It had seen considerable action in the war, attacking seaside Confederate forts in Georgia and South Carolina. In early 1863, the ship sank the blockade runner *Rattlesnake*, a side-paddle-wheel former passenger steamer, but was damaged by an underwater mine in Georgia's Ogeechee River.

In the late afternoon before going to Ford's Theatre, Abraham and Mary Lincoln toured the USS *Montauk* (left), a Passaic-class monitor that had seen considerable action, at the Navy Yard. *Wikimedia Commons*

? WHAT WE STILL DON'T KNOW

Were the papers found on the body of Union colonel Ulric Dahlgren, which appeared to authorize the assassination of Confederate president Jefferson Davis, authentic—or merely forgeries used to justify desperate, even illegal tactics on the part of the Confederacy? Historians differ. Some believe the papers were written by Dahlgren himself, not by his superiors. Yet recent handwriting analysis conducted by the Smithsonian Institution seems to support the view that the papers were authentic.

One of the men responsible for the *Montauk*'s success was a naval gunnery officer named John Dahlgren whom Lincoln had befriended and raised to the rank of admiral. He was famous for inventing the muzzle-loading cannon on board, nicknamed the Dahlgren gun, used throughout the U.S. Navy.

In one of the many eerie coincidences of the war, Dahlgren's son, Colonel Ulric Dahlgren, was killed a year earlier in a daring guerilla raid on the Confederate capital of Richmond. On Ulric's body Confederate soldiers found documents that appeared to order the assassination of Jefferson Davis, the president of the Confederacy. This alleged breach of the (at least implicit) rules of warfare by the Union, known as the Dahlgren Affair, may have led to an escalation of unconventional tactics and even atrocities in the final months of the war.

Those present this day when Lincoln and Mary toured the ironside were also struck by the president's good mood. "The president and wife drove down to the Navy Yard and paid our ship a visit, going all over her, accompanied by us all," wrote naval surgeon George Todd, assigned to the *Montauk*, in a letter to his brother. "Both seemed very happy, and so expressed themselves, glad that this war was over, or near its end, and then drove back to the White House."

Lincoln and Mary dawdled on board the ship, chatting with the crew. After about an hour, they returned to their carriage. They had to get back to the White House. Lincoln still had more work to do. And Mary had to get ready for a night out. They were going to the theatre.

6 | "THERE IS GOING TO BE SOME SPLENDID ACTING TONIGHT!"

Downtown Washington, 2:30 to 6:00 p.m.

From Surratt's boardinghouse on H Street, it was just five blocks south and west to Ford's Theatre. Sometime after 2:30 p.m., after leaving Surratt's boardinghouse, Booth entered Baptist Alley from F Street and walked to the stable he had rented located on the left side behind the theatre.

Two women who rented rooms in another building behind the theatre, Mary Ann Turner and Mary Jane Anderson, both saw Booth there, speaking for a long time with a woman.[1] A stagehand named John Morris, who was up in the theatre rafters at the time, saw Booth come into the theatre and walk across the stage at around this time.[2]

It's possible, although not certain, that Booth had advance preparations to make but had not been able to complete them when he had visited the theatre two hours earlier. At that time, rehearsals for the evening's performance had been in full swing. Had Booth walked up inside of the presidential box when he visited around noon, he would have been instantly noticed and perhaps challenged.

The official state box was actually two private boxes, numbers seven and eight, which were joined together whenever the president and his

91

The back of Ford's Theatre today looks much as it did when John Wilkes Booth entered and left it the afternoon and evening of April 14, 1865. The windows on the back have been covered over with bricks. *Photo by author*

guests attended the theatre. A temporary partition dividing the two boxes was removed whenever the president and his party attended. The boxes were located directly above the stage to the right as you entered the theatre. The two boxes were accessed through two sets of doors: an outer door on the right side off the first balcony—which the Ford brothers called the dress circle—that led to a short, narrow hallway; and then by two inner doors that opened up to the boxes themselves.

Booth knew this area very well. In addition to acting on this stage, he had personally sat in the box seats as an audience member at least three times that year.[3]

Rehearsals had just ended at two, shortly before Booth's meeting with Mary Surratt. But now stagehands were busy getting the state box ready. It was decorated with red upholstered walls, red carpets and, for the president's upcoming visit, bright American flags draped over the velvet-covered balconies.

Between two and three in the afternoon, a carpenter named Ned Spangler and a teenage stagehand named John "Peanut John" Burroughs began

The presidential box at Ford's Theatre, shown two days after the assassination. *Wikimedia Commons*

carrying chairs and other items up to the box, including an upholstered red rocking chair, the president's favorite. They also draped a U.S. flag on the balcony of the box openings and hung another flag on a pole at the right side of the box, closest to the stage.

Between the two boxes, at the base of the pillar dividing them, the carpenters placed a newly framed portrait of George Washington, facing out toward the stage. As they worked, the red-hot political differences among the crew members rose to the surface.

Spangler, a Southern sympathizer, exploded in rage.

"Damn the president and General Grant!" Spangler muttered.

"He's never done any harm to you," replied Peanut John.

"I don't care a damn. He ought to be cursed when he got so many men killed."[4]

These intemperate remarks, although widely shared among the Ford Theatre's crew members, would later help sentence Spangler to six years in prison.

All of this activity meant that Booth, if he did gain access to the presidential box that day, had to time his move just right so he could enter the boxes when no one was there.

Investigators would later discover that someone, long presumed but never proven to be Booth himself, had managed to carve a small niche in the plaster wall behind the outer door that led to the hallway to boxes seven and eight. Hidden behind the outer door was a three-foot-long wooden shaft, taken from a musician's stand. Booth would later use this wooden shaft to jam shut the outer door, fixing one end in the carved niche in the plaster and the other end up against the handle of the door. This presumably would give Booth the extra seconds he would need to leap onto the stage and make his getaway, were anyone to rush quickly to the president's defense from the dress circle.[5]

Investigators also later found a peephole just above the handle in the inner door, allowing someone to peek inside the presidential box at the inhabitants. There has long been a dispute about whether Booth made this or whether the hole was there already. The son of the theatre's owner, John Ford, would later claim that the hole had been drilled by theatre workers so they could peer in to see if the president needed anything.

★　★　🎩　★　★

Given the ferocity of John Wilkes Booth's loyalty to the Confederate cause, it's strange that the amount of time he actually spent in the South was not very long. Following his two-year apprenticeship in Richmond at the Marshall Theatre, Booth signed on with a Philadelphia lawyer named Matthew Canning—a theatrical manager who would accidentally shoot him in the thigh.

Canning's theatrical company kept Booth busy. They had numerous performances in Columbus, Georgia, where Booth was shot, and then later in Montgomery, Alabama. The shooting—which occurred on October 12, 1860, probably as a result of both men simply horsing around—left Booth gravely wounded and unable to perform for many weeks. The injury was a financial disaster for both men. Canning picked up Booth's expenses and Booth was unable to act or make much money.

When the company moved on to Montgomery, Alabama, Booth was only able to perform in a few plays as he was still very weak. Despite his guilt over the shooting, Canning did not renew Booth's contract, and Booth was soon out of a job. Nevertheless, he stayed in Montgomery through the month of November, playing Romeo in a benefit production of *Romeo and Juliet*, for which he received good reviews.

Events on the national stage, however, were moving quickly.

On November 6, 1860, Abraham Lincoln was elected the sixteenth president of the United States—an event that many believed made civil war inevitable. People in the South now openly spoke about secession. Politics were as heated then as they are today. Strangely, Booth during this period was both a raving political fanatic and, at the same time, opposed to the South leaving the Union.

All his life, Booth displayed the wild-eyed, fearless mania that today we associate with bipolar disorder. He could be sweet as a lamb and then, when someone said something he felt was not correct, explode in a manic rant that was disproportionate to the occasion at hand. Many people who knew Booth well thought he was slightly mad.

"I often thought that off the stage his mind was not just right," said the stunning Montgomery call girl, Louise Wooster, who was Booth's lover for a time. "I don't mean that he was insane, but there was something about him."[6]

No coward, Booth almost always said whatever was on his mind. He spoke boldly and without considering the reactions or feelings of his listeners. Later, this tendency would endanger his life when he gave voice to pro-Confederate sentiments in the North—and also when he loudly expressed pro-Union feelings in Montgomery, Alabama, after Lincoln's election.

Booth's position at this time was that both secessionists and abolitionists were extremists and that the country should, at all costs, avoid a civil war. This opinion, expressed in taverns and at parties all over the city, soon put the young actor's life in danger.

He was forced to flee Montgomery to avoid being murdered— traveling by train to Savannah, Georgia, and then taking a steamer north to New York City, where he arrived on December 9.

Now homeless, Booth was able to stay with his mother and sister in Philadelphia. Later, however, when his mother Mary Ann and sister Rose moved to New York City to live with his brother Edwin, Booth would no longer have any real home to visit. There was a fierce rivalry between

John and his elder brother Edwin, also an actor. There would also soon be strong political differences and fierce arguments.

Although not a combatant, Edwin was a strong supporter of the Union. John, for his part, after nearly three years in the South, had developed a passionate sympathy for the Confederacy.

As usual, John Booth did nothing to hide his political opinions. A five-thousand-word speech Booth wrote in late 1860 that was found years later by his brother Edwin shows that, while he was not in favor of secession, Booth hated abolitionists and blamed their "fanaticism" for the national crisis. He stated openly that the South's cause was just and insisted that slavery was a blessing, not a curse, for black slaves.

Events were moving quickly, however. The launch of Booth's acting career and the eruption of the Civil War occurred simultaneously. A year following John Brown's execution, and just a month and a half after Lincoln's election, on December 20, 1860, South Carolina became the first Southern state to declare its independence from the United States.

Over the next three months, Booth landed jobs at three theatres—the Metropolitan Theatre in Rochester, New York, beginning January 21, 1861, followed by performances in February, March, and April at the Gayety Theatre in Albany and the Portland Theatre in Portland, Maine. Now performing under the Booth family name as J. Wilkes Booth, Booth received some of the best notices of his career as he undertook roles in *Othello*, *Macbeth*, and *The Merchant of Venice* as well as some other plays.

But the political situation was worsening. In Montgomery, Jefferson Davis was inaugurated as president of the Confederate States of America on February 18, 1861. Lincoln was inaugurated three weeks later, on March 4. And on April 12, units of the new Confederate army opened fire on a Union outpost at Fort Sumter, an island fortress in the harbor of Charleston, South Carolina.

A week later, on April 19, riots erupted in Baltimore when Union troops marched through the city on their way to protect Washington, D.C., from possible attack. The long-dreaded war that Booth had thought impossible had now begun. The Baltimore riots were one of the events that further "radicalized" Booth, a proud Marylander. His natural Southern sympathies gradually turned to outright hostility against the Union cause. He spoke out boldly in Albany, declaring the rebel cause just—an opinion that was no more warmly received in the New York capital than his pro-Union, anti-war sentiments were received in Montgomery.

Yet the only combat Booth saw was on the stage. Booth's acting performances saw him wounded in some serious stage accidents, including one incident in which he accidentally stabbed himself with his own dagger.

Even off the stage, Booth was not entirely out of danger. Following a love affair with a fiery actress named Henrietta Irving, who played Juliet to Booth's Romeo at the Portland Theatre, Booth attempted to break off the relationship. The actress flew at Booth with a dagger, slashing his forehead at the hairline. She later tried to stab herself to death but failed. Booth retreated to his mother's home in Philadelphia to recuperate. There, on May 10, he celebrated his twenty-first birthday.

Given the events in Baltimore, Booth decided to return to his childhood home of Bel Air for the summer of 1861. He first stayed in the local Eagle Hotel, studied his lines for the upcoming fall season, and then joined a local militia unit sympathetic to the Confederate cause. There were skirmishes with Federal troops in the woods and many locals were facing a chilling decision: go south and join the rebels...or submit to an increasingly authoritarian Union government.

Union troops poured into the tiny hamlet of Bel Air, searching for militia members and weapons. They searched the Eagle Hotel, where Booth was staying, but let him go. After an incident in which Booth was shot at by Union troops, he decided to go stay at the family home, Tudor Hall.

Yet despite these perceived outrages and his unabashed sympathy for the South, Booth refused to join the Confederate military. This was not out of cowardice. If anything, he was too willing to fight. Rather, he had promised his mother that he would stay out of the war if it came.[7]

Booth was an accomplished horseman, a trained wrestler, and a crack shot. He would have been an asset to either side. Yet Booth's peripatetic lifestyle allowed him to avoid the draft in the North, and he never formally joined the Southern side. Booth's biographer believes that Booth knew he was the only realistic financial support for his mother, whom he sincerely loved, and that if he were killed, she would have no one to look after her.

With the Civil War now raging in earnest, Booth left Maryland and headed west for a series of acting gigs. He performed at DeBar's Theatre in St. Louis, Missouri, a border state. Like Maryland, Missouri sent men to fight on both sides of the conflict and maintained dual governments (one pro-Confederate, the other pro-Union).

Booth starred in eight or nine plays there, including *Hamlet, Macbeth,* and *Othello,* receiving rave reviews. He then began touring all around the eastern half of the country to larger and larger audiences. Booth opened in Chicago, Boston, Baltimore, and then New York City. The theatres were large, some holding as many as 2,500 patrons at a time. It was clear that Booth was becoming an enormous hit, even impressing the jaded New York critics.

Everyone remarked that he was one of the most handsome men to grace the stage. That, combined with his raw athletic energy, made up for his lack of polish. Many would say that Booth's performances, particularly of Shakespeare, were electrifying.

Booth's biographer tallied up his performances and concluded that, between October 1861 and June 1862, Booth gave 163 performances in 11 cities. He was a busy working actor. At his peak, Booth was earning close to $25,000 per year (about $400,000 in today's dollars).

★   ★   ▮   ★   ★

At 2:45 p.m., the Ford's property master Jimmy Maddox and call-boy Will Ferguson were surprised to see Booth back in the theatre, seated at the prompter's table.

Booth was talking with James Gifford, the fifty-one-year-old building contractor, who had supervised renovations of Ford's Theatre in 1863 and had built the Booth family home, Tudor Hall. With the two men were Spangler and the down-on-his-luck actor George Spear, a fifty-five-year-old alcoholic, who had worked with Booth's father and older brothers for years.

With his final preparations presumably finished in the minutes when Spangler and Peanut John were not in the state box, Booth invited the group to have a drink with him. Only Maddox and Ferguson agreed.[8]

At that time, Ford's Theatre was sandwiched between two popular saloons—both of which Booth frequented daily, sometimes several times a day, when he was in Washington. On the north side was Jim Ferguson's restaurant, the Greenback Saloon, located at 452 Tenth Street.[9] Booth ate lunch at Ferguson's most days.[10]

Ferguson was colorful character, a former soldier of fortune who strongly supported the Union. He regularly ejected from his premises anyone he didn't like or who voiced rebel sentiments. Yet for some reason, he and Booth got along. Ferguson had purchased two tickets to *Our American Cousin* for that evening with the hope of perhaps seeing the hero of the hour, General Grant.

From his seat in the audience directly opposite the president, Ferguson was looking out for Grant that evening when he saw Booth enter the presidential box—one of the few direct eyewitnesses to what happened next. He would later testify that Booth looked him directly in the eye as he fled the stage.[11]

To the south of Ford's was another establishment, the Star Saloon, owned by Scipiano Grillo[12] and run by Peter Taltavull. It was more broadminded in its opinions and tolerated the unconventional political views of Ford's actors, many of them distinctly "succesh." Booth fit right in there, too.

This was where Booth, Maddox, and Ferguson now headed. After drinking a quick glass of ale, Booth left the Star Saloon around three thirty and headed south down Tenth Street back to the stables. He had to retrieve his rented bay mare.

*   *   🎩   *   *

Booth moved quickly now. He still had a lot to do.

Around four in the afternoon, witnesses saw Booth riding his bay mare down Pennsylvania Avenue near the Willard Hotel and Brady's Gym, where he had recently begun working out. Minutes before, Booth had stopped in briefly once again at Grover's Theatre, double-checking if Mrs. Lincoln had answered the owner's invitation of the day before.

Yes, Booth was told, Mrs. Lincoln had definitely declined the offer. She was going to Ford's that evening. However, her son, young Tad Lincoln, would be at Grover's for *Aladdin! Or, The Wonderful Lamp.*

Back outside on Pennsylvania Avenue, Booth witnessed an event that no doubt steeled his resolve. He watched in horror as 440 captured Confederate soldiers[13] and eight generals[14] were marched, shackled, down the broad avenue. Thousands of Washington citizens had turned out to watch the event along the street. Captured just a week earlier, the bedraggled prisoners, worn out and humiliated, were being taken to a prison in Boston. Unusually, some people in the crowd shouted encouragement to the beaten men, showing mercy to vanquished enemies.

Booth knew some of the prisoners personally—such as John Pitt, who had gone with Booth to watch the execution of the abolitionist John Brown in 1859—although it's unlikely he recognized any of them or they him.

*   *   🎩   *   *

Although Lincoln is lionized today, during his lifetime he was often attacked as a dangerous autocrat too willing to dispense with the legal niceties in furtherance of his military agenda.

Ambivalence or open hostility towards the war was particularly strong in Maryland, where John Wilkes Booth was born and raised. A slave-owning border state that remained within the Union, Maryland's citizens bitterly disagreed about the war. The majority of its citizens did not want secession, yet they also disliked the crusading abolitionism of the Republican Party in general and Abraham Lincoln in particular.

During the 1860 election, Lincoln received only 2,294 out of a total of 92,421 Maryland votes cast—or just 2.5 percent of the total.[15] If given a choice, the people of Maryland would have wanted no part of "Mr. Lincoln's war." They had little desire to attack their neighbors and relatives to the south, and they knew that war would bring only death and destruction to their land.

As it turned out, Maryland was the site of the first bloodshed of the Civil War. Within days of the initial Confederate attack on Fr. Sumter, South Carolina, Lincoln moved quickly to defend Washington, D.C., from a presumed attack by Confederate forces. Volunteer militia units from the North flooded into Maryland on their way to defend the capital.

On April 19, 1861, a Massachusetts regiment disembarked from a train in one area of Baltimore and then had to march through the city to reach another train station miles away. As they were parading through the Baltimore streets, angry crowds of Maryland residents, who objected to what they felt was a vulgar show of force, began to pelt the soldiers with rocks. In a panic, a few of the soldiers opened fire, triggering a riot that eventually killed twelve soldiers and four civilians.

The Baltimore riot was eulogized in the lyrics of what became, and remains to this day, Maryland's official state song, which declares that "the despot's heel is on thy shore," a clear reference to Lincoln, and actually decries "Northern scum." Journalist James Ryder Randall penned the lyrics after learning that one of his close friends died in the Baltimore riot.

An open plea to his fellow Marylanders to join the Confederate cause, the poem includes the Latin motto *sic semper,* short for *sic semper tyrannis*—which means "thus always to tyrants." According to legend, the Roman aristocrat Marcus Junius Brutus uttered this declaration during the assassination of Julius Caesar in 44 BC, although historians doubt Brutus actually said the words. Nevertheless, the phrase became the official motto of the Commonwealth of Virginia and remains so to this day. In the poem, Randall writes:

> Dear Mother! burst the tyrant's chain,
> Maryland!
> Virginia should not call in vain,
> Maryland!
> She meets her sisters on the plain—
> "Sic semper!" 'tis the proud refrain
> That baffles minions back amain,
> Maryland! My Maryland!

The Booth family was intimately familiar with the assassination of Julius Caesar by Brutus. On November 14, 1864, all three Booth brothers—John Wilkes, Edwin, and Junius Brutus Booth Jr.— performed in Shakespeare's *Julius Caesar* at the Winter Garden Theatre in New York City.

The production was a fundraiser to collect money for a bronze statue of the Bard in Central Park. It was one of John Wilkes's last acting performances. John Wilkes played Mark Antony, Edwin portrayed Brutus, and Junius Jr. played Cassius.

In Shakespeare's play, Mark Antony delivers a final speech in which he praises the assassin Brutus as "the noblest Roman of them all" because he killed the tyrant Caesar for the good of the people of Rome.

"His life was gentle," Booth, as Antony, would say about the assassin Brutus, "and the elements/ So mix'd in him that Nature might stand up/ And say to all the world 'This was a man!'"[16]

In general, the Booth family avoided discussing politics amongst themselves. Although they were born and raised in Maryland, the Booth children spent much of their time in the North, performing in theatres across New England and the Atlantic seaboard. Except for John, they were supporters of the Union. The Booth parents, Junius Sr. and Mary

Ann, were both abolitionists and opposed slavery—although they weren't above occasionally "renting" slaves from their neighbors.

John Booth's hatred for Lincoln was widely shared, at least at first, by his fellow Marylanders—and not without good reason. One of the first acts of the war was the imposition of martial law on all of Maryland. The Maryland legislature had voted not to join the Confederacy, but it also voted to shut down Northern rail lines coming into the state to avoid having more troops sent into and through its territory.

As a result, a month after the riots, General Benjamin F. Butler quietly moved into Booth's hometown of Baltimore with a thousand

John Wilkes Booth (left, without mustache) as Mark Antony, Edwin Booth as Brutus, and Junius Booth Jr. as Cassius in a benefit production of Shakespeare's Julius Caesar in New York City in 1864. *Wikimedia Commons*

Federal troops, set up artillery cannons on Federal Hill, and threatened the city with destruction if the good citizens of Baltimore disobeyed his orders.

When Lincoln suspended the writ of habeas corpus, a long-standing legal principle whereby government officials must explain to a court their reasons for detaining someone, U.S. Supreme Court chief justice and native Marylander Roger B. Taney—author of the infamous *Dred Scott* decision—ruled that the Baltimore arrests were unconstitutional. "The President, under the Constitution and laws of the United States, cannot suspend the privilege of the writ of habeas corpus, nor authorize any military officer to do so," Taney wrote. Lincoln, and the mustering Union Army, simply ignored the ruling.

When Frank Key Howard, the editor of a Baltimore newspaper and grandson of the author of "The Star-Spangled Banner," criticized Lincoln for suspending the writ of habeas corpus, Secretary of State Seward simply ordered him arrested and held without trial for eighteen months. Mass arrests of other alleged Confederate sympathizers continued.

In early September, an estimated one-third of Maryland legislators were arrested en masse. Nine defiant newspapers were shut down and a dozen editors and publishers arrested and held without charges. A Maryland congressman, Henry May, was arrested. Judges and lawyers who tried to fight these actions in court were also arrested. When one judge ordered prisoners released due to lack of due process, he was himself arrested in his courtroom, beaten unconscious by Federal troops, and dragged out into the street.

The net result of these clumsy, brutal, and often unconstitutional suspensions of civil liberties was that many Marylanders who were not particularly sympathetic to the Confederate cause at the beginning of the war quickly became so. Even those who supported the Union bristled under what they saw as the heavy, authoritarian hand of the Federal government. In addition, the worst fears of the Marylanders, that the war would be fought on their land and that it would result in civilian casualties, were coming true.

In fact, some of the bloodiest battles of the Civil War were fought in Maryland. These included the Battle of Antietam on September 17, 1862, the most lethal single day of fighting in American history—including the D-Day landing during World War II. The Union suffered 12,401 casualties with 2,108 dead while the Confederates suffered 10,318 casualties with 1,546 dead.

★   ★   █   ★   ★

As the tide of war turned against the South, Booth became increasingly political and outspoken. Many Confederate sympathizers or those with anti-war sentiments were content to curse under their breaths or just make sarcastic comments. Actors especially understood that their livelihoods depended upon some discretion.

Yet Booth was different. He spoke out boldly—too boldly. Over time, Booth's many friends began to worry about his mental health. His support for the Confederacy was becoming a dangerous obsession. Friends, even those who shared his political views—such as the Ford brothers—would openly mock him when Booth began pontificating about the war. Many urged him to guard his tongue.

On the other hand, Booth was friendly with many stalwart supporters of the Union, too. The Civil War was like that. It divided families. Even Mary Todd Lincoln, the president's wife, came from a family of slave owners in Kentucky and lost half-brothers and brothers-in-law who died fighting for the Confederacy.

LINCOLN IN THE MEDIA

"The chief charge against the Administration, thundered in every key, is its despotism. It is incessantly asserted that personal liberty is destroyed, that original rights are annihilated, that we are all the cowering, shivering subjects of the bloody Emperor Abraham, who brings us all to our knees."
—Harper's Weekly, *October 15, 1864*

There were also Confederate supporters living and working peacefully in the North—including at Ford's Theatre in Washington, D.C. One of the theatre's workers, an actress named Helen Truman, had traveled north from Memphis to personally beg Lincoln for the life of her younger brother, who had been sentenced to death as a blockade runner. Lincoln, as was his practice, especially with younger soldiers, pardoned the boy—an act of mercy that made Truman a strong Lincoln supporter despite her loyalty to the South.[17]

★   ★   🎩   ★   ★

As soon as the group of Confederate prisoners passed by on Pennsylvania Avenue, Booth, atop his horse, spotted a fellow actor walking quickly toward him. His name was John Matthews. Months earlier, Booth had attempted to recruit him in the plot to kidnap President Lincoln, but Matthews had politely but firmly declined the insane offer.

Like most of Booth's friends in the theatre business, Matthews had a life and a future. In fact, Matthews was appearing that very night in *Our American Cousin* at Ford's Theatre. He played the role of the scheming accountant, Coyle, who was trying to cheat the Trenchard family out of their home. The actor, then thirty years old, lived upstairs at the Petersen's boardinghouse, across the street from Ford's Theatre.

Matthews asked Booth if he had seen the Confederate prisoners. Booth nodded yes, he had.

"Great God! I no longer have a country," Booth exclaimed with a melodramatic flourish. "This is the end of constitutional liberty in America!"

Suddenly, Booth reached down from his saddle and gripped Matthews's arm fiercely with his right hand, digging his nails into the other man's skin. Matthews could smell liquor on Booth's breath.

"I may leave town tonight, and I have a letter here that I desire to be published in the *National Intelligencer*," Booth told the startled actor. "Please attend to it for me unless I see you before ten o'clock tomorrow; in that case I will attend to it myself."[18]

Booth reached into his pocket and took out a sealed envelope containing a manifesto he had written earlier and handed it down to Matthews.

Given his difficulty in writing, and how many different places he had been that day, it is not known precisely when or where Booth actually wrote this document. He may have written the bulk of it over several previous days and only finished it during breaks at the National Hotel or at Grover's Theatre. It obviously took some time to draft. The lengthy essay outlined, in considerable detail, Booth's motives for what he was about to do.

Later that night, Matthews read the document. He is the only one besides Booth to have ever read it. Terrified that he would be implicated in the horrible events that had just taken place, Matthews broke his promise to Booth. He burned the pages in his room at Petersen's boardinghouse while the president was dying downstairs.

Twenty years later, Matthews would claim he was able to recreate much of the document from memory. However, his recreated version is virtually identical to an earlier (and later published) document Booth had written in November 1864, and left with his sister Asia, when his plan had been merely to kidnap Lincoln.

The reconstructed text alluded directly to the recent dramatic change in Booth's plans:

To The Editors of the National Intelligencer
Washington, D.C., April 14, 1865
    To My Countrymen: For years I have devoted my time, my energies and every dollar I possessed to the furtherance of an object. I have been baffled and disappointed. The hour has come when I must change my plan. Many, I know—the vulgar herd—will blame me for what I am about to do, but posterity, I am sure, will justify me. Right or wrong, God judge me, not man. Be my motive good or bad, of one thing I am sure, the lasting condemnation of the North. I love peace more than life.[19]

The rambling manifesto continued on for many pages.

Booth argued that the Civil War had been a war against the Constitution itself, and he proclaimed that he had always believed that the South was in the right.

"In a foreign war, I too could say, 'country, right or wrong,'" Booth wrote. "But in a struggle such as ours (where the brother tries to pierce the brother's heart) for God's sake choose the right."

He went on to say that the United States "was formed for the white, not for the black man," and argued that African slavery was "one of the greatest blessings, both for themselves and us, that God ever bestowed upon a favored nation."

He added that "Lincoln's policy is only preparing the way for their [black slaves'] total annihilation," and he denied that the South had been fighting for the continuation of slavery. Booth made it clear in the document that he believed the United States was "approaching her threatened doom" and that therefore he believed he had to act.

"Heartsick and disappointed, I turn from the path which I have been following into a bolder and more perilous one," he wrote, referring to his decision to shoot Lincoln rather than to kidnap him. "Without malice I make the change. I have nothing in my heart except a sense of duty to my choice. If the South is to be aided it must be done quickly."

Finally, Booth compared himself directly to his chosen role model, the man after whom his own father had been named, the Roman assassin Brutus who struck down the tyrant Julius Caesar. "When Caesar had conquered the enemies of Rome and the power that was his menaced the liberties of the people, Brutus arose and slew him," Booth wrote. "The stroke of his dagger was guided by his love of Rome."

Booth then signed the letter with Brutus's final words in Shakespeare's *Julius Caesar*: "He who loves his country better than gold or life. John W. Booth."[20] In a final act of cunning, Booth added the names of his few remaining co-conspirators to the tract: Lewis Powell, David Herold, and George Atzerodt.

Matthews promised he would do as Booth asked, placing the letter in the pocket of his own coat. Just then, however, Matthews glanced up. He told Booth that he believed that the carriage of General Grant himself had just passed by.

It was true! The general and his wife were racing to catch the late afternoon train to Baltimore, with the carriage top down to make room for their luggage. Having successfully declined Lincoln's offer to attend Ford's Theatre that evening, the general and his wife were heading home to New Jersey to see their young children.

"Goodbye," Booth said to his old friend, whom he had known since childhood. "Perhaps I'll see you again."

Booth then galloped off in pursuit of Grant's carriage.

In the lingering mud of Pennsylvania Avenue, Booth raced twenty yards past General Grant's carriage before he abruptly turned his horse around and proceeded to canter slowly back towards them.

Riding past the carriage, Booth, a maniacal look in his eyes, glared at the Union general widely celebrated for winning the Civil War. Inside, the general sat with his wife, Julia, and two friends. Booth's glares did not go unnoticed.[22]

Booth had a good reason to be upset. He now knew that the Grants would *not* be attending Ford's Theatre, as advertised. He likely feared that Lincoln, too, might not show up. Once again, one of his carefully constructed plots might be foiled at the last minute.

★　　★　　▮　　★　　★

Booth's maniacal hatred for Lincoln had only grown more intense as the war dragged on. The reason was clear: by 1864, it was not going well for the Confederacy.

Lincoln's decision to issue the Emancipation Proclamation on January 1, 1863—a historic presidential executive order that freed an estimated three million black slaves in the ten remaining rebel states of the Confederacy (but *not* in the border states remaining part of the Union)—heightened fears among supporters of the Confederacy that Lincoln was attempting to ignite a slave rebellion or outright race war.

Like many in the South, Booth saw the Emancipation Proclamation not as an act of liberation but as a cynical attack on the Confederacy's civilian population—and therefore a violation of the rules of "civilized" warfare.[23] Lincoln's call in the order for former slaves to avoid violence "except in self-defense" was interpreted by the Confederacy as a veiled call to rebellion from within. And from this point onwards, the war took

IN THEIR OWN WORDS

"I was at late luncheon with Mrs. Rawlins and her little girl
and my Jesse when these men came in [to the Willard Hotel
restaurant] and sat opposite us.... [O]ne, a dark, pale
man...seemed very intent on what we and the children
were saying. I thought he was crazy.... Afterwards, as
General Grant and I rode to the [train] depot, this same
dark, pale man rode past us in a sweeping gallop on a dark
horse—black, I think. He rode twenty yards ahead of us,
wheeled and returned, and as he passed us both, going and
returning, he thrust his face quite near the General's and
glared in a disagreeable manner."

—The Personal Memoirs of Julia Dent Grant *(Mrs. Ulysses S. Grant)*[21]

a more sinister turn. Atrocities began to occur on both sides. Black Union
soldiers captured by the Confederacy were sometimes summarily executed on the spot.

Lincoln responded to such atrocities by threatening to do the same to
captured Confederate officers, stating that "for every [Black] soldier of the
United States killed in violation of the laws of war, a rebel soldier shall be
executed"—a threat that appears never to have been carried out.[24]

However, the final straw for Booth and other Confederacy sympathizers was the series of events that became known as the Kilpatrick-
Dahlgren Raid in early 1864.

News reports began to reach the North of poor living conditions
suffered by captured Union soldiers, including tales of severe malnutri-
tion and even beatings by camp guards. One report even claimed that

President Lincoln's own brother-in-law—Captain David Todd, a Confederate warden—had slashed a prisoner's leg with his sabre merely because he was a Yankee.[25]

As a result of these reports, a series of daring raids was planned to rescue a large contingent of thirteen thousand Union soldiers being held in a camp near the Confederate capital of Richmond, Virginia. However, the raids may not have been simply rescue attempts but may have had an additional purpose.

Union military leaders called off the first raid, which was set to occur on February 6, 1864, when it became clear that Confederate intelligence agents had learned of the raid and rebel forces were preparing to meet it. A second raid was attempted in March, led by Brigadier General Judson Kilpatrick, commander of the Third Division of the Cavalry Corps, Army of the Potomac, and a young colonel, just twenty-one years old, named Ulric Dahlgren.

The plan was for Kilpatrick's main force of three thousand cavalrymen to attack Richmond directly from the northwest and then Dahlgren, with five hundred men, to slip into the city from the south and free the Union prisoners held at Belle Island prison.

Unfortunately, the raid was a disaster. After encountering fierce resistance, Kilpatrick aborted his attack from the northwest and Dahlgren fell into an ambush. The young colonel was shot dead by a Confederate marksman. On his body, recovered later, Confederate soldiers discovered written orders that would cause a sensation nationwide—and stir both the Confederacy and John Wilkes Booth to concoct a plot in retaliation.

The papers seemed to indicate that Dahlgren's men were to "destroy" the city of Richmond—burn the city. Written in Dahlgren's own handwriting, the papers summarized the unit's orders as being: "The [rescued] men must keep together and well in hand, and once in the city it must be destroyed and Jeff Davis and cabinet killed."

News of the secret orders spread quickly. Confederate officials photographed the captured documents and disseminated them to newspapers. They immediately caused a sensation. Whether or not the direct

The discovery on the body of Colonel Ulric Dahlgren of papers that seemed to authorize the assassination of Confederate president Jefferson Davis sparked outrage throughout the Confederacy. *Wikimedia Commons*

targeting of Davis and his cabinet was legal under the accepted rules of warfare, the apparent intention to burn down the city, thus directly harming the civilian population, was not.

Union generals immediately disavowed any knowledge of the raid. Some tried to pin the scandal on the dead Dahlgren, claiming it was a rogue operation. No one in the South believed that. Historians today differ. Many believe the documents were genuine but that Lincoln himself did not know about the raid. But that doesn't matter.

In retaliation for the perceived threat, the Confederacy began to plan "black flag" operations of its own—that is, unconventional warfare tactics that would today be classified as acts of terrorism or war crimes. For example, one plan involved biological warfare—an attempt by Confederate agents to deliberately infect civilian populations in the North with yellow fever, a highly contagious, often fatal disease, by distributing clothing from infected victims in Northern cities.

This part of the plot was apparently carried out by a Kentucky physician, Luke Blackburn, operating as a Confederate agent in Canada. Following an epidemic of yellow fever in Bermuda, Blackburn traveled to the island, offered his services as a physician, and then shipped back to Canada crates containing the soiled bedding and clothing of victims.

After the Dahlgren raid, Booth decided to get actively involved in the war effort—even though it meant breaking his promise to his mother to remain neutral.

Also, an event occurred in New Orleans that shook Booth to the core. Exhausted and still recovering from a bout of bronchitis, Booth had traveled down the Mississippi for an engagement on March 14, 1864, at the St. Charles Theatre in Union-occupied New Orleans. The city had been captured by Union forces early in the war, and the effects of the occupation were apparent. Booth was shocked by what he saw.

"I have never been upon a battlefield, but, O my country, could you all but see the reality or effects of this horrid war, as I have seen them, I know you would think like me," he wrote to friends a few months later. "And would pray the Almighty to create in the northern mind a sense of right and justice (even should it possess no seasoning of mercy), and that he would dry up this sea of blood between us—which is daily growing wider."[26] These sentiments burst forth from the impassioned actor's soul at a dinner at the home of Thomas Davey, manager of the St. Charles, as Booth denounced Lincoln and called the Union soldiers "all manner of evil names."

Unfortunately for Booth, a Union soldier and fervent patriot happened to be present at the dinner. His name was First Sergeant James Peacock of the Eighth Regiment, Indiana Volunteer Infantry. The combat veteran exploded in fury upon hearing Booth's words. He called the actor a "cowardly dog" who plainly didn't have the courage of his loud convictions.

"If Booth had one spark of manhood in him," the Union soldier bellowed in fury, "he would be in the Confederate ranks with a gun on his shoulder."

Booth, no coward, and possessed of a fiery temper of his own, reached for a pistol in his pocket. But the soldier was too quick for him, snatching a carving knife off of the dining room table and promising to "eviscerate" Booth if he made another move. Fortunately for all present, Davey and his wife, Lizzie, took advantage of the standoff to spring between the two combatants and calm them down before blood was shed.[27]

Whether this incident hardened Booth's resolve to become an active participant in his country's greatest crisis, or whether this resolve was already present, it's difficult to say. But it's clear that around this time Booth had made a fateful decision. "For four years I have lived (I may say) a slave in the north (a favored slave it's true, but not less hateful to me on that account)," he would later write in a letter to his mother.

"Not daring to express my thoughts, even in my own home. Constantly hearing every principle dear to my heart denounced as treasonable. And knowing the vile and savage acts committed on my countrymen their wives & helpless children, I have cursed my willful idleness. And begun to deem myself a coward and to despise my own existence. For four years I have borne it mostly for your dear sake. And for you alone have I also struggled to fight off this desire to be gone."[28]

Booth's mother read this letter days after the assassination. It was confiscated by Federal authorities and only rediscovered in 1977.[29] The letter revealed that Booth had decided he could remain a spectator no longer. He now had no choice but to take action.

7 | "MR. LINCOLN, ARE YOU GOING TO THE THEATRE WITH ME OR NOT?"

The White House, 6:00 to 8:00 p.m.

The short ride back to the White House was as relaxing as the ride out. The Lincolns were in great spirits when the dark green carriage, now splattered with mud, pulled into the White House grounds around five o'clock.[1]

Two dignitaries had been waiting for them: the recently elected governor of Illinois, Richard Oglesby; and General Isham Haynie, also of Springfield. They were walking away from the White House towards the Treasury Building as the Lincolns got out of the carriage.

"Come back, boys!" the president bellowed across the White House lawn. "Come back!"

Smiling, the men returned to the White House entrance. Lincoln invited them upstairs to the main White House reception area, where they spoke at length.

Richard Oglesby, then only thirty-eight, was one of Abraham Lincoln's best friends. They were both born in Kentucky and both moved to Illinois, dirt poor, and became lawyers. Oglesby had served in the

Clara Hamilton Harris (1834–1883) was an American socialite. She and her fiancé, Major Henry Rathbone, accompanied Abraham Lincoln and his wife to Ford's Theatre. *Wikimedia Commons*

Mexican–American War and as a major general under Grant in the Civil War, and became both Illinois's governor and its U.S. senator. As portly as Lincoln was thin, Oglesby was also responsible for marketing Lincoln as a "railsplitter" during the 1860 Republican Convention, shrewdly realizing that Lincoln's backwoods roots could be a political advantage rather than a liability.

After a time, Lincoln got out one of his humor books, David Ross Locke's *The Nasby Papers,* and began to recite some of his favorite passages out loud to his guests, chuckling as he did so. The book was low satire about a hypocritical country parson, Petroleum V. Nasby, the putative author. Lincoln offended some of his more pious visitors with the book's ribald mocking of pretentious preachers.

Reading funny passages from books like these was one of the president's favorite pastimes. On this occasion, Lincoln was enjoying himself so much that he ignored several summonses to dinner from the White House staff. Finally, around six o'clock, Lincoln could delay no longer. He bid farewell to his Illinois comrades.

Lincoln rejoined Mary in the downstairs dining area for a brief supper that lasted no more than half an hour. Robert did not join them. He was resting in his room. Young Tad had already left for Grover's Theatre and the play *Aladdin.*

Over dinner, Mary discussed with her husband the young couple who had agreed to join them at Ford's, Clara Harris and her fiancé Major Henry Rathbone.

Then thirty years old, a cultured and self-assured woman, Clara Harris was a Washington socialite, the daughter of U.S. senator Ira Harris of New York. Harris's mother had died when she was only eleven and her senator father had married Pauline Rathbone, the widow of a wealthy New York merchant who had two living sons, Jared Jr. and Henry.

Clara and her stepbrother Henry were thus raised in the same household. They had become formally engaged at the start of the war when Henry, three years her junior, had joined the Union Army.

Major Henry Reed Rathbone (1837–1911), a combat veteran, was badly wounded as he fought John Wilkes Booth in the presidential box. *Wikimedia Commons*

Despite the somewhat unusual relationship, the presidential couple had been friends with young Clara and her beau for some time.

With receding, wavy red hair, sporting the then-fashionable muttonchops whiskers, Rathbone served as a captain during the Battles of Antietam and Fredericksburg and had been promoted to major.[2]

Mary told her husband that the plan for the evening was for them to pick up Clara and Henry at the Harris residence on H Street near Fourteenth, just a few blocks from the White House.

Around six thirty, Mary got ready to leave for the theatre while Lincoln sandwiched in another last batch of meetings. He saw his good friend Noah Brooks, an old acquaintance from Illinois who was now the Washington correspondent for the *Sacramento Union*. He asked the reporter Brooks if he would like to go to Ford's Theatre with him to see *Our American Cousin*, but Brooks explained that he had a bad head cold and really didn't feel up to a night out. Lincoln replied that Mary had just found another couple to replace General Grant and his wife.

The bodyguard on duty at this time was a young man named William H. Crook, twenty-six, a former soldier who now served as a member of the Washington Metropolitan Police. Crook had been on duty since eight o'clock that morning. He was supposed to have been relieved by another bodyguard at four o'clock, John Parker, but, according to Crook, Parker was late.

According to Crook's later account, Lincoln decided to make one last visit to the War Department to check on the status of Sherman's advance. During that quick visit, Crook said, Lincoln spoke of the rumors that an assassination attempt was being planned. However, historians now view Crook's story, written forty years after the events he described, with skepticism if not outright disbelief.[3]

"Crook, do you know I believe there are men who want to take my life?" Lincoln supposedly asked.

When Crook expressed doubt, Lincoln said that other men had been assassinated. He also expressed the belief that if a determined killer was willing to give his own life in the attempt, "it would be impossible to prevent it."[4]

Crook would later write that he tried to talk Lincoln out of going to the theatre for security reasons. Lincoln replied that he had to go. With the war hero Grant not attending, all the people who came to the theatre would be very disappointed if neither of them showed up, the president said.

As Parker had still not shown up yet, Crook volunteered to stay with Lincoln on his ride to the theatre, but Lincoln said no—he had been on duty long enough. Standing at the portico of the White House after walking back from the War Department, Lincoln supposedly said, "Goodbye, Crook." Later, the bodyguard would recall that Lincoln normally said "Good night," and that this was the first and only time he had said goodbye.

$\star$ $\star$ $\blacksquare$ $\star$ $\star$

In 1843, after having served four two-year terms in the Illinois legislature, Lincoln ran for Congress—and lost. Ironically, given his genuinely impoverished background, his opponents portrayed him as an aristocratic snob due to his marriage to Mary Todd and connections with the wealthier citizens of Springfield.

But the young lawyer did not give up easily. Abraham Lincoln was always an ambitious, confident man, despite his lifelong bouts of depression, and he knew he was destined for higher office.

He got his first taste in 1846, at the age of thirty-seven, when he ran for, and won, a single term as a U.S. congressman from Illinois. The first photograph ever taken of Lincoln, a daguerreotype made shortly after his election, shows a serious, smooth-faced man with large ears and neatly combed hair peering intently at the camera, his eyes clear and strong.

The Lincoln family—Abe, his wife Mary, and their two young sons—moved to Washington, D.C., shortly before Christmas in 1847, for the thirtieth U.S. Congress. In his brief two-year stint in Congress, during which he and his wife and sons lived in a boardinghouse, Lincoln worked hard and hewed closely to Whig principles.

Whether Lincoln made a last trip to the War Department or not, his workday was not yet over. Sometime after seven o'clock, he was back upstairs in his office. He signed some papers and met with William Kellogg, chief justice of the Nebraska Territory, and young Robert Fraser, a friend of his son Tad who worked at Grover's Theatre.

A photograph taken of Abraham Lincoln in 1846. He was a thirty-seven-year-old up-and-coming lawyer and had just bought his first and only house in Springfield, Illinois. *Wikimedia Commons*

LINCOLN IN THE MEDIA

Fake news isn't a new phenomenon.

During the bitter presidential campaign of 1864, a pair of New York journalists sought to spread the false story that Abraham Lincoln planned a nationwide program of inter-marriage between poor whites and freed black slaves.

Republicans had no such plans. Instead, they merely said that marriage was a private matter. But Lincoln's opponents wanted to prevent his reelection at any cost.

"Lincoln is a worse tyrant and more inhuman butcher than has existed since the days of Nero," the Wisconsin newspaper editor Marcus M. Pomeroy fumed. "The man who votes for Lincoln now is a traitor and murderer.... And if he is elected to misgovern for another four years, we trust some bold hand will pierce his heart with dagger point for the public good."

Some Democratic politicians announced that Republicans had a secret plan to solve America's notorious racial problems through an ambitious campaign of interracial marriage that would result in a new American "super-race."

Their proof: a pamphlet entitled *Miscegenation: A Theory of the Blending of the American White Man and Negro.*

Supposedly written by a Republican, the pamphlet called on Republicans to make intermarriage between whites and blacks one of the central planks of Lincoln's reelection platform.

The pro-slavery Democrat Representative Samuel Cox of Ohio waved the pamphlet on the floor of the House, claiming he had dozens of letters from abolitionist Republicans supporting the pamphlet's program of aggressive intermarriage.

There was only one problem. The pamphlet was a fake.

The campaign behind the pamphlet—both its widespread publication and articles written denouncing it—was a journalistic hoax.

In an early example of journalists attempting to use fake news to influence a presidential election, two New York journalists in 1864 penned a pamphlet that pretended to be a Republican plan for interracial eugenics and the creation of an American super-race. The hoax was eventually exposed. *Library of Congress*[5]

Sold at newsstands for twenty-five cents, the seventy-two-page pamphlet was actually written by two journalists working for the *New York World,* a pro-slavery newspaper that supported the Democrats.

One of the journalists was David Goodman Croly, thirty-two, the managing editor and father of the cofounder of *The New Republic*. The other journalist was a regular reporter named George Wakeman.

Abolitionists and Republicans had been frenetic pamphle-teers before and during the Civil War, and the two journalists cleverly fashioned a pamphlet that sounded like something Republicans might write.

They even created the new term "miscegenation," which sounded vaguely scientific. In the past, writers spoke of "amal-gamation" between races. "If any fact is well established in his-tory, it is that the miscegenetic or mixed races are much superior, mentally, physically and morally, to those pure and unmixed," the pamphlet asserted, in a deliberate effort to rile up readers.

Thanks to the internet of the day—the telegraph—the hoax spread like wildfire across the country. Soon, Lincoln's opponents were calling Lincoln's Emancipation Proclama-tion the "Miscegenation Proclamation."

Lincoln had been smart enough to simply ignore the whole controversy, likely sensing it was all a setup. Shortly thereafter, victories on the battlefield in 1864 secured Lin-coln's reelection.

As for Croly and Wakeman, their hoax was eventually exposed.

Ironically, it was a pro-Southern newspaper, *The London Morning Herald*, that revealed the truth on November 1, 1864, with the headline, "The Great Hoax of the Day."

The British newspaper's U.S. correspondents reported that the miscegenation pamphlet had really been written by two New York journalists "who wanted to trick the Republicans into making damaging admissions that would hurt them with the voters."

Two weeks later, the *New York World* itself confirmed that the miscegenation story was indeed a hoax—neglecting to mention that its own managing editor and a *World* reporter had perpetrated it.

At seven thirty, just a half hour before *Our American Cousin* was to begin, Lincoln met again with House Speaker Colfax in his office. They chatted once more about the big trip out West—a trip that Lincoln very much wanted to emulate.

Just before eight o'clock, Mary Todd Lincoln appeared in the office doorway. She was wearing a black-and-white-striped silk dress and a matching bonnet. Over her dress, Mary also wore a black velvet, floor-length cloak that tied at the neck.[6]

"Well, Mr. Lincoln, are you going to the theatre with me or not?"

According to later accounts, Mary actually had a severe headache that evening and was only going to the play because she knew her husband had been looking forward to it. *Our American Cousin* was just the sort of lowbrow farce the weary president enjoyed.

"I suppose I shall *have* to go, Colfax," Lincoln said in reply, turning to the Speaker.

Lincoln gathered up his famous top hat and coat, both of which, stained with blood, still exist.

The silk hat, made by the hatmaker J. Y. Davis, had a three-inch black mourning band around it, which Lincoln wore in memory of his beloved son Willie. The president's Brooks Brothers wool coat, a gift for his second inauguration, had the design of an eagle sewn into the lining. In the eagle's beak was a banner that held the words, "One Country, One Destiny."

Before going downstairs, Lincoln walked over to his son Robert's room.

"We are going to the theatre, Bob," Lincoln announced. "Don't you want to go?"

The young Army captain politely but firmly begged off. He was, he said, exhausted from his recent military exploits, even though he had not really seen combat in person. He told his father he just wanted to get some sleep.

"All right, my boy. Do just what you feel most like. Good night."

"Good night, Father."

That was the last time Robert ever spoke to his father.

A final visitor appeared just as Lincoln was walking Colfax down the elaborate stairway of the White House. His name was George Ashmun, a sixty-one-year-old Massachusetts lawyer who had presided over the 1860 Republican Convention that had nominated Lincoln as the party's presidential candidate. He was waiting to see Lincoln in the Red Room downstairs. Ashmun was there on behalf of a client who had a claim on some cotton production.

As they walked together into the Red Room, Colfax again mentioned that people up north were very worried when they heard Lincoln had recently visited Richmond. They were worried that an angry Southerner might shoot him.

Lincoln shrugged off the concern.

"I would have been alarmed myself if any other man had been President and gone there, but I, myself, did not feel any danger whatever," he said.

As he said goodbye, Lincoln asked Colfax for the second time and Ashmun for the first if either of them would like to accompany him and Mary to the theatre, but both the Speaker and Ashmun, like everyone else that day, begged off. The Speaker was leaving for his big trip the following morning, he explained, and a night at the theatre was not a good idea. Ashmun had a previous engagement.

For some reason, the Lincolns couldn't pay people to go with them to the theatre that evening. In the end, Mary and the president invited that day no fewer than *fifteen*[7] people to accompany them who declined. Only young Clara Harris and Major Rathbone said yes.

Lincoln and Ashmun found Mary Lincoln waiting for the president just inside the main doorway where their carriage was standing ready. As he helped Mary up into the carriage, the White House doorman informed the president that two more visitors, Senator William Steward of Nevada and his former law partner, Judge Niles Searles, were waiting to see him upstairs.

Lincoln paused and dashed off a note to the two men, explaining that he was off to the theatre with his wife and inviting them to return the next morning. He also wrote a quick note, his final piece of writing besides his autograph, for Ashmun to return at nine. Ashmun wanted to bring a friend to see Lincoln, Judge Charles Daly of New York.

Just as Lincoln was stepping into the carriage, Steward and Searles appeared outside, as did another supplicant, Congressman Isaac Arnold, a friend. Lincoln quickly shook hands with Steward and Searles, apologizing and repeating what he had said in his note, and told Arnold the same thing, that he simply had to leave for the theatre.

The Lincolns' trusted household servant, Charles Forbes, was holding Lincoln's long black overcoat. A thirty-year-old Irish American with long muttonchop whiskers who looked older than he was, Forbes functioned as Lincoln's personal assistant and occasional babysitter for young Tad.

As Forbes helped Lincoln put on his coat, Forbes said, "Mr. President, Tad gave me a photograph this afternoon, and I wish you would put your name on it."

"Certainly, Charlie," Lincoln replied. He scrawled his name on the photograph.[8]

At long last, Lincoln swung into the carriage seat next to his wife, and the door to the carriage was slammed shut.

It was past eight o'clock, and the play had already begun. The evening had turned suddenly cold and damp, and rain seemed likely.

Lincoln's driver, Ned Francis Burke, also Irish-born, sat up ahead of them in the driver's seat with Forbes next to him. He wore a stovepipe hat and a long gray coat to keep out the cold.

There was no security detail on the trip. The two-man cavalry escort that had accompanied the presidential carriage to the Navy Yard was nowhere to be seen. Despite the protestations of his staff, Lincoln had himself forbidden the practice of having an armed military escort whenever he went to the theatre. However, he had agreed to the presence of less conspicuous bodyguards.

There were four police bodyguards assigned to protect the president. The one on duty this night was a Washington Police detective named John Parker who had gone ahead of the carriage separately to Ford's Theatre.

Parker, then thirty-five, was a poor choice for presidential bodyguard. He had a fondness for the bottle and had been reprimanded numerous times for being drunk and visiting brothels while on duty. Assigned to guard the presidential box at the theatre, Parker was not at his post when John Wilkes Booth appeared outside the president's door. He was last seen next door at the saloon, drinking with Forbes and Burke.[9] Parker would eventually be charged with dereliction of duty for his conduct, yet remained on the force for three more years and even continued to function as a White House bodyguard for months afterwards. In 1868, he was finally dismissed for sleeping while on duty, thus disappearing from history.

8 PREPARING FOR THE PERFORMANCE OF A LIFETIME

Ford's Theatre, National Hotel, 4:30 to 9:00 p.m.

A fter rushing at General Grant's carriage and unnerving its occupants, Booth continued down Pennsylvania Avenue back to Tenth Street and then headed north again. It was now four thirty or so.

Booth raced up the street and stopped right in front of Jim Ferguson's Greenback Saloon, the restaurant next door to Ford's Theatre where he often ate lunch. There, Booth bragged to Ferguson about his feisty new horse. "She can gallop and can almost kick me in the back," Booth said, before he raced off.[1]

Witnesses would later testify seeing Booth repeatedly riding this horse in and out of the alleyway behind Ford's Theatre around this time, practicing, investigators would later surmise, his escape route. A black maid, who lived in a building behind the theatre, noticed Booth galloping out of the alley and thought it strange when she saw him do it twice in a row.

Booth finally dismounted behind the theatre, where two theatre employees, Jim Maddox and Ned Spangler, came out to speak with him.[2] Another theatre hand and Spangler took the reins from Booth and began to remove the saddle from his horse, but Booth told them to leave it. He told the men that the horse was a "bad little bitch" before leading her

IN BOOTH'S OWN WORDS

"I know how foolish I shall be deemed, for undertaking such a step as this."

—*November 1864*[3]

into the stable stall behind the theatre that he rented.

After locking the stall, Booth took the men back over to the Star Saloon for yet another drink. He had been drinking all day.

When Booth walked into the lobby of the National Hotel a short while later, Merrick noticed he looked worn out.

The desk clerk asked him if he had made a thousand dollars that day.

"No, but I have worked hard enough to have made ten times that amount," Booth replied under his breath.

Once again, Booth began writing. It appears he was penning letters to a number of people.

At one point, Booth asked Merrick what year it was. "Is it 1864 or 1865?" he asked.[4]

"Surely you are joking, John," the desk clerk blurted out. "You certainly know what year it is."

"Sincerely I do not," Booth replied.[5]

On the evening of April 14, Booth placed his chosen weapon into his pocket: a .44-caliber single-shot derringer made by Henry Deringer of Philadelphia, only 5.87 inches long and weighing just 8 ounces. *Wikimedia Commons*

? **WHAT WE STILL DON'T KNOW**
Did John Wilkes Booth meet with Mary Surratt one
final time on the night of April 14, after she returned
from Surrattsville around 8:30 p.m.?

Booth continued writing furiously and then, when he finished, slid the pages into an envelope and dropped a letter in the hotel's mailbox.

Booth asked a colleague of Merrick's, a man named George Bunker, if he planned on attending Ford's Theatre that night. "You ought to go," he told Bunker. "There is going to be some splendid acting tonight!"[6]

Booth returned to his room and changed for the evening. He chose a dark business suit, boots and spurs, and a quilted slouch hat.

In his pocket, Booth placed his carefully chosen weapon: a large-bore, .44-caliber single-shot derringer with a curved walnut stock. It was very small and lightweight—just 5.87 inches in length—fitting easily in the palm of Booth's hand. Yet it was a deadly weapon, capable of blowing a hole through a man's body at close range.

Booth knew that if the gun misfired he wouldn't have time to reload.

As a result, he also carried a backup weapon, a 10-inch Manson Sheffield double-edged dagger with a horn handle and the words "America" and "Liberty" engraved on the blade.

★   ★   🎩   ★   ★

The incident in New Orleans in which a Union soldier had questioned both Booth's courage as well as his dedication to the Southern cause had had a profound effect on the egotistical actor.

From that time on, it appears, Booth began to brood about what he could do for the war effort. He began to have informal contacts with members of the Confederate secret service, perhaps in New Orleans and Boston, definitely later in Montreal.[7]

Booth met Michael O'Laughlen in Balti-more when he was seven and O'Laughlen only five. The actor talked his old friend into joining his madcap plot to kidnap Abraham Lincoln. *Wikimedia Commons*

Booth had talked long enough, both on and off the stage. The time for action had come.

As a result, in August 1864, Booth invited two of his oldest and closest friends to visit him at the Barnum's City Hotel in Balti-more. One was Michael O'Laughlen, then twenty-four years old, the other Samuel Arnold, twenty-nine. Booth knew them both from childhood, but they did not know each other—even though both had served in the same Confederate unit, the 1st Maryland Volunteer Infantry.[8]

Booth and O'Laughlen had been friends almost their entire lives. They had met sometime around 1845 when Booth's father, Junius Sr., had purchased a modest townhome on Exeter Street, near Fayette, in Baltimore. At the time, Booth was around seven, O'Laughlen five.

As for Arnold, Booth had met him as a student at St. Timothy's Hall and hadn't seen him since. Arnold was a big, well-built man with gray eyes, even more robust than Booth. He had sided with the Confederacy when the war broke out, serving briefly with the Maryland Volunteer Infantry and then, later, as a civilian clerk. He had returned home to Maryland only that February 1864, to care for his sick mother.

After a long period of drinking, smoking cigars, and reminiscing about their past together, the three men got down to discussing the war. They focused on the plight of captured Confederate prisoners. In the earlier stages of the war, prisoner exchanges had been common. How-ever, the Union soon found itself facing again on the battlefield the same soldiers it had just recently released.

As a result, General Grant ordered that all prisoner exchanges cease. At that point, the Union held some sixty-six thousand Confederate soldiers in various military prisoner-of-war camps across the country. The conditions were harsh, with meagre food, little medical care, and rampant disease.[9]

In addition, the Confederacy desperately needed these soldiers if it were to have any hope of surviving. General Robert E. Lee had already attempted to break out some fifteen thousand prisoner soldiers held at Point Lookout Prison in southern Maryland, to no avail.

John Wilkes Booth met Samuel Arnold when they were students together at St. Timothy's Hall, a Maryland boarding school both attended as teenagers. Booth recruited Arnold into a plot to kidnap Lincoln. *Wikimedia Commons*

And then Booth made an announcement to his two friends that would astound and enthrall them. He insisted that he had an idea that might make prisoner exchanges possible again—in fact, it would virtually guarantee them. Rather than the Confederate Army attempting difficult and dangerous breakout efforts, there was a much simpler way.

Booth proposed that they—he, O'Laughlen, Arnold, and a few more Southern patriots—simply *kidnap* Lincoln, "convey him to Richmond, turn him over to the Confederate States government, to be held as a hostage for the exchange of prisoners."

Booth smiled. O'Laughlen and Arnold just stared. They were speechless. It was an insane, audacious plan—and historians debate to this day where Booth got the idea for it. Was he given the idea by Confederate

IN BOOTH'S OWN WORDS

"Our cause being almost
lost, something decisive
& great must be done."

—*Booth's diary, April 17, 1865*[10]

secret agents he met in Boston and in Canada? There is some evidence that the Confederacy was already making kidnap plans on its own, following the Kilpatrick-Dahlgren Raid. Did Booth know about these plans...or was his an independent plot?

As a habitué of Washington, D.C., and someone who moved in the same general social circles as the president, Booth claimed that a kidnap plan was far more realistic than his old friends might think. The actor argued that Lincoln was surprisingly unguarded. Booth knew from personal experience as an actor at Ford's Theatre that the president would frequently slip into his private box at the theatre—sometimes with, sometimes without Mrs. Lincoln—accompanied by only a friend or an official.

Booth added that on Lincoln's regular trips to his summer cottage at Soldiers' Home, the government-run hospital for disabled soldiers just north of Washington, the president rode in a carriage or on his own horse, usually with one or two soldiers accompanying him but occasionally alone. Lincoln's route north along Seventh Street took him through isolated stretches of farmland where the fifty-six-year-old president could be easily waylaid, bound and gagged, bundled into a carriage, and then ferried across the Potomac, Booth said.[11] From there, it would be an easy ride straight to Richmond and into the waiting arms of Confederate forces!

Alternatively, they could kidnap Lincoln on one of his visits to wounded soldiers at St. Elizabeth's Hospital in Washington, as on these trips he was usually joined only by his driver, Booth said. On this latter point, Booth exaggerated. In fact, Lincoln often traveled with a full military escort of thirty or more armed cavalrymen.[12]

Unbeknownst to Booth, just a week after his meeting with his old friends, a would-be assassin would take a pot shot at Lincoln as he rode alone along Seventh Street at dusk, shooting his famous stovepipe hat off

WHAT WERE THEY THINKING?

JOHN WILKES BOOTH'S PLAN to kidnap the president of the United States may seem insane today, but military planners in the Confederacy also considered a similar plot. However, when a seasoned intelligence agent came to Washington to study the plausibility of kidnapping the president, he decided the plan had little hope for success. Despite appearances, Lincoln was too well-guarded. Nevertheless, Booth was at first able to attract dozens of people who expressed interest in participating in his scheme. Yet as it became clear that the Union would win the war and prisoner exchanges began again, the original purpose of the plot, to free Confederate soldiers in exchange for Lincoln, became moot. In the end, Booth was left with only a tiny handful of co-conspirators, all impoverished, desperate men who, with one exception, lacked the resolve to take action.

his head—an incident that resulted in Lincoln's never again being able to ride without an armed military escort.[13]

However, Booth was adamant that the plan could succeed—and his enthusiasm was contagious. He told his two boyhood friends that he would personally finance the entire plot himself. To prove to them that he could afford it, Booth showed the two men his diary with different entries for his acting fees. Arnold, nearly destitute himself, later estimated that Booth made between $25,000 and $30,000 a year—almost $400,000 in today's terms.

The problem they faced, Booth added, was not money but time. The Confederacy was running out of it. The presidential election was only a few months away, in November. It would be better if Lincoln could be snatched before then.

As a result, the three men made a solemn pact: they would undertake the dangerous mission of kidnapping the president of the United States. Booth told his friends that it would take him about a month to wind up his business affairs. He would then return to Baltimore and, together, they would set everything in motion.

★   ★   🎩   ★   ★

However, there were numerous unexpected delays. Booth moved into his older brother Edwin's house in New York City, where his mother now lived, and promptly contracted a bad case of erysipelas, a streptococcal infection that, in an era before antibiotics, could be fatal. For three weeks, Booth was in bed, delirious. As he gradually recovered, he and his brothers inevitably talked politics.

Edwin refused to take John Wilkes's political opinions seriously— and this, naturally, only enraged the hotheaded young man all the more. In the end, the political arguments became so heated that Edwin kicked John Wilkes out of the family home he had helped to buy.

Soon it was October. After packing up his theatre gear in trunks— costumes, swords, and fifty-six volumes of scripts—Booth traveled to Montreal by train. At this time, Montreal was a kind of Switzerland in the Civil War—neutral territory crawling with spies, smugglers, escaped prisoners from both camps, and blockade runners. Booth checked into the Confederacy-friendly St. Lawrence Hall, a hotel where dozens of Southern refugees and Confederate agents made their home.

He was only in Montreal for nine days, but he was busy. Booth arranged to have his trunks shipped to Richmond via Nassau, Bahamas, to circumvent the Union blockade. Booth then set about arranging his financial affairs for a future escape, opening up a Canadian bank account and arranging for a bill of exchange, a kind of nineteenth-century traveler's check, that could be redeemed virtually anywhere.[14]

Finally, Booth made contact with well-known Confederate agents. These included Patrick Martin, a notorious blockade runner; the St. Lawrence Hall owner Henry Hogan; and George Sanders, a professional provocateur who once plotted to assassinate Napoleon III.

By the time Booth left Montreal on October 29, he had the names of Confederate agents on the way to Richmond including two Catholic physicians from Maryland, Dr. William Queen and Dr. Samuel A. Mudd. Both of the doctors loathed abolitionists in general and Lincoln in particular. Mudd was later found guilty of being a knowing accomplice of Booth, a charge he firmly denied. Through Mudd, Booth would later be introduced to other Confederate agents operating in Maryland, Thomas Harbin and John H. Surratt.[15]

*   *   🎩   *   *

The presidential election of 1864 was held on November 8. Until the weeks just prior, Lincoln's reelection had been very much in doubt.

The war, more horrible and bloody than anyone could have imagined, was dragging on with no end in sight. In addition, the radical abolitionists in Lincoln's own Republican Party thought slavery was not ending quickly enough. The loyal but anti-war Democrats in the North, known by the nickname "Copperheads" and led by a former Union general, George B. McClellan, campaigned for immediate peace negotiations and an end to the slaughter. They called themselves "Peace Democrats."

It was quite possible that Lincoln could have been defeated, and with him any hope of maintaining the United States as it had been.

But then, in September, the Union general William Tecumseh Sherman, in a series of brilliant and bloody tactical maneuvers, managed to capture the city of Atlanta, giving the North a big boost in morale. Sherman's "March to the Sea," from Atlanta to the Carolinas, left a swath of destruction American soldiers would not see again until World War I.

By early November, in the face of Union victories on the battlefield, Lincoln was winning newspaper endorsements all across the country

Union general William Tecumseh Sherman's capture of Atlanta helped win Lincoln's reelection in November 1864. *Wikimedia Commons*

amid calls to "stay the course." Booth's brother Edwin proudly voted for Lincoln. "I voted (for Lincoln) t' other day—the first vote I ever cast," Edwin wrote to his friend Emma Cary, "and I suppose I am now an American citizen all over, as I have ever been in my heart."

There is no evidence if or how John Wilkes voted, but when he found out that his older brother had voted for Lincoln, he declared Lincoln would soon be made "king" of America—a sentiment widely shared in the South.

When the ballots were counted, Lincoln and his vice president, the former Democrat Senator Andrew Johnson of Tennessee, won 2.2 million votes against the Democrats' 1.8 million. In the electoral college they won 212 of 233 electoral votes, with the Democrats carrying only the three states of Delaware, New Jersey, and Kentucky. It was a landslide reelection, one that gave little hope to those wishing for a negotiated peace.

Following the election, Booth traveled from Washington to Bryantown, a small town in Maryland, to make the acquaintance of the Confederate contacts he was given in Montreal. However, he was shocked by how much the atmosphere had changed. Although Maryland had remained in the Union, there was once strong sympathy for the Confederacy. But that sympathy was largely gone now, as his old friend Samuel Arnold had discovered.

Just two weeks earlier, the state's legislators had adopted a new constitution that voluntarily abolished slavery without providing any compensation to slave owners. What was even worse, Lincoln now had strong support in the Old Line State, receiving 55 percent of the total vote in the recent election compared to just 3 percent in 1860.[16]

The parts of the state where sympathy for the Confederacy remained were the southern counties, particularly in the Catholic enclave of Charles County. Booth would return to this area again and again over the coming months, attending Mass with Dr. Queen at St. Mary's Church, near Bryantown, and with Dr. Mudd.

Planning for the kidnapping would proceed in earnest now that Booth had a realistic escape route available to him via the contacts the blockade-running doctors would provide. But first, he had one last family commitment to honor.

Despite his earlier banishment, Booth returned to the Booth household in New York City in mid-November to appear in the lavish production of Shakespeare's *Julius Caesar* with both of his brothers, Edwin and June.

The production, twice postponed, was a benefit to raise money for a massive statue of the Bard in Central Park, a statue that still stands today. The play would be performed on November 25 at the Winter Garden Theatre, where Booth's brother Edwin was a manager together with Edwin's brother-in-law John Sleeper Clarke and friend William Stuart.

The play was widely advertised. The "three sons of the famous Junius Booth" under one roof and in one play were a substantial draw. Tickets sold for as much as five dollars apiece, an outrageous sum, and yet the show sold out.[17] Scalpers would eventually be able to charge many times the price of admission for a single seat.

When it came time for John Wilkes Booth, playing the Roman Mark Antony, to deliver his funeral oration over the body of the slain Caesar, some audience members would later swear they heard John Wilkes ad-lib the famous words, "Sic semper tyrannis," the motto of Virginia.

Incredibly, John also took the opportunity to tickle, as a prank, the actor who was playing the dead Caesar—showing the gentle, playful side that would perplex historians for generations. When the play was over, the three Booth brothers received standing ovations, with the *New York Times* noting that John Wilkes possessed a fire that "electrifies the audience."[18]

By mid-December, Booth had returned to Charles County where he would again meet with the Catholic doctors and attend Mass. Dr. Mudd introduced Booth to Thomas Harbin, a Confederate secret agent and courier, who had recently engaged in a daring gunfight with Union soldiers and somehow managed to escape.[19]

Booth told Harbin his plans. He explained that he didn't need any help with the kidnapping itself, only with the considerable task of transporting the president through Union lines in Maryland and south to Richmond.

Harbin reluctantly agreed to help. Both Harbin and Mudd had mixed feelings about this self-proclaimed Confederate patriot. They both found Booth a bit manic, perhaps slightly crazy, and an obvious drinker. To a professional spy like Harbin, this was not a good combination. Yet Booth's plan was too good for a Confederate loyalist to pass up.

In Washington, two days before Christmas, Mudd introduced Booth to another Confederate courier, John H. Surratt, a twenty-year-old former Catholic seminarian, and planning began in earnest. John's mother, Mary Surratt, a widow, owned both a tavern and small farm in Prince George's County and a town house in Washington that opened its doors to boarders.

Unlike Booth, John Surratt knew rural Maryland backwards and forwards. He would be an invaluable guide who could navigate the dirt roads even at night. After much hesitation and suspicion on both sides, Booth confided his plan to Surratt. Surratt thought it a crazy undertaking but also conceded that it might actually work. Young Surratt knew, like Booth, that only with an event such as this—kidnapping Lincoln— could the Confederacy have any chance of surviving the war. Surratt agreed to join the conspiracy.

At this point, the plan was to waylay Lincoln at Ford's Theatre in Washington, where he was a frequent attendee and where the security was minimal. They planned to use chloroform to keep Lincoln unconscious and for the conspirators to dress in Union uniforms to get by military checkpoints.[20]

★   ★   🎩   ★   ★

Heartened by his success in gaining some initial supporters, Booth now set about recruiting more people for his ambitious plan. He approached quite a few Confederate sympathizers, but many were terrified even to hear about Booth's plans.

Booth needed people inside at Ford's for the "abduction team." Yet even though many of the stagehands and actors at Ford's were notorious rebels, at least in spirit, he had little success finding anyone willing to help.

As a result, Booth returned to his home county of Harford, where he was well known, and openly talked to local farmers about his plan. Many were receptive but few agreed to take an active role. Booth faced the same reaction in New York City. He approached an actor friend and drinking buddy, Sam Chester, who worked with his brother at the Winter Garden Theatre, asking outright if he would help cut the gaslights at Ford's Theatre, plunging the place in darkness.

It would be, Booth said, an enormously lucrative assignment. The actor, horrified, flat out refused—as he would do many times again over the coming months. Unlike Booth, many of these men had families and futures, and they knew both would be placed in jeopardy by any plot against the president.

However, Booth was getting desperate. "I have facts in my possession that will ruin you for life," he snarled at the actor, adding the threat that he carried a pistol "to shoot every one that betrays us."[21]

In January 1865, Booth returned to Washington, staying, as he usually did, at the National Hotel. He met frequently with O'Laughlen, Arnold, and young Surratt, and began spending money on the plot in earnest.

He purchased a buggy and weapons, managing, with Surratt's help, to smuggle the guns one by one into the capital. Surratt also took an active role in the plot. He negotiated for $250 the purchase of a flat-bottomed boat that could carry fifteen men, to be hidden at King's Creek, a waterway that fed into the Potomac River. He sought two more just like it to be placed at fixed points along the Potomac.

With the help of serious-minded Confederate agents such as Harbin, the kidnapping plot grew from a small group of four or five men into a much larger conspiracy. The plan was for the "abduction team" to bundle Lincoln into a carriage and then, as fast as possible, race to one of the boat-launching points, changing horses if necessary along the way for greater speed.

To get across the Potomac, the group needed an experienced river smuggler. The Potomac is a wide and fairly deep river that extends four hundred miles from its headwaters in the Allegheny Mountains near Fairfax Stone, West Virginia, east and south to the Chesapeake Bay, where it widens to a distance of eleven miles across. Given that the Potomac passed through the Confederate heartland of Virginia, it was constantly patrolled by heavily armed Union gunboats.

Surratt and Harbin found the river smuggler they needed in the person of George A. Atzerodt, a good-natured German immigrant, then thirty years old, who came to America from Thuringia when he was only eight. He worked as a blockade runner and smuggled goods in both directions. Strong, muscular, not very bright, and a bit scary-looking, with long hair and a black goatee, Atzerodt was one of the few early conspirators who stayed with Booth until the very end.

Harbin also recruited Charles Yates, another skilled boatman, and Benjamin B. Arnold of King George County, Virginia. A Confederate courier, Arnold agreed to take Lincoln to the rebel capital of Richmond once the boat crew managed to cross the river. Harbin also talked his brother-in-law, Thomas A. Jones, who assisted the Confederate couriers, into helping out if needed. He would eventually hide Booth and get him across state lines into Virginia.

Clearly, there may have been some truth to Booth's boast, recalled by the contemporary journalist George Townsend, who knew Booth

CRITICAL MINUTES

Witnesses claimed to have seen John Wilkes Booth meet with his secret fiancée, Lucy Hale, both on the morning and late afternoon of April 14. If one or both of the meetings did occur, they would have been a moment of decision for the conflicted actor: Did he keep his promise to marry the young woman and return to his life of fame and fortune as an actor, as he had told his mother he wanted...or did he stay on the path he had set himself, a path that would certainly lead to infamy, exile, and perhaps even death? In the end, Booth's desire to make a name for himself, to "live in history" as he once put it, was too great. He chose infamy.

personally, that "a party of fifty or a hundred" were involved in the kidnapping plot.[22]

★   ★   🎩   ★   ★

Booth must have looked around room 228 one last time. He left quite a few items behind, including a letter from a woman begging him to give up his crazy plan.

At around 6:30 p.m., Booth was back downstairs in the lobby, drinking tea and preparing to check out.[23] Witnesses reported seeing him with Lucy Hale and her mother at the time.[24] Before he left the hotel forever at seven, however, Booth pounded on the hotel bar for a brandy, plainly agitated.

"Make it snappy!" he barked, uncharacteristically.[25]

It's not known where Booth was for the next forty-five minutes or so. He may have had a last-minute meeting with his fellow conspirators.

? **WHAT WE STILL DON'T KNOW**
When was the final meeting between Booth and his three co-conspirators held at Herndon House—at 8:00 p.m. on April 14? Or at the same time the night before, April 13?

Booth's biographer Terry Alford and historian Edward Steers Jr. both believe that Booth held a last-minute meeting at 8:00 p.m. at Herndon House, the hotel where Lewis Powell had been staying.[26]

However, Alford admits that the Herndon House landlady, Martha Murray, later testified under oath that Powell checked out of the hotel at 4:00 p.m. on April 14, making it difficult but not impossible to see how the final meeting was held there.[27]

Both Powell and Atzerodt later claimed that the final "briefing" to kill Lincoln, Johnson, and Seward was held at an 8:00 p.m. meeting at this hotel.[28] An alternative hypothesis is that the final planning meeting was indeed held at Herndon House but on the evening before, Thursday, April 13.

In any event, by nine on Friday Booth may have been sitting in Mary Surratt's parlor, waiting for her to return from her meeting with her tenant John Lloyd in Surrattsville. Booth may have wanted her report on the presence of military guards on the roads south. Witnesses later would testify that they *heard,* but did not see, Booth speaking briefly with Surratt upon her return. If he did meet Surratt at her home, he left quickly, after only a brief meeting.[29]

9 | A CHANGE IN PLANS

Washington, D.C., late March 1865

In March 1865, with the main pieces of the kidnapping plan in place, Booth and his associates began following the president closely to learn his routines and whereabouts. They quickly discovered that there were occasions, despite the increased security, when the president's carriage moved about with only Lincoln and a guest or two inside.

Yet inexplicably, Booth decided that it would be easier to snatch Lincoln while he attended a play, surrounded by hundreds of people, than to waylay him on an isolated road when he might have an armed escort. And it was true: Lincoln usually had a single bodyguard when attending the theatre and not the more formidable cavalry escort that followed him when he was moving about the city in his carriage.

Also, Booth became fascinated by the idea of cutting off the gaslights in a theatre, plunging the building into total darkness. In the ensuing chaos, he believed, the so-called "abduction team" could then easily subdue Lincoln, drug him if necessary, and carry him out to a waiting carriage. The kidnappers would vanish before the theatre lights were restored.

In reality, the plot to kidnap Lincoln constituted a series of missed opportunities, botched plans, delays, and amateur mistakes. John Wilkes Booth was a self-absorbed actor with dreams of fame and glory, not an experienced field agent. Although an expert shot and horseman, he had no military training except for the two weeks he spent with the Richmond Grays. What's more, Booth lacked the most basic information any real kidnapping scheme would require, such as the location and daily schedule of the target.

For example, the first attempt at kidnapping the president was set for January 18, 1865, at Ford's Theatre. That was when the actor Edwin Forrest would perform in the play *Jack Cade*. Forrest was considered the greatest living American actor since the death of Booth's own father, Junius Sr.

Booth was certain that Lincoln would show up for this performance, one of Forrest's most famous. As a result, he and the kidnapping team got ready. Booth repeatedly inspected the escape route through southern Maryland, stopping at Mary Surratt's tavern along the Brandywine Road in what is now Clinton, Maryland. He also visited Dr. Mudd's home and made friends with Mudd's parish priest, Fr. Peter Lenaghan.

Yet on January 18, nothing happened. The play went on as scheduled. For many different reasons, the plot didn't go forward. For one thing, on that day there were torrential rains, making the roads virtually impassable. In addition, it appears Lincoln didn't actually attend the performance but may have gone to the National Theatre instead. In any event, no one did anything. Booth quickly left Washington for New York City, discouraged.

Having already spent nearly $4,000 of his own money on the plot—nearly $100,000 in today's money—Booth was now short on funds. He told associates that he was considering abandoning the whole thing. Also, Booth now had a new distraction: Lucy Hale, the twenty-four-year-old daughter of Senator John Hale. Despite the fact that Lucy, like all her family, was a dedicated abolitionist, Booth was smitten. Lucy Hale complicated matters for Booth. By all accounts, Booth's ardor was shared by the young woman.

Yet as the war dragged on, the ill feeling on both political sides increased markedly. At the end of February 1865, a swashbuckling Confederate secret agent named John Yates Beall was arrested. He was a notorious privateer who raided Union ships on the Great Lakes and on the Chesapeake Bay. Recently, Beall had been engaged in a plot to free Confederate prisoners by derailing a passenger train carrying them to a new location.

The military tribunal that tried Beall sentenced him to death for being a spy and a saboteur. However, a sizable portion of the public urged clemency, including eighty-five members of the Union House of Representatives. Booth had met Beall briefly years earlier at the hanging of John Brown and admired his recent exploits. As for Lincoln, although he was known for his frequent acts of clemency, in Beall's case the president deferred judgment to the head of the military tribunal who tried Beall, General John Dix. Dix ignored all pleas for mercy.

Beall was promptly hanged by the neck on February 24 in a particularly gruesome way, yanked upwards by a spring-activated machine of some kind. His last words were recorded: "I die in the service and defense of my country."[1]

Booth was very upset by Beall's execution. He had joined those petitioning for clemency and, when news of the execution reached everyone at the National Hotel, Booth had some sort of mental breakdown over it. His sometime roommate at the hotel, John McCullough, reported later that Booth denounced Lincoln as a murderer and predicted that "somebody would one day give it to him."[2]

★   ★   ▮   ★   ★

Beall's execution may have pushed Booth closer to the edge, despite his new romance with Lucy Hale, and made him rededicate himself to stopping Abraham Lincoln by any means necessary.[3] As a result, Booth immediately set out to enlist new recruits for what his earliest followers found to be an increasingly insane plot.

A photograph of the second inauguration of Abraham Lincoln on March 4, 1865. Some experts claim John Wilkes Booth may be visible in the crowd just above Lincoln's left shoulder. *Wikimedia Commons*

He found one in David Herold, a handsome but aimless young man. Herold was only twenty-two years old, a native of the District of Columbia who had attended Georgetown College and worked occasionally as a pharmacy clerk.

Booth also discovered another young recruit, Lewis Powell, a tall, well-built young man, just twenty-one, who had served in the Confederate army until he was wounded and captured at Gettysburg in 1863. Powell, after somehow managing to escape, briefly joined a unit of famous Confederate guerrillas, but then, tired of the fighting, posed as a refugee and crossed Union lines back into Baltimore.

Apparently he felt guilty for being a deserter to the Confederate cause, and Booth's associates were able to recruit him. Powell would be the only one of Booth's associates courageous enough, or ruthless enough, to take action along with Booth on the fateful date.

Throughout this entire period, the early months of 1865, the members of Booth's odd gang of misfits continued to shadow Lincoln, monitoring his movements. In Washington at this time, it was relatively easy to both see and get close to the president. Lincoln had long maintained an "open door policy" at specific times when supplicants, including those seeking clemency, could see him in person. The citizens of Washington often saw the president riding about the city in his carriage.

On March 4, a rainy and blustery day, much of Washington turned out to watch Lincoln's second inauguration, held as usual on the steps of the Capitol, where the president delivered what has long been considered one of the finest speeches in American history. Booth and some of his co-conspirators were present.[4]

In fact, Booth would later boast that he could have shot Lincoln then and there, standing just feet away from him. There is even a photograph of the event that some have claimed shows Booth just behind Lincoln, up to his left.

However, the man usually pointed out in this photo appears to have parted his hair on the right side of his head, and Booth, as many contemporary photos prove, always parted his hair on the left. Another candidate nearby, a man with a mustache and in a top hat, may be more likely. Booth did have a ticket to the inauguration, which he got from Lucy Hale, and he likely did get within shooting distance of Lincoln.

He first witnessed the swearing in of Vice President Johnson; then, in a mad attempt to get close to Lincoln, broke through police lines just as Lincoln was exiting the Capitol rotunda to go outside on the east steps. Capitol Hill police immediately tackled the wild-eyed Booth, whom no one recognized at the time, and subdued him. The officers understandably thought he was a madman but released him with a warning and told him to get lost.

Lincoln, unaware of any of this, proceeded down the massive Capitol steps, was duly sworn in, and delivered his second inaugural address. He promised to finish the work the nation had begun with the war, to bind up its wounds, and to achieve "a just and lasting peace among ourselves and with all nations."

The inauguration had disrupted, but did not end entirely, Booth's budding romance with Lucy Hale. It appears the young woman, perhaps frightened by Booth's increasingly manic behavior, wanted some distance. She was about to leave for Spain, where her father, his term as senator over, had just been appointed ambassador. Hale wrote a Dear John letter of sorts to Booth, of which only the outer envelope survives.

On it was inscribed a line from the famous poem by John Greenleaf Whittier about the saddest words being "it might have been." Booth was chivalrous and tender in his reply, which he penned on the outside of the envelope above her words:

> Now in this hour that we part
> I will ask to be forgotten never.
> But in thy pure and guileless heart,
> Consider me thy friend, dear, ever.
> J. Wilkes Booth

The envelope was dated March 5, 1865, just thirty-nine days before one of the most notorious crimes in American history would be committed.

Booth was now running out of money. The benefit in New York City was just that, a benefit, and he had no regular acting gigs providing him with fast cash, as in the past. The high-living actor had spent considerable sums on travel and on buying horses, a carriage, and weapons for the conspiracy—not to mention cash payments to some of the conspirators to keep them actively engaged.

Booth implied and, in some cases, outright told his associates that the kidnapping would net them all "a fortune," even promising the penurious Atzerodt the gigantic sum of $20,000 when it was all over.[5] It was this promise of enormous financial rewards that led the Union government later, and writers ever since, to assume the involvement of the Confederacy in the plot—since the South was known to have financed and planned a number of irregular military operations, up to and including kidnapping Lincoln.

We will return to the issue of the Confederacy's possible involvement in the final chapter of this book. But in the meantime, if Booth was financed by the Confederacy, there was little evidence of it. He borrowed money—quite a lot of money—even from his co-conspirators. Booth had additional funds available—bonds stashed for his mother, and the money he had deposited in a Canadian bank for a getaway—but his access to ready cash was limited.

And he was getting desperate. When he was down to the last twenty-five dollars in his checking account, Booth agreed to smuggle medicines, specifically quinine, south to the Confederacy—for which he earned a thousand dollars for a single trip.[6]

★　★　▮　★　★

On Wednesday, March 15, 1865, Booth called a fateful meeting of all the main conspirators, the first and only time this ragtag crew met all at once. The meeting was held at Gautier's restaurant on Pennsylvania Avenue in Washington, D.C.

For someone so short on funds, Booth splurged: he ordered a private dining room with oysters, food, whiskey, and cigars for all. They were all there: Arnold and O'Laughlen, John Surratt, Lewis Powell, George Atzerodt, and David Herold. Facing an increasingly skeptical and ambivalent group of malcontents, Booth told them that everything was now ready. They only had to identify the ideal date and time to snatch Lincoln at the Ford Theatre. Booth still insisted on taking Lincoln at the theatre instead of at other locations, such as during his occasional walks at night around the White House.

Booth could see that many of his fellow co-conspirators were getting cold feet. John Surratt, for example, was sure the Union government was on to them. What's more, the entire point of the kidnapping plot was to force the Union to begin prisoner exchanges once again—but that had already happened. As a result, there was no longer a good reason to kidnap Lincoln.

Booth ignored all these objections. Instead, he outlined how the kidnapping would go in detail, assigning roles to each of the conspirators then present. Members of the group had thoroughly cased the Ford Theatre, with Surratt and Powell even going so far as to sit in the presidential box during plays (which was free when the president was not using it).

As Booth outlined it, the plan was for Arnold to accost Lincoln in his box. Booth and the burly German Atzerodt would then handcuff him and lower him onto the stage below, where Powell would catch him. The entire group would then join Powell onstage and they would proceed to hustle the handcuffed and gagged president out of the back door of the theatre to a waiting carriage. Surratt and Herold would guide them through the countryside to the waiting boats on the river.

It was, plainly, an insane plan. There would likely be dozens, perhaps hundreds of combat-hardened soldiers in the audience, some of them armed and well-trained, who would instantly leap to the defense of the bound president. The sheer lunacy of the plot is what leads some historians to conclude that it originated with Booth personally and not with seasoned Confederate agents. This would also be the opinion of the war correspondent George Townsend, who was one of the first journalists to investigate in detail the events and who had met Booth personally.

There had indeed been a Confederate plan to kidnap Lincoln, led by a Confederate secret service agent, Thomas N. Conrad. Yet it was quickly abandoned when Conrad, reconnoitering in Washington, saw for himself just how well-protected the president actually was.[7]

As the members of Booth's gang discussed the details of the plot over drinks at Gautier's, some began to voice serious objections. Most wanted to survive the undertaking; a few were going along solely for the alleged fortune that Booth promised they would make from it. Also, as the dinner dragged on, it slowly began to dawn on some that perhaps Booth had no real intention of kidnapping Lincoln at all. His real plans might actually be something more sinister.

One by one, the members of Booth's group of conspirators bowed out of the plot. The former Catholic seminarian John Surratt stated flat out that he wasn't going to murder anyone, if that was what Booth had on his mind. Others agreed. The meeting almost broke up in complete disarray. But then Booth did his best to calm everyone and stress that he was open to their ideas and willing to consider other kidnapping plans. As the meeting came to an end early in the morning, Booth promised everyone present that he would have an alternative course of action for them in the next day or two.

Booth found it the very next day at the Campbell Hospital on Seventh Street, a military facility that Lincoln had visited in the past and would again that Friday. On that day, St. Patrick's Day, the president supposedly would attend a production of *Still Waters Run Deep* performed by a troupe of actors from the Washington Theatre.

Booth had visited the hospital right after Lincoln's most recent appearance there. As a result, he sent messages to everyone in his group that the plot was on. They would kidnap the president at the hospital during the performance and then make a run for it, in the carriage, for the riverbank.

Despite their increasing reservations, the members of the team dutifully gathered their supplies—the carriages and horses, the weapons—and met at a rendezvous point on the way to the hospital. Identifying himself as an actor, Booth rode his horse to the hospital and went inside to chat with the theatre company.

But once again, Booth's amateurish intelligence gathering utterly failed him. He was shocked to discover that the entire area was heavily guarded. He began to suspect that perhaps John Surratt was correct that the government was on to them. Booth quickly called the plan off, alerting his men to return to the city.

And as it turned out, it didn't matter. Lincoln had had no intention of showing up to Campbell Hospital that day. Instead, he was delivering a speech at Booth's own hotel, the National, celebrating the recent capture of a Confederate flag. The bumbling would-be kidnapper Booth made it back to town just in time to witness another Lincoln speech, standing just a few yards from the verandah of the White House where Lincoln spoke.

Witnesses reported seeing Booth's face twitch as Lincoln spoke about black soldiers being forced to fight on behalf of the Confederacy. "They have drawn upon their last branch of resources, and we can now see the bottom," Lincoln said, referring to the Confederates. "I am glad to see the end so near at hand."[8]

★　★　🎩　★　★

The conspiracy was plainly falling apart due to Booth's incompetence more than anything else. The members of the group were now scared.

Incredibly, Booth showed up the next night at Ford's Theatre for the final acting performance of his life. It was another benefit, this time for the actor and Booth's sometime roommate John McCullough. Booth played the character of Pescara in Richard Lalor Sheil's 1817 tragedy, *The Apostate*. Some members of the gang were in the audience. By all accounts, Booth delivered a masterful performance.

Yet after the show, the members of Booth's gang went their separate ways. They were beginning to draw the attention of the police. Booth had been named as a Confederate sympathizer. Surratt was wanted for questioning. Even worse, some of the members had been arrested—including Powell, who was banished from Washington for being a "spy."

But Booth wouldn't give up. After a quick trip to New York to visit his brothers and mother, he returned to Washington and discovered that Lincoln and his wife would supposedly attend an opera at Ford's on Wednesday, March 29. Once again, he summoned the ragtag remnants of his gang. And once again the befuddled group was foiled by its poor knowledge of the president's actual movements. In reality, Lincoln wasn't attending the theatre but was visiting troops at the front, making a dangerous journey south to inspect the captured Confederate capital of Richmond. He didn't return to Washington until April 9.

By this time, virtually all of the conspirators had had enough. Despite his seeming wealth and overwhelming confidence, Booth was beginning to look like a clown who plainly had no idea what he was doing. It was beginning to dawn on the more intelligent members of Booth's conspiracy that their fearless leader might just be crazy, drawing them all into something from which they, and their families, would never recover. His old friend Sam Arnold wrote Booth a letter, which he would soon bitterly regret sending, in which he pleaded with Booth to "desist," urging him to first seek "Richmond's" approval.

Even Booth appeared ready to give up. He spoke about returning to acting, and implied that his romance with Miss Lucy Hale had been reignited.

And yet, it also appears that it was around this time, in early April, that Booth began to consider seriously a major change of plans. He realized that kidnapping Lincoln was no longer realistic given the president's uncertain schedule and security. In addition, the original purpose of the exercise—forcing the renewal of prisoner exchanges—was now moot because such exchanges had started up again.

However, what *was* realistic was something much simpler and potentially just as effective: shooting Lincoln. A talented marksman, Booth had now been within easy shooting distance of Lincoln at least three or four times, not counting appearances on the stage. He had hinted at this during the final meeting of his gang at Gautier's restaurant but then backed off when he saw the horrified reactions of his co-conspirators. Yet it appears this thought was now very much in the forefront of his mind.

Visiting New York one last time the first week of April, Booth was drinking with his old friend Sam Chester at the House of Lords bar when he revealed his true plans. "What an excellent chance I had to kill the President, if I had wished, on Inauguration Day!" Booth blurted out, to Chester's horror. "I was on the stand, as close as I am to you."

Chester was stunned. "You're crazy, John," he replied. "What good would that do?"

Abraham Lincoln and his son Tad toured the ruins of vanquished Richmond, the capital of the Confederacy, on April 4, 1865. They were rowed up the James River in a small boat with twelve sailors and marines as their sole escort. *Wikimedia Commons*

Booth smiled. He then confessed his real motives for all the scheming and planning these past months. "I could live in history," he said.[9]

★   ★   🎩   ★   ★

To the horror of Booth and his fellow Confederate sympathizers, the war was getting increasingly desperate. Clearly, something dramatic would have to be done, and soon, or the war would be utterly lost.

On April 1, General Ulysses Grant's forces struck what remained of the Confederate line southwest of Petersburg, Virginia, and the next day the Confederate government and what was left of its army fled the capital of Richmond. The retreating troops set fire to strategic bridges and the armories, hoping to slow the enemy's advance. Unfortunately, the fires spread uncontrolled. Thousands of buildings were burned to the ground. On April 3, as victorious Union troops marched into the capital, Richmond was a smoldering wasteland.

IN THEIR OWN WORDS

"The next day after our entry into the city, on passing out from Clay Street, from Jefferson Davis's house, I saw a crowd coming, headed by President Lincoln, who was walking with his usual long, careless stride, and looking about with an interested air and taking in everything. Upon my saluting he said: 'Is it far to President Davis's house?' I accompanied him to the house, which was occupied by General Weitzal as headquarters."

—*Thomas Thatcher Graves*

President Lincoln, who had been visiting Grant at his headquarters, insisted on seeing the Confederate capital in person. Despite warnings about the dangers he faced, Lincoln traveled up the James River with his young son Tad and spent hours walking through the devastation, visiting Jefferson Davis's former executive mansion and the Confederate capitol building.

As Lincoln was surveying the damage at Richmond, what was left of Robert E. Lee's army was driving west towards Lynchburg. He hoped to join up with General Joe Johnston's Army of Tennessee in North Carolina and then go back on the offensive. But lack of supplies and a string of lost engagements finally convinced Robert E. Lee to surrender.

By this time, Lee's army was surrounded, outnumbered five or six to one.[10] On April 9, following the last major battle of the Civil War at Appomattox Court House, Lee met his old comrade Ulysses S. Grant to discuss the terms of surrender.

The meeting was held at the home of Wilmer McLean, who, as fate would have it, had fled to this rural location after his previous home had been fired upon in the early stages of the war.

Lincoln's eldest son Robert, who served briefly on General Ulysses S. Grant's staff and gave his father a report on the morning of April 14, noted the differences between the Union general (left) and Confederate general Robert E. Lee (right). *Wikimedia Commons*

Grant was generous. He told Lee that his men, upon swearing an oath to cease fighting, would receive a full pardon, would not be prosecuted as traitors, and would be allowed to return to their homes with their horses for the spring planting. The Confederate officers would even be allowed to keep their sidearms. Grant also offered immediate provisions so Lee could feed his by-then starving troops.

Upon hearing the news, the Union troops erupted in joyous cries of victory, shooting off their cannons in salutes, but Grant ordered them to stop, insisting that the defeated Confederates were once again their fellow countrymen. As we saw earlier, Lincoln's eldest son, Robert, serving a brief tour in Grant's entourage as a lieutenant, witnessed all this.

★   ★   🎩   ★   ★

Both President Lincoln and Booth returned to Washington around the same time, on the evening of April 9, Palm Sunday. As was his custom, Booth checked back into the National Hotel. Lincoln and Tad arrived in Washington on the steamer *River Queen* just as official word reached the War Department of Lee's surrender.

On his way back to the White House, Lincoln stopped to visit Secretary of State Seward, who had been badly injured in a carriage accident. He only received General Grant's telegram about Lee's surrender when he returned to the White House that evening.

The next day, Monday, April 10, the citizens of Washington awoke to newspaper headlines blaring the good news. A week-long drunken party erupted. Although Jefferson Davis was still at large along with a considerable number of Confederate fighters, Lee's surrender meant the war, which had cost 623,000 American lives, was effectively over.

Booth, for his part, observed Lee's surrender by visiting a pistol range on Pennsylvania Avenue he often frequented, getting in some target practice.[11] He visited the Surratt boardinghouse and ran into an acquaintance, Lou Weichmann. His friend asked Booth if it was true that he was going back into the acting business, and Booth pointedly replied that, no, he had no intention of returning to the theatre. He then said that the only play he wanted to be in now was *Venice Preserv'd*, a cryptic reference that Weichmann missed entirely. It was a play about a man, married to a Venetian senator's daughter, who assassinates the leaders of Venice.[12]

?

WHAT WE STILL DON'T KNOW

What made John Wilkes Booth change his plans from attempting to kidnap Lincoln to killing him? Some historians are skeptical that Booth was persuaded to do so simply by hearing Lincoln's speech on the evening of Tuesday, April 11, when the president spoke of voting rights for freed slaves. For one thing, the report that Booth whispered to his accomplice, David Herold, "That means nigger citizenship," is based on hearsay: Herold's attorney, Frederick Stone, told the journalist George Townsend that this is what Booth said. Respected historians such as Michael Kauffman seem satisfied that it is likely true. Yet even if Booth did say this, he had already strongly hinted at killing Lincoln at his famous dinner meeting with his larger gang a month earlier, when many of them, including John Surratt Jr., backed out as a result.

Booth spent the next day, Tuesday, April 11, trying to sell the expensive carriage he had purchased for the kidnapping plot—a further sign that he had changed his plans in a dramatic way.

The city had planned a special treat for that evening, a "Grand Illumination" in which many public and private buildings would be illuminated at night by gaslight, but this was postponed. Instead, a large crowd gathered outside the White House to hear Lincoln speak. In the very front row, just yards from the president, stood John Wilkes Booth and one of his few remaining loyalists, David Herold.

Lincoln was solemn. He spoke of the work of Reconstruction ahead. Lincoln then touched on a controversial topic: what would happen with the country's recently emancipated slaves. Lincoln made clear that he would press for greater rights. "It is also satisfactory to some that the

WHAT WERE THEY THINKING?

JOHN WILKES BOOTH was obsessed with the idea of kidnapping Abraham Lincoln at Ford's Theatre. His plan was to have an accomplice douse the lights, and then, in the subsequent confusion, somehow lower a bound-and-gagged president to the stage and carry him out the back door. That a significant portion of the audience would be combat veterans still in the Army, and likely armed, never seemed to deter him.

elective franchise is not given to the colored man," the president said. "I would myself prefer that it were now conferred on the very intelligent, and on those who serve our cause as soldiers."

The next day, Booth finally sold his carriage. He went over to Ford's Theatre to pick up his mail, as he usually did, and got into an argument with Harry Ford and some friends about Lincoln's plan for extending franchise to some former slaves. "We are all slaves now," Booth spat out, launching into a rant. The other men, resigned former supporters of the Confederacy, merely shrugged. Booth's fanaticism was getting old.

★ ★ 🎩 ★ ★

On Thursday morning, April 13, General Grant arrived in Washington along with his wife and assistants. They checked into the Willard Hotel, still located today at 1401 Pennsylvania Avenue NW.

Grant was busy most of the day at the War Department, taking dramatic steps to end the war. This included halting the hated military draft and lifting trade restrictions against the South.

All Thursday, as most of Washington prepared for a grand celebration, John Booth and what was left of his followers were busy. In the

The Willard Hotel, located just a block from the White House, as it appeared during the Civil War when General Grant was a frequent guest. *White House Historical Association*

morning, Lewis Powell proceeded to "case" the home of Secretary of State Seward, who lived in a three-story building facing Lafayette Park on Madison Place near Pennsylvania Avenue.

Booth traveled to Baltimore in a failed effort to re-enlist his old friend Mike O'Laughlen in the conspiracy. Horrified and frightened, O'Laughlen would have no part of it. Booth returned to Washington.

Booth held a final meeting with the tiny handful of his die-hard followers at the Herndon House hotel, located on the corner of Ninth and G Streets. The hotel was torn down in 1891 to make room for a new office building. Two of those present, Powell and Atzerodt, would later testify that this final planning meeting was held at 8:00 p.m. in this hotel. As noted earlier, what isn't resolved is whether the meeting was held Thursday or Friday night.

They met in Lewis Powell's room, room 6 on the third floor. Present were Booth, Powell, George Atzerodt, and David Herold. Booth laid out his final plan. They would all strike at once and eliminate the key leaders of the U.S. government in one fell swoop. They would decapitate the government leadership in an era before a clear line of succession was established. Booth would personally assassinate the president. Powell would kill Secretary of State Seward. Herold and Atzerodt would kill Vice President Johnson.

Apparently, this latter part of the plan was news to Atzerodt, who announced that he wanted no part in murder. Booth, now furious, merely replied that Herold had the guts and would do it alone.

Booth told the men to be on the alert. He would notify them soon when to strike. He had to find out where Lincoln would be Friday evening to put their plan into motion.

Booth left the Herndon House hotel late. If, as is likely, the meeting was held Thursday night, it's possible Booth stayed with a call girl, Ella Star. It later appeared that he hadn't slept in his room at the National Hotel on Thursday night. Wherever Booth was, long after midnight he sat down and wrote what would be a farewell letter to his mother.

> April 14, 2 a.m.
> Dearest Mother:
> I know you expect a letter from me, and am sure you will hardly forgive me. But indeed I have nothing to write about. Everything is dull; that is, has been till last night.
> Everything was bright and splendid. More so in my eyes if it had been a display in a nobler cause. But so goes the world. Might makes right. I only drop you these few lines to let you know I am well, and to say I have not heard from you [lately]. Had one from Rose. With best love to you all,
> I am your affectionate son ever,
> John[13]

10 | HAIL TO THE CHIEF

Ford's Theater, 8:00 to 10:15 p.m.

With Lincoln and Mary huddled in the back seat, the dark green presidential carriage swung down the circular driveway of the White House and exited the grounds. It clattered northeast towards the Harris home at the corner of H and Fourteenth Streets, just four blocks away.[1] Major Rathbone lived nearby in a red brick town house at 722 Jackson Place, right off Lafayette Square. The Harris home is long gone, but Rathbone's house still stands.

After stopping to pick up Clara Harris and Rathbone around 8:20 p.m., the presidential carriage raced towards Ford's Theatre about a mile away on Tenth Street NW. Major Rathbone was dressed in civilian clothes, a dark suit, while Clara was dressed in a gown.

It was now beginning to drizzle, yet there was plenty of light. Washington had had gas street lighting since the 1850s, and there were eight hundred public gas lamps throughout the city. What's more, the city was still in the midst of the Grand Illumination begun the night before, so buildings throughout the city were lit up with extra lighting to celebrate the coming end of the war. At Ford's Theatre, the contractor James Gifford had installed a special "limelight" on a pole outside, flooding the theatre's outside entrance in extra light.[2]

The Lincolns were very late. The carriage pulled up to the main entrance of Ford's Theatre on Tenth Street at about 8:35 p.m. The entrance was made up of five double doors, each below a curved archway. There was a special wooden platform built to help patrons alight from their carriages without having to step into the muddy street. Two men were out on the street waiting for the carriage: the theatre's dapper doorman, John Buckingham, thirty-seven, and presidential bodyguard John Parker.

After helping the women and the president out of the carriage, Buckingham led the party into the theatre's small inner lobby. The usher, a man named James O'Brien, led everyone to the curving staircase on the left side of the theatre, which led up to the second-story balcony overlooking the stage.

Young Joseph Hazelton, the boy assigned to hand out programs, handed one of the printed sheets to Lincoln and to each member of the party. The president smiled at the boy, whom he had met before. The group moved up the staircase with Forbes and the bodyguard Parker accompanying them.

★　★　🎩　★　★

The theatre was crowded, despite its being Good Friday, but not entirely full. Many of the patrons had come in anticipation of the arrival of Lincoln and his guests (wrongly assumed to be General Grant and his wife). About four hundred people could fit into the second-story balcony, each paying seventy-five cents for a ticket.

Below them, on the ground floor, was the orchestra level with six hundred seats costing a dollar each.[3] Above them, on the third floor, was a family circle balcony that seated another six hundred people who sat on wooden benches (price: twenty-five cents per person). In addition to the general seating, the theatre also had eight private boxes, four (numbered 1 through 4) on the orchestra level and four (numbered 5 through

8) on the dress circle level. The cost for a box was ten dollars. In deference to the president, none of the other boxes were in use that night.

To reach the state box, the Lincolns and their guests crossed the back of the dress circle balcony from left to right and made their way along the right wall. It's not entirely clear precisely when this occurred—a crucial fact for working out a definitive timeline for what was about to happen next.

The actors on stage would later disagree about what point in the play was interrupted by the arrival of the Lincoln party. As was his custom and inclination, and painfully aware that he was late, Lincoln was trying to slip inconspicuously into his box without interrupting the play. That wasn't going to happen. Once Lincoln was spotted, the theatre patrons began whispering loudly as the presidential party entered—and the actors, who could see what was happening from the stage, immediately paused.

As Lincoln and his guests reached the outer door that led to the two private boxes, the president stopped. For the first time at Ford's, the orchestra leader, William Withers, led the musicians in a rendition of "Hail to the Chief" as the houselights were raised to full. With a pained smile on his face, Lincoln bowed humbly as the audience rose to their feet and gave the president a standing ovation. As the applause continued, the president put his hand over his heart and bowed a second time. On stage, the British actress Laura Keene curtsied.

Reviled by millions and revered by millions more—including many in the theatre—Lincoln no doubt relished this moment. It had been a very long four years.

The audience continued clapping for some minutes as the members of the presidential party made their way to their seats inside the state box. Once inside, Lincoln drew open the draperies that hung from above and bowed once again. He took his seat in the red upholstered rocking chair placed at the right-hand side of the box and closest to the audience, looking at it from the stage. The chair was only four feet from the second door that led into the state box.[5] Mary sat next to him while Clara Harris and Major Rathbone were seated on the other side of the pillar dividing the two boxes, about seven feet from Lincoln.

IN THEIR OWN WORDS

"The President entered the theater at 8:30 amid deafening cheers and the rising of all. Everything was cheerful, and never was our magistrate more enthusiastically welcomed or more happy. Many pleasant allusions were made to him in the play, to which the audience gave deafening responses, while Mr. Lincoln laughed heartily and bowed frequently to the gratified people."

—*Jason S. Knox, Orchestra Level, Second Row, in a letter to his father, April 15, 1865*[4]

Finally, the houselights were lowered. The actors on stage began the play from where they had left off. Having escorted the Lincolns to their seats, John Parker, the presidential bodyguard, left the presidential box. He found an empty seat in the family circle, perhaps at the president's suggestion. Parker would later leave the theatre with Charles Forbes, Lincoln's personal assistant, to have a drink next door during the intermission.

In honor of the president's visit, the cast improvised a little. There was a line in the play that spoke of cold drafts, but Laura Keene, aware that the government had declared an end to conscription only the day before, ad-libbed, "The draft has been suspended."[6] The audience laughed appreciatively. Filled with good cheer now that the bloody war was finally coming to an end, the audience was putty in the hands of the veteran actors on stage.

Everyone could tell that Lincoln, too, was enjoying himself immensely. They could hear their war-weary leader chuckle at the play's many corny one-liners. These were just the sort of lowbrow plays that Lincoln enjoyed, as they took his mind off his problems.

Witnesses sitting across from the presidential box would later testify that Lincoln and his wife appeared to enjoy the play tremendously. During part of the play, Mary Lincoln held the president's hand. As it was a cold night and the theatre had no heating, both Clara Harris and Mary Lincoln wore their bonnets and cloaks.

Around nine o'clock, the first act ended. The theatre's stagehands lowered the curtain and raised the houselights once again. There was a brief intermission as Ed Spangler and the crew changed the sets on stage.

Around 9:10 p.m., as the second act was about to begin, the call boy Will Ferguson went out the back door to fetch any actors smoking or getting some fresh air. While there, he saw it was raining—and noticed that the stage carpenter and scene changer Edman Spangler was outside talking with the famous actor John Wilkes Booth.

11 SIC SEMPER TYRANNIS

Ford's Theatre, 9:10 to 10:30 p.m.

Booth had entered the alleyway that led to the back of Ford's Theatre around ten minutes after nine, just as Act II was about to begin.[1] *Our American Cousin* had been underway for more than an hour. He had already retrieved his bay mare from his rented stall in the stables located to the right behind the theatre.

Booth checked the saddle and bit thoroughly and then, holding the reins, led the horse to the back door of the theatre. He called softly for the carpenter and scene changer Ned Spangler. While he was speaking to Spangler, the call boy, Will Ferguson, appeared in the back doorway of the theatre, announcing that Act II of the play was about to begin. He overheard Booth speaking with the carpenter.

"Ned, help me all you can, will you?" Booth asked Spangler, according to a witness. This remark, overheard by other crew members as well, would cost the hapless carpenter dearly in the months and years ahead.

Once Act II began, Spangler, the prompter John DeBonay, just seventeen years old, and a man named John Selecman went outside to speak with Booth again. Booth handed the reins of his horse to Spangler and

CRITICAL MINUTES

One reason why Booth was able to bluff his way past Lincoln's aide, Charles Forbes, and gain entrance to the hallway leading to the presidential box was because others had done it just minutes before him. An eyewitness, Alexander Crawford, told investigators on April 14 that a messenger had brought a dispatch to the presidential box about twenty minutes before Booth appeared on the scene and gained immediate entrance. This relative lack of security at least contributed to what happened next.

asked him to hold them for a while, and then he, DeBonay, and Selecman went to the far right of the back stage.

With the play going on, they couldn't move across the stage even with the back curtain down. As a result, Booth lifted a trapdoor at the right corner of the back stage, just inside the outside door, that led to a passageway under the stage and near the orchestra pit. Booth and DeBonay were able to cross underneath the stage to the other side without being seen, coming up in the wings beneath the presidential box.[2]

Spangler, who was needed for the many scene changes in the play, didn't have time to stand there holding the reins of Booth's horse, so he asked another stagehand to do it, who refused, and then finally laid eyes on young "Peanut John" Burroughs, who was in charge of the back door. "Hold Mr. Booth's horse," he told the boy. Spangler promised him that Booth would pay him fifty cents if he did what he was told. Burroughs agreed. For the next forty-five minutes or so, Burroughs would sit outside in the light rain, holding the reins of Booth's horse.

Reproduction of Ford's Theatre tickets from the night of the assassination. *Author's collection*

From the wings of the theatre, Booth and DeBonay headed down the narrow side passageway that ran along the south wall of the theatre and came out on Tenth Street, directly in front of the Star Saloon. Witnesses saw Booth enter the saloon and order a whiskey and water, drinking it down in one big gulp. Yet if he was nervous, no one seemed to notice.

Booth sauntered out of the saloon's front door, smoking a cigar, and then strutted into the theatre's front lobby. Once there, Booth chatted amiably with the doorman, John Buckingham, and asked him what time it was.[3] By this time, Booth was likely a little drunk. He had been drinking most of the day, off and on.

As it was getting close to ten o'clock, Booth ambled over to the ticket window on the right side of the lobby where young Harry Ford was counting the evening's receipts. Even at this late stage, when most people would be extremely nervous, Booth was capable of having a little fun. He placed his cigar on the ledge of the ticket window, and, according to Ford, announced in a mocking way, "Whoe'r this cigar dares displace must meet Wilkes Booth face to face."[4] It was an obscure allusion to a comedy both men knew, and Booth got a laugh out of Ford.

Booth walked back to the center of the lobby, brushed off a young ticket taker who demanded a ticket from him, asked again what time it was, and then walked to the back of the ground-floor orchestra seating. He stared over the heads of the audience at the presidential box diagonally opposite. Incredibly, Booth was heard humming quietly to himself.

Still, his actions did arouse some suspicion. A former Metropolitan policeman who helped out in the ticket booth, Joe Sessford, thirty-two, walked over to the boy taking tickets. "I wonder what he's up to," the ex-cop muttered out loud. "He was in here this afternoon, too."[5]

Act II came to an end around 9:50, the houselights came up, and the play's second, briefer intermission was announced. Half of the house, it seemed, and more than a few members of the cast, jumped up from their seats and quickly repaired next door to the Star Saloon for another quick drink.

As Spangler and other stagehands rearranged the set, Booth walked over to the ticket boy and bummed a plug of tobacco off of him. He was also watching the large clock in the lobby closely. Although likely tipsy, Booth had planned his move down to the minute. Booth knew the play by heart, and he knew that, at roughly 10:15, there would be only one actor on the stage—his rival in romance, Hawk—and that this was the moment when Hawk would deliver the biggest laugh line of the evening.

The abstemious Lincoln stayed in his seat during the second intermission, looking nonchalantly over the balcony of his box at the audience below.

Shortly before this, two of Booth's few remaining followers, the muscular Confederate soldier Lewis Powell and the pudgy former pharmacist David Herold, were about one mile away, executing another part of Booth's plot to decapitate the leadership of the Union. They stood outside of the home of the secretary of state, William H. Seward, located ten blocks away from Ford's Theatre in what is now Lafayette Square, across from the back side of the White House.[6]

Seward, then sixty-four, was widely considered the most powerful man in the country after the president—and, for some, the most powerful man in Washington. A lawyer, committed abolitionist, the former governor of New York State, and a friend to Catholics and immigrants, Seward nevertheless had a reputation for ruthlessness. He was widely hated by Confederate sympathizers for his willingness to arrest and, in many cases, execute couriers and blockade runners. Seward had been badly injured in a carriage

Lewis Thornton Powell (1844–1865), also known as Lewis Payne, was only twenty-one when he joined John Wilkes Booth's plot to kidnap Abraham Lincoln. The son of a Baptist minister in Alabama, Powell was an experienced Confederate guerilla fighter and member of Mosby's Rangers. *Wikimedia Commons*

accident just a week before. He had broken his jaw and required a special metal splint. The secretary was now recuperating at his home near the White House.

Booth had ordered Powell to kill Seward, but the country boy from Maryland didn't know his way around the capital. As a result, David Herold, who was born and raised in Washington, guided Powell to Seward's house. The plan was for Herold to hold their horses outside while Powell took care of things inside.

Powell knocked on the front door of the Seward home. Although the young and handsome Powell was just twenty-one, he was undoubtedly the most dangerous member of Booth's gang, a hardened Confederate guerilla fighter who knew how to kill. Powell used the only excuse he could think of for such a late-night call and claimed to have some medicine for the secretary. However, the servant who answered the door would not let him pass.

Ignoring him, Powell simply barged through the front door and up the stairs. Frederick Seward, the secretary's son, confronted the intruder immediately, demanding to know what he was doing there. After a brief, surreal conversation on the landing outside of Seward's bedroom door, with Powell still using his lame excuse about the medicine, Powell suddenly drew a gun, a formidable .38 caliber Whitney revolver. He aimed it directly at Fred and pulled the trigger.

But nothing happened. The gun misfired. Without hesitating, the well-trained combat soldier Powell instantly smashed the wooden handle of the gun into the young man's skull, slicing open a gash and causing him to bleed profusely. Inside Seward's room, the secretary's twenty-year-old daughter, Fanny, and a male Army nurse named George Robinson opened the bedroom door to see what the commotion was all about.

When they did so, Powell sprang at Robinson with a large knife. The Army private instinctively deflected the blow, which slashed his forehead, but the force of the blow knocked him to the ground. Powell then moved quickly toward Seward in his bed, lying weak and helpless. Powell jumped on the bed and began slashing repeatedly at the injured man, badly cutting his face, neck, and arms. He then tried to slit the secretary's throat or slice an artery in his neck. Fanny screamed.

In the meantime, Robinson had managed to get back to his feet and leapt onto Powell's back, pulling Powell away and allowing Seward to roll off of the bed. Within seconds, Augustus Seward, Frederick's brother, burst into the room. He had been asleep in the bedroom next door.

The Army nurse and Augustus managed to pin Powell down briefly. Augustus stood up with the idea of retrieving his own gun next door. But then Powell broke free, leapt through the bedroom door, and barreled down the stairs towards the exit, stabbing a State Department messenger in the back as he did so. He then flew out the door and into the night.

Powell was expecting to find David Herold waiting for him, holding his horse for a getaway. But Herold was nowhere to be seen. He had vanished.

★　　★　　🎩　　★　　★

The vice president, Andrew Johnson, who would later be the first president to be impeached, was asleep in his room at the Kirkwood House hotel when all this was happening. Within minutes, word of the attack on Seward reached the Ford Theatre.

Upon hearing the news that Seward had been almost killed, a member of the audience, Leonard J. Farwell, the former governor of Wisconsin, instantly recognized a possible plot against the U.S. government. As a result, he hurried over to Kirkwood House to warn the vice president.

After waking Johnson and telling him what had happened to Seward, Farwell convinced someone to post a guard outside of Johnson's room as a precaution. He need not have bothered. Despite the fact that Johnson's rooms at Kirkwood House were unguarded and easily accessible, the man Booth assigned to assassinate Johnson, George Atzerodt, had no intention of carrying out Booth's orders. Atzerodt, who had checked into the hotel that morning, was in a nearby saloon, getting drunk.

★　　★　　🎩　　★　　★

During the intermission, Booth was back in the Star Saloon, drinking again. Incredibly, so were all three of Lincoln's attendants—police bodyguard John Parker, carriage driver Ned Burke, and footman Charles Forbes.

The audience members only had a few minutes for refreshments, however. At around ten o'clock, they were called back to the theatre for the start of the third and final act.

Apparently only Charles Forbes, Lincoln's trusted valet, had enough sense of duty to return to his post outside the door leading to the

IN THEIR OWN WORDS

"Somewhere near ten o'clock, during the second scene of
the third act of *Our American Cousin*, I saw Booth pass
along near the President's box, and then stop and lean
against the wall. After standing there a moment, I saw
him step down one step, put his hands on the door and
his knee against it, and push the door open—the first
door that goes into the box."

—*James P. Ferguson, saloon keeper*

presidential box. No one knows for sure, but the police bodyguard Parker
likely tarried in the saloon.

Parker would only discover what had happened to the president
when he staggered into the Washington Police Station, sometime after
midnight, with a prostitute named Lizzie Williams whom he had arrested
(allegedly for not granting him free favors[7]). Burke would eventually
return to his carriage outside, like Parker oblivious to what was happening inside the theatre.

As the patrons hurried out of the saloon to their seats, Booth ran
into an old friend, Edwin Brink, who was the last person to speak
with Booth before what came next. "Ted, old fellow, I'm going to
have my name hung in a place where my father's never was," Brink
would later claim Booth said.[8] The two men walked back into the
theatre lobby together. Brink went to the left, and Booth followed
him up the narrow staircase to the balcony seats in the dress circle.

At the top of the stairs, Booth walked quickly along the south wall
of the theatre towards the presidential box. He passed by a friend, Abner
Brady, who owned the gym on Pennsylvania Avenue where Booth had
been working out, but he didn't even give him a nod in greeting.

A reconstruction of the outer door leading to the presidential box at Ford's Theatre. While the outside of the theatre was left intact, the interior was gutted following the assassination and used as a federal office and storage facility. The interior was rebuilt with modern materials in the 1960s to serve as a museum. *Wikimedia Commons*[9]

Directly in front of the outer door of the presidential box, watching the play, sat two Army officers, Alexander Crawford and Theodore McGowan. The chairs of the two men were blocking Booth's way.[10] In his diary later, Booth would, with characteristic exaggeration, refer to these men as a "thousand" of the president's friends he had to somehow pass through. Booth insisted on going by and the two men reluctantly moved their chairs so he could pass, one of them thinking to himself that Booth was drunk. "There was a glare in his eye," Crawford told Stanton later that night.[11]

Booth paused for a moment, removed his hat, and looked down at the play in progress. The distance was not great, perhaps twenty feet. For a brief moment, Booth caught the eye of an actress he knew onstage, the southern belle Helen Truman playing the character of Augusta, who subtly nodded a greeting.[12]

On the opposite side of the theatre, another witness, James Ferguson, the owner of the Greenback Saloon on the north side of the theatre where Booth often ate lunch, was watching Booth's every move. He had come to the theatre precisely to see General Grant and, with the help of his girlfriend's opera glasses, had been eyeing the presidential box all evening. He knew Booth well and was now perplexed about what the actor was doing there outside the door to the presidential box.

The police bodyguard Parker was not present (probably still in the saloon next door), but loyal Charles Forbes was back in his seat outside the outer door leading to the presidential box. There was a single step down from the aisle where Booth stood to the level of the doorway entrance, and Booth took it. Forbes, the burly immigrant from Ireland,[13] looked up at the bleary-eyed actor. He was not a guard, but his expression no doubt expressed the question of what Booth wanted.

"This is the president's box, sir, no one is permitted to enter," Forbes whispered to Booth.

"I am a senator," Booth reportedly replied, not missing a beat. "Mr. Lincoln has sent for me."[14]

Booth then reached into his pocket and took out a calling card of some kind as a pretext. Lucy Hale, Booth's secret fiancée, believed it was one of her senator father's calling cards. In any case, the pretext worked. Forbes, assuming Booth did have permission to enter, nodded for Booth to pass. In Forbes's defense, two other men had come to the presidential box in the past hour, bearing messages for the president—one merely a newspaper reporter. Both had been allowed to enter without incident.

Booth reached for the doorknob, on the left side closest to the stage, and tried to open the door. But it was stuck. He had to lean against it and give a little shove with his knee, forcing it open. Booth quickly entered the narrow passageway leading to the private boxes and closed the outside door behind him.

He then found the wooden shaft lying behind the door along the base of the wall. Putting one end of the shaft in the small niche cut in the plaster wall behind the door to the left, Booth jammed the other end tight against the doorknob, effectively blocking the door from being opened from the outside. Later, the shaft had to be removed by Rathbone before anyone could enter.

It was now almost 10:20 p.m.[15] Booth was inside the short, narrow passageway, or vestibule, which was about four feet wide and eight feet long, that led to the two inner doors that opened to the two boxes.[16] Both of these inner doors normally had locks on them, but at least one of them was broken. The theatre crew had mislaid the keys and, just a few days earlier, found it necessary to force the locks to get into the boxes.

Booth stood silently in the dimly lit passageway. At the end of the passage were the doors to the boxes, one on the left and one straight ahead. The door on the left, which was closed and probably locked, led to box number 7.

The door directly ahead led into box 8; it was open and slightly ajar.[17] Booth could hear the actors on stage through the open doorway. He stepped silently down the carpeted passageway, pausing in front of the door.

Peering in and looking slightly to his left, Booth could see that Lincoln sat just a few steps, about four feet,[18] from the doorway opening. He was in his upholstered rocking chair, set back a small distance from the balcony.

The back of Lincoln's head was directly in front of Booth. Mrs. Lincoln sat next to him on his right. To the right, sitting on the other side of the column that divided the two boxes, about ten feet from Lincoln, sat Clara Harris and her fiancé, Major Rathbone. Harris sat in an upholstered chair and Rathbone on a small sofa next to her. All were transfixed by the action on the stage.

No one noticed Booth hovering silently in the doorway. The moment had finally arrived, the moment when, Booth's biographer would later write, Booth would deliver the "performance of a lifetime."

Booth held the single-shot .44-caliber derringer in his right hand. In his left, he clutched the long dagger with the word "Liberty" engraved on it, a backup weapon in case the single-shot derringer misfired. As usual, Booth was waiting for his cue, the moment when Hawk would say his laugh line.

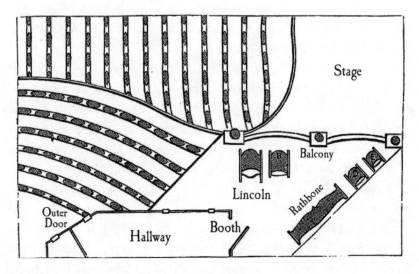

Booth entered the hallway to the presidential box, blocked the outer door with a stick of wood, and proceeded silently to the inner door, slightly ajar, opening to the box itself.

Moments later, Booth heard Hawk shout the words, "Don't know the manners of good society, eh," and, as he knew would happen, the audience erupted in laughter at the following insult: "You sockdologizing old man-trap!"

It was time.

At the sound of the laughter, Booth pushed the narrow door open further. He glanced to his right at Major Rathbone, took two steps forward, and reached out so the derringer was just six inches[19] or less from the back of Lincoln's head.

Lincoln may have heard him enter, because witnesses testified that the president turned his head slightly to the left, looking down towards the orchestra below, with his hand leaning on the balustrade railing.[20]

Booth squeezed the trigger. A loud gunshot ricocheted throughout the theatre. The president immediately slumped forward, his head dropping to his chest.

THE ASSASSINATION OF PRESIDENT LINCOLN.
AT FORD'S THEATRE WASHINGTON.D.C.APRIL 14TH 1865.

A contemporary illustration of Booth's attack upon Lincoln, showing the president's hand on the flag (as mentioned by an eyewitness) and Booth's derringer only inches from the back of Lincoln's head. *Wikimedia Commons*

The slow-moving .41 caliber bullet, traveling at just four hundred feet per second, had entered the lower half of Lincoln's skull slightly to the left of the centerline, lodging behind one of his eyes. The physicians who examined Lincoln and later performed an autopsy did not agree on where the bullet came to rest, behind his left or right eye, and so the path the bullet took remains uncertain to this day.[21]

The explosive laughter in the theatre had dulled the sound of the shot but white smoke filled the box, briefly blinding Rathbone. Nevertheless, the major instantly leapt to his feet and sprang at Booth, grabbing him from behind and pulling him back from the railing.[22]

Booth dropped the derringer on the floor of the presidential box and, twisting around, raised his dagger. There was a brief struggle. "Let go of me, or I will kill you!" Booth hissed at the major.

?

WHAT WE STILL DON'T KNOW

At what time did John Wilkes Booth shoot Lincoln? Estimates vary. The saloon keeper James Ferguson, an eyewitness, said "just about 10 o'clock." Jason S. Knox, who was in the orchestra level, also said it was "at 10 o'clock." However, another eyewitness, known only as Basset, said it was at "half past 10 o'clock." And a fourth eyewitness, Frederick A. Sawyer, agreed with Basset, saying it was "not far from ½ past 10 o'clock." The contemporary historian Edward Steers Jr. splits the difference and says Lincoln was shot at 10:20 p.m. Lincoln's acclaimed biographer David Donald is even more precise: he places the shooting at 10:13 p.m. The best guess is that Lincoln was shot sometime between 10:15 and 10:30 p.m., leaving enough time for Booth to reach the long bridge across the Potomac by 11:00 p.m.

"No, I will not!"

The major grabbed for Booth's throat but the actor, who worked out regularly at Brady's gym, was able to break free from the major's grasp.

"I might as well have attempted to hold a giant," Rathbone would say later. "He seemed endowed with sinews of steel."[23]

Booth stabbed at Rathbone's chest with the razor-sharp, double-edged dagger. The major instinctively raised his left arm to parry the blow upward, but that only resulted in Booth's knife slicing through Rathbone's forearm and bicep from his elbow to his shoulder, narrowly missing his brachial artery. Within seconds, there was blood everywhere.

Without hesitating, Booth then quickly stepped up on the velvet-covered balustrade that overlooked the stage. He did not, as later illustrations would portray it, "vault" over the ledge like a gymnast but rather

awkwardly lowered himself partially down the front side of the
box, gripping the decorative flags
with both hands and dropping
down only the last six or seven
feet onto the stage.[24]

Yet Rathbone managed to
catch hold of Booth's coat as he
went over the balustrade, knocking him off balance, and then one
of Booth's spurs caught on the
decorative flag draped over the
balcony. As a result, Booth landed
hard on the green stage carpet, his
boots making a loud crash that
was heard backstage. He quickly
stood up. "Sic semper tyrannis!"
Booth bellowed—"Thus always to
tyrants"—the motto of the Commonwealth of Virginia.

In an entry in his diary, written a few days later when he was
on the run, Booth claimed he had
said these words *before* he had

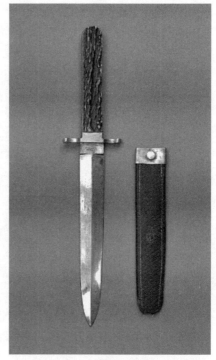

The horn-handled dagger Booth used to
attack Major Rathbone and brandished
on stage is engraved with the words "Liberty" and "America." It is on display at
the Ford's Theatre National Historic Site.
Wikimedia Commons

fired.[25] Booth was responding to newspaper denunciations of him as a
coward who had shot an unarmed man. Yet this scenario is unlikely.
Such a shout would have startled the unsuspecting Lincoln.

Hawk, the actor closest to Booth but facing away from him at the
moment the shot was fired, yelling his insult off stage right, thought he
heard Booth say the whole phrase from the box.

Yet one eyewitness, James Ferguson, who claimed to have witnessed
the entire event, insisted Booth said the words from the stage. Another
patron who sat only a few feet away from the outer door, Army captain

IN THEIR OWN WORDS

"I heard the discharge of a pistol behind me, and looking round, saw through the smoke a man between the door and the President. The distance from the door to where the President sat was about four feet. At the same time I heard the man shout some word, which I thought was 'Freedom!' I instantly sprang toward him and seized him. He wrested himself from my grasp, and made a violent thrust at my breast with a large knife. I parried the blow by striking it up, and received a wound several inches deep in my left arm, between the elbow and shoulder.... The man rushed to the front of the box and I endeavored to seize him again, but only caught his clothes as he was leaping over the railing of the box."

—*Major Henry R. Rathbone, May 16, 1865*

Theodore McGowan, writing three days later in the *New York Tribune*, also reported that Booth had yelled the words from the stage.

In any case, the leap from the stage did not go well. In a diary entry after the assassination, Booth wrote that he broke his leg during the fall and that, as he rode away later, he could feel "the bones of my leg tearing the flesh at every jump"—a slight exaggeration.

In later testimony, Dr. Samuel Mudd stated that he examined Booth's leg later that night and found only a simple fracture two inches above the left ankle, not a compound fracture that pierced the skin.[26]

Yet once on the stage, his natural habitat, the young actor couldn't resist an encore. Booth spun around, faced the audience, and raised the

IN BOOTH'S OWN WORDS

"I struck boldly and not as the papers say. I walked with a
fine step through a thousand of his friends, was stopped,
but pushed on. A colonel was at his side. I shouted Sic
Semper *before* I fired. In jumping broke my leg. I passed
all his pickets, rode sixty miles that night, with the bone
of my leg tearing the flesh at every jump. I can never
repent it, though we hated to kill. Our country owed all
her trouble to him, and God simply made me the
instrument of his punishment."

—*Booth's diary entry, likely written April 17*

bloody dagger dramatically in the air, as he had done in many plays over
the years. "The South shall be free!" he yelled out, according to the actor
Hawk, standing just feet away from him on the stage.[27] Others heard
him say, "The South is avenged!"

Above the stage in the box, Major Rathbone, who saw Lincoln
slumped over in his chair and instantly realized what had just happened,
screamed, "Stop that man!"[28]

Yet almost no one moved. Not realizing what was happening, the
audience simply froze in astonishment. Some in the audience were Union
officers fresh from combat, a few carrying revolvers on them. Yet many
assumed that both the gunshot and Booth's dramatic entrance were
simply part of the play.

Booth then turned to his right, toward Hawk, his dagger still in his
hand, and walked diagonally across the stage toward him. As he did so,
Booth glanced up at the audience in the dress circle and at the seats
opposite. According to saloon keeper Ferguson, Booth caught Ferguson's

IN THEIR OWN WORDS

"At the moment the President was shot, he was leaning his hand on the railing, looking down at a person in the orchestra; holding the flag that decorated the box aside to look between it and the post, I saw a flash of the pistol right back in the box. As the person jumped over and lit on the stage, I saw that it was Booth. As he struck the stage, he rose and exclaimed, 'Sic Semper Tyrannis!' and ran directly across the stage to the opposite door, where the actors come in."

—*saloon keeper James Ferguson, who was sitting directly across from the presidential box*

eye and even raised his dagger above his head in a kind of victory salute, mouthing or whispering the words, "I have done it!"

For his part, Hawk took one look at the wild-eyed actor and, not yet realizing what had happened and assuming Booth had found out that he was still seeing the call girl Ella Starr, fled for his life off the stage and up the stairs that led to the dressing rooms at the far left of the theatre.

Booth walked quickly offstage to the wings on the left side of the theatre, bumping roughly into Laura Keene as he passed her. He leaned for a second with both hands against the brick wall that formed the north side of the theatre, catching his breath, before he bolted down the dark, narrow, side passageway along the north wall, heading for the outside door to the alley.

Yet another obstacle stood in Booth's path. Blocking the outside door was the twenty-eight-year-old orchestra leader William Withers Jr. and his girlfriend Jeannie Gourlay—neither of whom had a clue about what had just transpired.

"Let me pass!" Booth screeched at Withers.

The orchestra leader froze and Booth plodded into him. "Damn you," the actor bellowed, slashing at Withers with his dagger and just nicking him slightly on the neck before Withers fell to the floor.

Another stagehand, the twenty-four-year-old French carpenter Jacob Ritterspaugh, stood in Booth's way but backed off when the actor slashed at him with the knife.

Booth then burst through the outside door to the alley, where a cold rain was falling. He was looking around desperately for Spangler, the stage carpenter with whom he had left the rented bay mare. But the busy Spangler, with scenery to change between acts, had handed the reins to the teenage stagehand "Peanut John" Burroughs.[29] Booth spotted the mare.

"Give me that horse!" Booth yelled, startling Burroughs. The boy hesitated, not knowing who Booth was. As a result, the actor reached out, and, with the butt of his dagger, cracked the befuddled teenager hard on his head, tearing the reins from his hands as he did so.[30]

His left foot throbbing from the fall onto the stage, Booth then struggled up into the saddle, a process he later said took "five minutes" but which probably only took a few seconds. Only at that moment did someone try to intervene.

One of the few audience members who instantly understood what had just happened, an Army colonel named Joseph B. Stewart, had leapt to his feet the moment he saw Booth crossing the stage with the dagger in his hand.

A lawyer and former Army officer who stood six feet six inches tall, taller even than Abraham Lincoln, Stewart had clambered up on the stage and proceeded to chase after Booth down the dark passageway that ran along the north wall. He saw Booth go through the outside door but, unfamiliar with his surroundings, and unable to see clearly with the dim light backstage, it took Stewart a few seconds to open the outside door. Once outside, however, as Booth struggled to gain control of his skittish horse, Stewart just barely missed grabbing the reins of the bay mare.

But Booth spotted him, jerked the reins hard to the right, and kicked his spurs into the horse's muscular sides. A lifetime of dedicated horsemanship kicked in. The spirited mare exploded down Baptist Alley at full gallop.

Within seconds, Booth disappeared into the cold rain…and was gone.

12 BELONGING TO HISTORY

Ford's Theatre, 10:30 p.m.

Within seconds the theatre erupted in pandemonium. Mrs. Lincoln issued a piercing shriek that echoed off the theatre walls as she caught Lincoln from falling forward. His left arm bleeding profusely, Rathbone turned toward the stricken president. He saw that Lincoln was unconscious, his head drooping on his chest, and understood immediately what had happened.

Rathbone rushed to the hallway, where theatre patrons were already banging loudly on the outer door. The major saw the door had been jammed shut with a piece of wood. With considerable effort, due to his badly wounded arm and the force of patrons outside trying to push open the door, Rathbone finally succeeded in knocking loose the wood plank and opened the door.

Providentially, one of the theatre patrons closest to the outer door was a young Army surgeon named Charles Leale, only twenty-three years old. He was an ardent admirer of Lincoln and had come to the theater that evening with the express purpose of seeing the president in person. With the lower orchestra seats all taken, Leale had been

Charles Augustus Leale (1842–1932) was a surgeon in the Union Army and the first doctor to reach the stricken Lincoln. Shown here in 1865, he was only twenty-three years old at the time. *Wikimedia Commons*

forced to take a seat in the dress circle balcony.

Leale didn't hesitate. The moment he heard screams from Mrs. Lincoln and Clara Harris, the doctor bounded toward the outer door leading to the two boxes. Right behind him was a second physician, Dr. Albert King, who also was sitting in the balcony seats very near the outer door. Leale reached Lincoln within minutes. Mary Todd Lincoln, nearly fainting with panic, was still holding her unconscious husband in the rocking chair, preventing him from falling. The doctor felt for a pulse and was immediately alarmed when he couldn't feel one. With the help of another man, Leale lifted Lincoln from the rocking chair and lay him flat on the floor of the box.

Right at that moment, a third doctor, Charles Taft, an experienced Army surgeon standing below on the stage, announced himself and was boosted into the box from below by patrons. Taft wasted no time. Using a borrowed penknife, he cut off Lincoln's collar and tore open the president's shirt. But the doctors could see no bleeding or sign of a wound.

Leale examined Lincoln's eyes by lifting the eyelids and saw that the president's pupils were dilated, not a good sign. With his fingers, Leale then felt around the president's head and quickly found the wound: a clean hole in the back of his head. Using his finger, Leale probed the bullet hole, removing a blood clot and thereby relieving the building pressure on Lincoln's brain. The doctors saw immediately that Lincoln began breathing more easily as a result.

Right at this moment, one of the more bizarre incidents of the evening occurred. Laura Keene, the theatre producer and one of the stars of *Our American Cousin,* inexplicably appeared in the president's box.

Down below on the stage, Keene had heard Clara Harris scream for water. With a professional actor's natural instinct for publicity, Keene had grabbed a water pitcher from the theatre's greenroom and directed Thomas Gourlay, the stage manager, to get her upstairs to the box by any means necessary. Gourlay likely took the actress up a hidden stairway that led from the right side of the theatre, next to the saloon, up to the dress circle balcony. However she did it, Keene somehow managed to get through the crowd and pushed her way right to where Lincoln was lying unconscious on the floor.

Keene then knelt on the floor, and, asking permission of Leale to do so, cradled Lincoln's head, oozing blood and brain fluids, in her lap. Knowing she was witnessing history before her very eyes, Keene would keep the bloodstained dress for years, proof that she had held Lincoln's head as he was dying.

However, the doctors were determined that Lincoln should not die on Good Friday in the disreputable environs of a theatre. Yet any attempt to move the president to the White House, across the muddy and pothole-filled streets of Washington, would only hasten his demise. As a result, the doctors decided to move Lincoln to any nearby building they could find. Under Dr. Leale's orders, the physicians and some other men lifted Lincoln off the floor of the presidential box. Barking commands to soldiers to clear a path, they very carefully carried Lincoln, feet-first, down the narrow stairway of the dress circle to the theatre lobby.

With surging masses of angry and sorrowful people all around them, the group moved slowly outside, stopping every few feet as Dr. Leale, in the dark, rainy street, desperately searched for a place to take the president. As the group moved slowly forward, the doctor would occasionally pause to pick open the scab forming on the bullet hole, allowing it to

The Petersen boardinghouse (middle building), where Lincoln was taken, was located directly across the street from Ford's Theatre. Now a museum, it is shown here in 1918. *Wikimedia Commons*

drain. Finally, Dr. Leale spotted a narrow, three-story brick townhouse across the street and screamed for the soldiers to make a path there.

This was a boardinghouse, owned by a German tailor named William Petersen, where many of the actors, including John Matthews, had taken rooms. The house still exists, one of the few buildings from that era that remains substantially untouched. Ironically enough, John Wilkes Booth had just the week before visited the same first-floor room toward the back, and lounged on the very same bed, where the doctors now carried the mortally wounded president.

The bed was too short for the tall president, so he was placed diagonally across it with his feet near the wall. The doctors shooed all visitors, including Mrs. Lincoln, out of the room while they began a more thorough examination. They removed all of Lincoln's clothes and went over his naked body inch by inch, looking for trauma. Only the bullet hole in his head was found. The doctors later marveled that Lincoln seemed in good shape for a man of his age, his arms still thick with muscles.

Satisfied that there was no other injury than the bullet wound, the doctors then covered Lincoln's near-lifeless body with mustard plasters, to keep him warm, drew blankets up to his neck, and did their best to make him comfortable. Mrs. Lincoln was then allowed to return to the room and sit in a chair by Lincoln's head, where she begged him to speak to her one last time and collapsed in tears.

★　　★　　🎩　　★　　★

Meanwhile, all hell was breaking loose on the streets of Washington. Word of the assassination attempt on Lincoln, and the attack earlier on Secretary of State Seward, had spread like wildfire across the city. Large drunken crowds that had been celebrating the end of the war suddenly appeared outside Ford's Theatre, with enraged hotheads screaming that they should burn the place to the ground. Despite the rain, thousands of people were now flooding the streets.

Young Tad Lincoln, watching the play about Aladdin at Grover's Theatre, heard the manager announce that President Lincoln had been shot. Aides rushed the young boy back to the White House—even though Mary Lincoln had begged that he be brought to Petersen's boardinghouse so he could see his father one last time. Robert Lincoln, asleep at the White House, was awoken with the news, and he was able to hurry to Petersen's and was there all night.

There were rumors that all of the telegraph wires out of the city had been cut.[1] Some citizens feared that they were witnessing a coup d'état against the government in progress, almost certainly engineered by the vanquished Confederates. Indeed, had George Atzerodt not lost his nerve and killed the vice president as Booth had instructed him, a coup would have seemed very plausible.

Six hundred thousand men had died in a civil war that led to atrocities on both sides. The political leadership of the Confederacy was on the run, certain they would be executed for treason. It seemed plausible that this was a last-ditch effort to destabilize the Union government, to throw Union forces into chaos so that the remaining military forces of the Confederacy might escape and live to fight another day.

Secretary of War Stanton had already received a report of the attack on Seward and had rushed to Seward's home. He found him badly wounded but still alive, so he left him and the other victims in the hands of doctors already there and proceeded directly to Ford's Theatre. Within thirty minutes of the attack, Stanton was in the parlor of Petersen's boardinghouse, setting up a de facto war room and seat of the executive government. For all intents and purposes, he was functioning as the acting president. When Vice President Andrew Johnson arrived, he stood aside and let Stanton run the country for the time being.

Stanton's first objective was to figure out what exactly had happened. He quickly found and conscripted a transcriptionist who knew shorthand, a young clerk named James Tanner, and he created a three-man board of inquiry—made up of top judges—who proceeded to interview witnesses one after the other throughout the night. From the testimony of literally dozens of eyewitnesses, the interrogators quickly identified John Wilkes Booth as the likely suspect.

★   ★   ▮   ★   ★

Booth had spent months planning his escape from Washington in the event he succeeded in kidnapping Lincoln. He had traveled along the roads south of the capital numerous times. As a result, Booth knew precisely where he wanted to go. His plan was to get out of Washington as soon as possible, ride south into rural Maryland, and then cross the Potomac to Virginia.

After exiting Baptist Alley in the rain, Booth must have turned onto F Street (to the right or left, no one knows for sure which) before quickly heading south across the Mall. Booth was headed for the long bridge across the Potomac River that lay next to the Navy Yard, where Lincoln and his wife had spent the afternoon. This bridge, closely guarded by sentries, was one of the few exit points out of the city. We have photographs of what it looked like at the time.

Booth appeared at the Washington side of the bridge around 11:00 p.m., just over half an hour after he pulled the trigger. The sentry on duty immediately challenged him, and then called for his sergeant. Although the situation was inherently suspicious—the late hour and a horse breathing heavily from a hard ride—Booth seemed completely relaxed. Once again, his actor's training and careful planning came to his aid.

Booth was, as usual, well dressed and looked like a gentleman. What's more, he was wearing a hat. As strange as this may seem, the hat was important. At that time, men usually wore hats in public—and appearing without one would make you seem somewhat disreputable. Booth had been wearing a cloth hat when he entered the presidential box, but it had fallen off when he leapt onto the stage. Incredibly, it

The Long Bridge across the Potomac was rebuilt in 1863, as shown here, to create a new span that could hold heavier rail traffic. Booth crossed over the old bridge (left) designed primarily for horses and pedestrians. *Wikimedia Commons*

appears Booth had planned for even this eventuality and had stored a backup hat in the saddlebag of his rented horse.

The bridge sentry, Sergeant Silas T. Cobb, asked Booth why he wanted to cross so late at night.

"I am going down home, down in Charles," Booth said casually, referring to Charles County in Maryland.

"Didn't you know, my friend, that it is against the laws to pass here after nine o'clock?"

"No," Booth lied. "I haven't been in town for some time, and it is new to me."

Sergeant Cobb was suspicious. He looked Booth over closely. Then he asked Booth his name—and, incredibly, Booth told him it was John Booth.

"What is your object to be in town after nine o'clock when you have so long a road to travel?" Cobb pressed.

Booth remained cool and nonchalant. "It is a dark road," he said, quite plausibly, "and I thought if I waited a spell I would have the moon."

Cobb didn't look convinced but also figured Booth was harmless. "I will pass you but I don't know as I ought to."[2]

Booth smiled and nudged his horse forward. The rules required that he walk his horse across the bridge.

Within minutes, another rider suddenly appeared out of the darkness. This was David Herold. He had callously abandoned his co-conspirator, Lewis Powell, to his fate, and was now desperate to escape Washington. Unlike Booth, Herold didn't give the guards his real name but said his name was "Smith."

As with Booth, the guards told Herold that he wasn't allowed to cross the bridge after nine o'clock. However, since the war was almost over, and Herold, too, had a plausible explanation for his late-night appearance—he said he had been visiting a woman on Capitol Hill—the guards let him pass over the bridge as well.

Herold caught up with Booth on the dark road beyond the bridge at a designated meeting place. Together, the two men headed south towards the tiny crossroads hamlet of Surrattsville (now Clinton, Maryland) and

Booth and David Herold's first stop after crossing the Potomac was Mary Surratt's tavern, located in Surrattsville (now Clinton, Maryland), fourteen miles from the Long Bridge. It still stands and is now a museum. *Wikimedia Commons*[3]

Mary Surratt's tavern. It was fourteen miles to the tavern from the bridge. The rain had let up, and with the help of a bright moon, Booth and Herold made the trip in record time. The Surratt tavern still exists and is now a museum.

After midnight, Herold knocked loudly on the side door of the tavern house, used by paying customers. He woke the proprietor, John Lloyd, from a deep and drunken sleep. Lloyd staggered to the door and found Herold standing outside and a mounted horseman a few feet away in the darkness. Herold told Lloyd that he was there to collect the items that Mary Surratt had given him earlier in the day. Lloyd nodded. He had already removed the "shooting irons" from their hiding place in the walls upstairs.

Lloyd let Herold come inside while he went upstairs for the guns. Coming back down the staircase, Lloyd then handed Herold one of the carbines, a bottle of whiskey, and the binoculars that Booth had given

Mary Surratt to deliver earlier that day. Booth remained seated on his horse. When Lloyd announced that he would go get the second carbine, Booth replied that he didn't want it. He had broken his leg, Booth said, and wanted to know if there was a doctor nearby. Lloyd said that he didn't know of any.

Before the two men rode away, however, they couldn't resist revealing their secret. "I will tell you some news if you want to hear it," Booth said.

Lloyd grunted assent. "You can tell me if you think proper."

Booth smiled. "We have assassinated the president and Secretary Seward," he said.

Lloyd was speechless. As steeped in alcohol as his brain was, it quickly dawned on him, as the two men rode off into the darkness, that this was *not* good news. For aiding Booth, he realized, Lloyd could very well face a hangman's noose himself.

★   ★   🎩   ★   ★

John Lloyd wasn't the only person worried about what the attack on Lincoln would mean for his future prospects. Within hours, one of the largest manhunts and criminal investigations in the history of the United States began.

The Federal government, convinced that it was under attack, likely by its hated and desperate enemies in the Confederacy, reacted with remarkable speed under the circumstances. Armed guards were immediately stationed outside the homes and offices of cabinet members and some other major officials. All transportation in and out of the city was immediately halted.

Within an hour and a half of the shooting, around midnight, Stanton's aide Major Thomas Eckert—the man with the iron arm whom Lincoln had asked to attend the theatre with him—fired off a telegram to General Grant:

April 14, 12 p.m. 1865
Washington D.C.
To Lt. Genl Grant
On Night Train to Burlington
    The president was assassinated tonight at Ford's Theatre
at 10 30 tonight & cannot live. The wound is a pistol shot
through the head. Secretary Seward & his son Frederick were
also assassinated at their residence & are in a dangerous
condition. The Secretary of War desires that you return to
Washington immediately. Please answer on receipt of this.
    Thos. T. Eckert, Maj.

Thanks to a military bureaucracy well-honed by the war and a net-
work of thousands of telegraph wires that now crisscrossed much of the
United States, a considerable investigative apparatus sprang into action.
    Many hundreds of people were arrested and interrogated over the
coming days and weeks, often with little or no cause. That included most
(but not all) of the cast and crew of Ford's Theatre, including the owner,
John Ford himself. Those arrested were held in Washington's prisons—
either the Old Washington Penitentiary (torn down in 1867) or the Navy
Yard—and interrogated repeatedly.
    Yet in the end, the government showed considerable restraint. Most
of those arrested were released relatively quickly. Only those who were
Booth's companions at the very end faced severe justice.

★   ★   🎩   ★   ★

    After recovering the carbine, field glasses, and bottle of whiskey,
Booth and Herold left the crossroads of Surrattsville and headed south
along the main road. The road was clear of patrols. They didn't see a
soul as they rode silently on. Around four in the morning, less than six
hours after Booth had fired a steel ball into Abraham Lincoln's brain,

Booth sought refuge in the home of Dr. Samuel Mudd, whom he knew, early on the morning of April 15. Located about five miles from Bryantown, the home is now a museum. *Wikimedia Commons*[4]

the two riders approached a farmhouse just outside the village of Bryantown in Charles County, Maryland.

Booth knew exactly where he was going. It was the home of Dr. Samuel A. Mudd. He had been there before. Herold dismounted and took the reins of Booth's horse, edging toward the dark farmhouse. There was no light whatsoever and all was quiet. Not even a dog barked to break the silence. Even today, the country road that passes the farmhouse has very little traffic.

Herold pounded on the front door of the two-story wood farmhouse, which still exists. After some minutes, Herold heard a voice on the other side of the door demanding to know who was there at this time of night.

Herold may have explained that they were two travelers heading to Washington and that one of their horses had reared, throwing the rider to the ground and breaking his leg. They desperately needed a doctor.

Dr. Mudd, thirty-two years old, with a bald head and a thick goatee mustache, was a respected physician in the area and a well-known

Confederate sympathizer. He had
earned his M.D. from Georgetown College. With his wife
Sarah, with whom he had four
young children, Mudd farmed a
218-acre tobacco farm with the
help of eleven slaves he had no
intention of giving up willingly.

Mudd would later claim that he
didn't know or recognize Booth
when he treated his broken leg that
night—yet the evidence was overwhelming, his attorney would later
admit, that he knew Booth well and
at the very least knew about his plot
to kidnap Lincoln. Booth had traveled to Bryantown twice in the past
six months, attending Catholic
Mass with Dr. Mudd and his family
in the nearby parish church. It was
Dr. Mudd's obvious lies, evasive-
ness, and nervousness that made
investigators suspicious at once.

Dr. Samuel Mudd (1833–1883) set Booth's
broken leg. While during his trial he
denied that he knew who Booth was,
Mudd later admitted that he had known
all along. He narrowly escaped being
hanged for his role in Booth's escape.
Wikimedia Commons

Whether he recognized Booth or not, Dr. Mudd helped the injured
man off his horse and, grasping him around the waist, slowly moved him
inside the farmhouse. After making Booth comfortable in a chair, Dr.
Mudd proceeded to examine him. He tried to remove Booth's boot, but
it wouldn't budge an inch. The swelling from the break above Booth's
left ankle made the boot almost impossible to pull off. As a result, Dr.
Mudd simply took a scalpel, cut gently through the leather, and removed
the boot that way. He quickly saw that Booth's injury was a clean break,
not a compound fracture. The doctor found some wood to use as a splint.
Later, he fashioned some crude crutches from an old plank.

Dr. Mudd invited the two weary travelers to rest at his home. Booth was anxious to press on. He knew that one of the greatest manhunts in the history of the United States was almost certainly underway. Yet he also knew that traveling the roads now, as dawn was just breaking, would be a serious mistake.

As a result, Booth decided to accept Dr. Mudd's offer. Mudd and Herold helped Booth to the stairway and, with great effort, Booth managed to climb the stairs to the second floor. Booth and Herold would share the Mudds' guest bedroom. It was now about six in the morning.

★   ★   🎩   ★   ★

Back in Washington, Stanton and the doctors were on a death watch around Abraham Lincoln's bed in the Petersen boardinghouse.

Detectives had visited Booth's room at the National Hotel, scouring it for clues, and had found a letter from Booth's childhood friend, Sam Arnold, that made it clear that there had been a conspiracy of some sort against the president. "Do not act rashly or in haste," Arnold had written to Booth from his home in Baltimore. "I would prefer you first query, 'go and see how it will be taken at R___d,' and ere long I shall be better prepared to again be with you."

The meeting at Gautier's restaurant a month earlier, in which Booth had hinted at assassination, had filled Arnold with dread. Along with most of the other kidnapping conspirators, he wanted nothing to do with murder, and yet he knew that if Booth did do something crazy and somehow killed the president he would almost certainly be implicated. Now Arnold's worst fears had been realized, and the reference in the letter to the capital of the Confederacy—"see how it will be taken at R___d"—convinced Stanton there was a vicious Southern conspiracy against the government. It made sense: their capital recently invaded, their president and other officials on the run, why wouldn't the Confederacy strike at the leadership of the Union government?

By six in the morning, just as John Wilkes Booth was easing himself into a soft bed in Dr. Mudd's guest bedroom, the doctors were watching anxiously as the life drained out of Abraham Lincoln. Thousands of people were gathered outside, black and white, to await news of what was happening. The president's pulse was failing and his breathing increasingly rapid.

By seven o'clock, the doctors were all conscious that they were witnessing history. All three present had their hands on Lincoln's body, measuring his pulse and watching their pocket watches. They thought death had come many times; but even at fifty-six years old, Lincoln was a strong man, and a fighter. He clung to life. At the end, the doctors recorded everything: Lincoln's heart stopped beating at 7:22 and ten seconds. The doctors all looked at one another. He was gone.

IN THEIR OWN WORDS

"The Surgeon General now held his finger to the carotid artery, Col. Crane held his head, Dr. Stone who was sitting on the bed, held his left pulse, and his right pulse was held by myself. At 7:20 a.m., he breathed his last and 'the spirit fled to God who gave it.'"

—*Charles A. Leale*

No one said a word for at least five minutes. Finally, Stanton turned to Lincoln's pastor at the New York Avenue Presbyterian Church where he attended services regularly, the Reverend Phineas Gurley, and asked him to say a prayer, which no one recorded. It was then that Stanton, openly weeping, pronounced Lincoln's passing.

Like so many aspects of this tragic story, Stanton's precise words are a matter of dispute. Most Lincoln biographies, including the one written in 1890 by his two personal secretaries, John G. Nicolay and John Hay, record the secretary saying, "Now he belongs to the ages." James Tanner, the shorthand transcriptionist who had been recording testimony all that night from witnesses and was in the room when Lincoln died, believed Stanton said, "He belongs to the angels now."[5] However, Tanner wasn't certain: his pencil had broken by that time and he only recalled what he heard from memory.

Robert Lincoln and Rev. Gurley left the room to break the news to Mary Todd Lincoln. She couldn't bear to see her husband's dead body. After about an hour and a half, Mary Lincoln and Todd left the boardinghouse. The presidential coachman, Francis Burke, who had been waiting all night outside in the rain, drove Mary Lincoln back to the White House. Soon after, a detachment of soldiers appeared carrying a plain pine box. It was only then that the crowd outside finally realized that Lincoln was dead.

The soldiers entered the boardinghouse and, under Stanton's watchful eyes, wrapped Lincoln's still-naked body in a large American flag, placed it in the coffin, and screwed the lid down. The box was then loaded onto a plain horse-drawn wagon. The wagon, accompanied only by a few soldiers and some members of the cabinet, then took Lincoln's body back to the White House. It was taken upstairs to a guest bedroom of the White House for a primitive and pointless autopsy.

The huge gathering of people inside Petersen's boardinghouse slowly drifted away. The bed where Lincoln had been placed was left just as it was. The man who rented the room in which Lincoln died, William Clark, would return later that day to retake possession. He would sleep that night in the same bed in which Lincoln had died, under the same covers. When Stanton and everyone else had left, a professional photographer named Julius Ulke, who also rented a room in the boardinghouse, came downstairs, set up his camera, and took a photograph of the bed where Lincoln died.

★　★　🎩　★　★

John Wilkes Booth and David Herold spent all day Easter Sunday at Dr. Mudd's home. Herold got up early for a hearty breakfast, but

Booth, his broken leg throbbing, spent all day in bed, ignoring the plates of food that Mrs. Mudd brought up to him. Later in the day, Dr. Mudd and Herold rode over to the farm of Dr. Mudd's father to see if they had a carriage he could rent out to transport the now-crippled Booth. Dr. Mudd's younger brother told him they had no carriages to spare and suggested they go into town, nearby Bryantown, to see if they could rent one there.

The two men did precisely that. However, before they got to Bryantown David Herold suddenly yanked his horse to a dead stop. He could see up ahead a unit of soldiers in blue, the Thirteenth New York Cavalry. These men were precisely what Herold feared: a posse hot in pursuit of the man or men who had assassinated the president of the United States. Without saying a word, Herold simply turned his horse around and galloped at full speed back to Mudd's farm.

Incredibly, Mudd simply shrugged and continued on into town. At this point, Mudd may not have known what Booth had done and thus saw no reason to fear the soldiers. However, he was about to find out. As he ambled about the small settlement, long known as a hotbed of rebel sentiment, he could see the Union soldiers strutting from building to building, asking pointed questions. Finally, someone told him the shocking news: the actor John Wilkes Booth had murdered President Lincoln.

David Herold raced back to Mudd's farm, said hello politely to

David Edgar Herold (1842–1865), a twenty-three-year-old former pharmacist's assistant, stayed with his hero John Wilkes Booth to the very end. Born into an affluent Washington family, Herold attended Georgetown College. *Wikimedia Commons*

Mrs. Mudd as she was preparing the Easter dinner, and then bounded up the stairs to the guest bedroom.

Within moments, Booth and Herold appeared downstairs, dressed for travel, gun belts around their waists. If Dr. Mudd betrayed them to the authorities, the Union soldiers could be at the door within half an hour. Yet Booth hesitated. It was still light out, and he and Herold had no idea where they should head next. They took a big chance and decided to wait anxiously for Dr. Mudd to return.

He finally did return around six o'clock in the evening. Dr. Mudd, a Confederate sympathizer and slave owner, did not betray Booth. But Mudd understood the mortal danger in which Booth had placed him and his entire family by showing up at his farm just hours after killing the president of the United States.

Yet for some reason, Dr. Mudd decided to help Booth escape. He told Booth that he, Mudd, had to report his visit to the authorities, because they would soon discover that Booth had visited the farm. However, he could let Booth and Herold have a good head start. Dr. Mudd gave Booth the names of two people who might help him, local Confederate sympathizers, and told him how to get to their farmhouses.

Booth and Herold left Dr. Mudd's farm after dark, circumventing Bryantown, where the troops were actively searching farmhouses, and headed toward the farmhouses Dr. Mudd had described. They missed the first one, owned by a man named William Burtles, but eventually made their way to the farmhouse of Colonel Samuel Cox, a Confederate courier, aided by a half-black local man named Oswell Swann. Long after midnight, they approached Cox's farmhouse on horseback. Cox came out to meet the two men and, it appears, Booth decided that on this occasion honesty was the best policy.

He told Cox who he was, what he had just done, and openly asked for his help. Like Dr. Mudd, Cox understood immediately the danger he was in, aiding and abetting the assassin of the president. Yet he, too, couldn't resist one last act of defiance for the rebel cause. Cox told Booth and Herold that they couldn't stay at his farmhouse, but that they could hide out in a pine thicket nearby where they could probably avoid detection.

Knowing that he was already implicated, Dr. Mudd sent his cousin to military headquarters in Bryantown on Monday to tell them about the two strange visitors who had stopped by the farm on Saturday morning. When investigators searched the farmhouse, Mudd showed them the boot he had removed from the injured man's leg. Inside the boot the investigators found a name engraved on the leather, J. Wilkes.

Colonel Cox sent his son to visit a neighbor, a local widower named Thomas A. Jones, who was one of the most successful river smugglers the Confederacy had. The boy brought Jones to his father's estate, Rich Hill, and Cox explained the situation. Jones, like Cox, was intrigued by the challenge of helping the killers of the tyrant Lincoln escape Yankee justice. Yet he also knew the odds were against them.

Jones rode out to the pine thicket to meet Booth and Herold in person. Cox taught Jones the special coded whistle that the men had all agreed upon so that Booth wouldn't mistakenly shoot a friend or ally. Jones rode out to the thicket, whistled the special whistle, and found Booth lying on his blanket on the cold, wet ground, deep in the trees. Booth was in considerable pain. Yet he greeted Jones warmly and confessed that he had, indeed, killed Lincoln. He asked if Jones could help him escape.

Jones realized that Booth's only chance, as Union troops fanned out across the entire area, was to hide in plain sight until the search parties had exhausted themselves and moved on. He told Booth and Herold that he or one of his associates would keep them provisioned with food and supplies if they promised not to light a fire or draw attention to themselves. Jones told them where there was a freshwater spring nearby, where they could fill their canteens, and promised that he would arrange for food to be brought daily. Once the coast was clear and the search parties had moved on, then and only then could Jones transport them across the Potomac to Virginia.

And that is precisely what happened. While the largest manhunt in history swung into full gear, and literally thousands of soldiers and detectives searched every nook and cranny for hundreds of miles around Washington—storming into farmhouses, arresting anyone they suspected of aiding the assassin—Booth and Herold simply lay down in the densely wooded pine thicket and kept quiet. Jones's strategy was eerily prescient.

A day after they had hidden themselves, Booth, Herold, and the visiting Jones crouched nervously on the ground as a unit of Union cavalry raced past, coming within two hundred yards of their hiding place. The two fugitives later made the difficult decision to get rid of their faithful but starving and noisy horses to evade detection. Herold may have taken the animals to a nearby patch of quicksand and shot them in the head, allowing their bodies to sink into the slime.

Booth asked only one special favor from Jones: newspapers! Yes, the actor Booth's greatest desire, second only to his wish to escape, was to read his reviews. He wanted to know what the country thought of his greatest performance, especially his comrades in the South. A bit taken aback by this strange request, Jones promised that he would buy some newspapers and bring them along with food.

★   ★   🎩   ★   ★

Just as Jones had predicted, Booth's hiding in the wooded Maryland thicket gave the illusion that he had vanished into thin air without a trace. The country assumed that he was racing to Virginia in a mad dash to escape to the South, and, perhaps, escape the country. But after being seen at Mary Surratt's tavern on the night of the assassination, Booth's trail had gone cold. Stanton and other government officials were frantic.

But then, on Monday, they got their first break. One of the conspirators accidentally walked right into their arms. Now that the trail had gone cold, Stanton and the other top men searching for Booth began to go over what they knew—and they kept coming back to the mysterious boardinghouse run by the equally mysterious Mary Surratt. Booth had visited there many times, the detectives knew, and Mary Surratt's son, John Jr., was a suspect along with Booth.

The authorities decided to pay Mary Surratt another visit. They arrived at her home at 541 H Street around eleven o'clock at night on Monday, April 17. Their intention was to arrest every man, woman, and child in the place—including the eleven-year-old girl who boarded there alone, Appolonia Dean. Led by Major W. H. Smith, a contingent of soldiers arrived at the boardinghouse, knocked hard on the door, and informed Mary Surratt that they were arresting everyone on the premises. The soldiers also began another thorough search.

However, something unexpected happened. While everyone was waiting for a carriage to transport the prisoners to the military headquarters for interrogation, an unknown man walked up the stairs to Mary Surratt's boardinghouse, oblivious to the large contingent of soldiers loitering about on the street. He was dressed in relatively nice clothes, but he was filthy and unshaven and carrying a large pickaxe. The man, young and strong, knocked on the boardinghouse door and was immediately allowed inside.

There he stood face to face with five armed soldiers and knew instantly that he had made a very bad mistake. It was none other than Lewis Powell, the tough Confederate soldier who had attempted to murder the secretary of state and had almost killed two of his sons. After Powell's bizarre attack on the secretary, he had fled out the front door of Seward's home only to discover that David Herold had panicked and ridden off, leaving Powell to his fate.

For the past two days, the hapless Powell had wandered the streets of Washington aimlessly, hiding out in a cemetery. Now, near midnight, cold and hungry, he had decided to look for shelter at the only place in Washington he knew: Mary Surratt's boardinghouse. Yet he chose just the exact wrong moment.

Thinking quickly, Powell claimed that he was at the boardinghouse to arrange for a time to dig a trench for Mary Surratt. But Surratt, alarmed, insisted she had never seen the ominous young man in her life. After brief but intense questioning, Major Smith decided that Powell was sufficiently suspicious to be taken into custody with all the others. Although Powell could have made a break for it—he was armed with a pickaxe and could have theoretically taken out two or three soldiers in a matter of seconds—he gave up without a fight.

Within hours, the detectives investigating the case knew exactly who he was. Without any work on their part, the most wanted man in the country after Booth had literally walked into their arms.

The same thing would almost be true of another of Booth's Gang of Four conspirators, the dim-witted alcoholic George Atzerodt. Like Powell and even David Herold, Atzerodt could have just hit the road, moved out West, and vanished into the nameless multitudes roaming about the countryside in the wake of the Civil War. In an age without fingerprinting or other scientific methods of identification, he would have been difficult to apprehend. But he didn't. After George Atzerodt lost his nerve and

IN THEIR OWN WORDS

"On the evening of the 14th of April, I met Booth and Payne [Powell] at the Herndon House, in the city, at eight o'clock. He said he himself should murder Mr. Lincoln and General Grant, Payne should take Mr. Seward, and I should take Mr. Johnson. I told him I would not do it; that I had gone into the thing to capture, but I was not going to kill. He told me I was a fool; that I would be hung anyhow, and that it was death for every man that backed out; and so we parted."

—*George Atzerodt, statement at trial*

abandoned Booth's plan for him to kill Vice President Andrew Johnson at the Kirkwood House hotel, he spent the night of the assassination getting drunk.

He eventually stumbled into another Washington hotel, the Pennsylvania House, sometime after midnight. He rented a shared room, at first declining to sign the register, and spent the night there. Early the next morning, now a bit sobered up, Atzerodt walked down F Street just a block or two from Ford's Theatre and attempted to throw away his knife, which he must have felt would implicate him. Unfortunately for him, someone saw him toss the knife, retrieved it, and gave it to the police. Atzerodt then traveled to nearby Georgetown

George Atzerodt (1835–1865) was a thirty-year-old German immigrant and carriage maker who joined Booth's circle of conspirators in 1864. He ignored Booth's order to kill Vice President Andrew Johnson and got drunk instead. *Wikimedia Commons*

where he attempted unsuccessfully to borrow money and was forced to pawn his revolver for ten dollars.

With that money, the German immigrant was able to travel twenty miles north of Washington to the home of a friend in Montgomery County, Maryland. After Easter dinner, Atzerodt left the house and went to stay with his cousin, Hartman Richter, who lived nearby. He stayed there for the next four days, oblivious that he was being hunted by half of the policemen in the country.

Atzerodt's own brother, John, alerted police of his possible whereabouts. On April 20, a unit of six cavalrymen arrived at Hartman Richter's home and found Atzerodt asleep in an upstairs bedroom. He was arrested without incident and proceeded to confess to everything he knew—the kidnapping plot, Booth's last-minute decision to kill rather than capture Lincoln, everything.

Only one co-conspirator got away: John Surratt Jr. Although he left Booth when it became clear that the actor was plotting murder and not merely kidnapping, Surratt was initially suspected of being one of the assassins. The famous wanted poster that Stanton had made, promising a $100,000 reward for the capture of the assassins, listed Surratt along with Booth and Herold as the three men wanted. The government was offering $25,000 for his head. As a result, Surratt knew he had to get out of the country, and fast.

★   ★   ▰   ★   ★

John Wilkes Booth and David Herold stayed hidden in the pine thicket for five days and four nights, from Easter Sunday, April 16, until Thursday, April 20. They were damp, cold, hungry, and miserable. Booth was dressed in the clothes of a city dandy, utterly unprepared for camping out in the woods. The Confederate smuggler Jones faithfully brought the two men both food and newspapers as he had promised he would, and Booth devoured both.

But when he read his "reviews," Booth was devastated. Rather than being celebrated as the savior of the South, the slayer of a tyrant, a modern incarnation of the noble Roman Brutus, Booth found himself denounced as a cold-blooded assassin. The *Baltimore Sun,* Booth's hometown newspaper, asked how it could be possible that the republic could have given birth to "men capable of the vilest crimes which blot and disgrace the pages of history."[6]

A few defiant newspapers in the South dared to assert that Lincoln got what he deserved. For example, the *Chattanooga Daily Rebel* wrote that "Abe has gone to answer before the bar of God for the innocent blood which he has permitted to be shed, and his efforts to enslave a free people."[7] But for the most part, even in the South, the newspapers damned Booth as an amoral coward.

Even worse from Booth's point of view, the whole world was now speaking about Abraham Lincoln, the hated tyrant—the man who started a war that killed 600,000 Americans and imprisoned anyone who dared to question his actions—as the savior of democratic government itself. Incredibly, historians know how Booth took all this because he wrote down his thoughts in two lengthy diary entries that still exist, one written while he was lying on the cold ground in the pine thicket. Booth carried with him an old datebook for 1864, and he used the blank pages to pen his responses to his critics.

In his first entry after the assassination, dated April 17, Booth bluntly contradicted what the newspapers said about his motives:

> For six months we had worked to capture, but our cause being almost lost, something decisive and great must be done. But its failure was owing to others, who did not strike for their country with a heart. I struck boldly, and not as the papers say. I walked with a firm step through a thousand of his friends, was stopped, but pushed on. A colonel was at his side. I shouted Sic Semper before I fired. In jumping broke my leg. I passed all his pickets, rode sixty miles that night with the bone of my leg tearing the flesh at every jump. I can never repent it, though we hated to kill. Our country owed all her troubles to him, and God simply made me the instrument of his punishment.

★　★　**I**　★　★

On Tuesday, April 18, Lincoln's body lay in state in the East Room of the White House. The coffin was placed on a raised platform beneath a canopy.

The next day, an elaborate funeral was held in Washington. Lincoln's casket was carried down Pennsylvania Avenue in a specially outfitted carriage to the Capitol rotunda. Thousands lined the streets, including many freed slaves, to say goodbye to "Father Abraham." A committal service was held at the Capitol, and then thousands passed by his open casket for a viewing of Lincoln's body.

On April 21, Lincoln's body was transported on a special train to his final burial in Springfield, Illinois. It would be a final goodbye tour, as the train would stop in eleven cities on the way, with open-casket viewing ceremonies held in each. Out of respect for Lincoln's widow, Stanton refused to permit photography of Lincoln's body. In New York City on April 24, the only known photograph of Lincoln in death was taken—and Stanton promptly ordered all prints and plates destroyed. However, the photographer managed to keep one in a secret file. This final photograph of Abraham Lincoln was only discovered ninety years later, in 1952, by a fourteen-year-old boy visiting the Lincoln Home in Springfield.

13 "TELL MOTHER, I DIE FOR MY COUNTRY"

homas Jones's strategy of hiding Booth in plain sight worked like a charm. Just as he had predicted, after a week of intense house-to-house searches, the military units that converged on the rebel stronghold of Maryland quickly concluded that Booth had eluded their grasp and was now well on his way to Virginia.[1]

For five long days, Booth and Herold lay quietly in the dense thicket, shivering, with Booth in great pain but safe. Finally, on the afternoon of Thursday, April 20, Thomas Jones appeared and announced that the moment had arrived.[2] Like the seasoned intelligence operative that he was, Jones had passed the time at the local general store, eavesdropping on what the troops searching for Booth would say as they ordered drinks and supplies. He had just overheard that there had been a report that Booth and Herold were seen in another county—and that the entire force was moving out in hot pursuit.

As a result, Jones bundled up the two fugitives and, after dark, led them three miles down forest paths and marshlands to the banks of the Potomac, where he had a boat hidden. Along the way, they stopped at Jones's own farm. Jones went inside and brought out some food for the hungry men.

CRITICAL MINUTES

Booth was able to escape justice as long as he did due to the steely nerves of Thomas Jones, the Confederate agent who helped Booth and Herold survive in a pine thicket and then gave them a boat to cross the Potomac. Had Booth and Herold not waited until the Federal troops had exhausted their searches of the nearby farmhouses, they would almost certainly have been captured. Jones's strategy of hiding in place bought the fugitives more time. Jones had been offered a $100,000 reward if he helped capture Booth, but, Jones later wrote, had he betrayed the fugitive for money, he would have been "of all traitors the most abject and despicable."

When they got to the banks of the river, Jones instructed Booth and Herold on how they were to cross the formidable Potomac. He gave them a candle, matches, and a compass. He instructed Booth to keep to a specific heading and promised that, if they did so, they would reach Machodoc Creek on the Virginia side. There they would find help at the home of a Confederate sympathizer, a woman named Elizabeth Quesenberry, who lived in a farmhouse along the creek. Jones then pushed the small skiff off from the makeshift dock and waved goodbye.

David Herold, who was an experienced oarsman but didn't know this area of the river, rowed with all his might. Sitting in the stern, Booth did his best to navigate in the dark with a flickering candle that he tried to keep hidden below the gunwale so it wouldn't be spotted. The voyage on the river was a disaster. The two men spent most of the night out on

IN THEIR OWN WORDS

"We placed Booth in the stern with an oar to steer; Herold took the bow-seat to row. Then lighting a candle which I had brought for the purpose—I had no lantern— and carefully shading it with an oil cloth coat belonging to one of the men, I pointed out on the compass Booth had with him the course to steer. 'Keep to that,' I said, 'and it will bring you into Machodoc Creek. Mrs. Quesenberry lives near the mouth of this creek. If you tell her you come from me I think she will take care of you.' I then cautioned them to keep the light hidden and said, 'Goodbye.'

"As I was in the act of shoving the boat off, Booth exclaimed, 'Wait a minute, old fellow.' He then offered me some money. I took eighteen dollars, the price of the boat I knew I would never see again. He wanted me to take more, but I said no, what I had done was not for money. In a voice choked with emotion, he said, 'God bless you, my dear friend, for all you have done for me. Good-bye, old fellow.' I pushed the boat off and it glided out of sight into the darkness."

—*Former Confederate agent Thomas Jones,* J. Wilkes Booth, *1893* the mighty Potomac, with naval patrol boats on the watch for them, and ended up going in the wrong direction. They eventually came ashore in an inlet called Nanjemoy Creek, northwest of where they had started. In other words, they had gone sideways.

However, Herold knew a Southern sympathizer in the area, a man named John Hughes, who took them into his home, gave them a hot meal, and told them where they could hide in the marshlands near the river. It was here, a full week after the assassination, on Friday, April 21, that Booth got out his trusty diary and wrote another entry, frankly expressing his dismay at the treatment he had received from an ungrateful population:

> After being hunted like a dog through swamps, woods, and last night being chased by gunboats till I was forced to return wet, cold, and starving, with every man's hand against me, I am here in despair. And why? For doing what Brutus was honored for. What made Tell a hero? And yet I, for striking down a greater tyrant than they ever knew, am looked upon as a common cutthroat. My action was purer than either of theirs. One hoped to be great himself. The other had not only his country's but his own wrongs to avenge. I hoped for no gain. I knew no private wrong. I struck for my country and that alone. A country that groaned beneath this tyranny, and prayed for this end, and yet now behold the cold hands they extend to me.

Booth went on to describe his plans. Acknowledging that he had been "abandoned, with the curse of Cain" upon him, Booth wrote that this night, Friday, he would "try to escape these bloodhounds once more," although, he added, his fate was in the hands of God.

One thing Booth wanted to make clear: he had no intention of dying like a criminal. He prayed that God would let him "die bravely." The self-centered actor even spared a thought for his pathetic follower, Herold.

IN BOOTH'S OWN WORDS

"For my country I have given up all that makes life sweet and holy, brought misery upon my family and am sure there is no pardon in Heaven for me since man condemns me so. I have only heard of what has been done (except what I did myself) and it fills me with horror. God try and forgive me, and bless my mother. Tonight I will once more try the river with the intent to cross; though I have a greater desire and almost a mind to return to Washington and in a measure clear my name, which I feel I can do. I do not repent the blow I struck. I may before my God but not to man. I think I have done well, though I am abandoned, with the curse of Cain upon me...."

—*Booth's diary entry, April 20*

He wrote that Herold "often prays (yes, before and since) with a true and sincere heart."

Finally, Booth concluded that while he did "not wish to shed a drop of blood," he must nevertheless "fight the course." By that Booth appears to have meant that he intended to go down fighting, that he had no intention of surrendering and suffering the humiliation of a public trial and execution, like he had seen with his own eyes John Brown suffer through.

Booth and Herold should have pushed off that night and tried the crossing again. But for some unknown reason, they didn't. They chose to stay hidden in the marsh for another twenty-four hours, allowing the

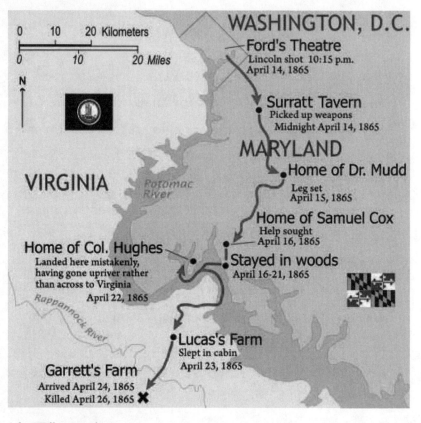

John Wilkes Booth's escape route. *Wikimedia Commons*

man hunters to catch up and study valuable clues. The next night, however, they were better prepared. They knew where they had to go.

As a result, right after sundown on Saturday, April 22, Booth and Herold once again shoved off in the little skiff and headed out into the icy waters of the Potomac, narrowly missing another Union gunboat patrolling the shoreline. After rowing for hours, this time in the right direction, the little boat managed to cross the river, although Herold missed his target destination of Machodoc Creek and instead beached the boat a little bit short on Gambo Creek.

Nevertheless, the two fugitives were now in long-sought Virginia—the state with the motto Booth had loudly proclaimed from the stage, sic semper tyrannis. It was early Sunday morning, April 23, 1865.

What happened next was a series of bizarre chance encounters that would eventually set the stage for Booth's final capture. Amazingly, the fugitives were helped by many people and likely could have escaped were it not for a number of small incidents that literally locked the door on them.

On early Sunday morning, Herold left Booth at the boat and set out to find Elizabeth Quesenberry's farmhouse on the shore of Machodoc Creek. Herold quickly found both the farmhouse and Mrs. Quesenberry herself. He appealed to her sense of Southern hospitality—and her even stronger sense of Confederate loyalty. Unsure of what to do, Mrs. Quesenberry immediately sent for the top Confederate agent in the area—none other than Thomas Harbin, a man who had agreed to help Booth with his kidnapping plot months earlier.

Along with a colleague named William Bryant, Harbin agreed to help Herold and Booth, even though to do so could mean execution. They quickly arranged for some horses and brought them, along with food Mrs. Quesenberry prepared, to the boat landing spot just after dark. Their mission now was to find some place where Herold and Booth could hide out. The first place they tried, the home of another physician, Dr. Richard Stuart, was the opposite of welcoming. Dr. Stuart quickly figured out who they were and wanted nothing to do with Booth and Herold.

As a result, they left and then forced their way into the cabin owned by a free black family, William Lucas and his wife. The men more or less terrorized the old couple and stayed the night there. Lucas and his wife sat outside on the porch all night rather than share their quarters with Booth and his comrades.

The next day, the fugitives forced Lucas to have his son, Charles, drive Booth in their buggy to Port Conway, a ferry crossing on the Rappahannock River, about ten miles further south. Booth agreed to pay twenty dollars in greenbacks for the trip. The trip was uneventful, and the group arrived at Port Conway around midday. Booth took the opportunity to pen a sarcastic letter to Dr. Stuart upbraiding him for his lack of Southern hospitality.

At Port Conway, Booth and Herold tried to talk a fisherman into taking them across the river and perhaps all the way to the train station just beyond Bowling Green, where they could catch a train to Richmond; but the fisherman was too slow mending his nets, and the men decided to make other arrangements. At the same time, a trio of Confederate soldiers suddenly appeared out of nowhere. They were not just any Confederate soldiers, either, but members of the feared guerilla unit known as Mosby's Rangers, the Forty-Third Battalion of the Virginia Calvary.

After spinning unconvincing tales of being Confederate soldiers themselves on their way back home—tales that the Mosby veterans could see right through—Herold decided to take a chance and told them point-blank who they were. The young soldiers were startled but impressed. Booth told them he was worth $175,000 to the man who captured him, a considerable exaggeration. Yet the soldiers agreed to help.

After dismissing Charles Lucas and sending him back home with the wagon and Booth's letter to Dr. Stuart, Booth, Herold and the three soldiers boarded the flat-bottomed ferry that crossed the river to Port Royal on the other side. From there, the three soldiers, like Thomas Harbin before them, took on the onerous task of finding a farmhouse that would house the two fugitives—who were now posing as returning Confederate soldiers and cousins, both with the last name of Boyd. Two farmhouses rebuffed their requests for help because the men of the establishments were not at home and it was not proper, not to mention unsafe, for women to take strange soldiers into their homes.

But finally, late in the afternoon of Monday, April 24, the soldiers found a farmer willing to help. His name was Richard Garrett, owner of a 500-acre spread known as Locust Hill. Garrett's two sons had recently returned safely from fighting in the Confederate army, and he felt it was his duty to help two Confederate soldiers returning home from the war. Booth and Herold certainly looked the part. Although not in uniform, Booth had been on the run for ten days. He had shaved his signature mustache but now had a thick, week-old beard, and looked like he had spent many nights sleeping outside on the ground, as indeed he had. Garrett agreed to take Booth in for a day or two.

Their mission accomplished, the three Confederate soldiers said goodbye to Booth. They were heading to the nearby town of Bowling Green. Herold said he would go with them to a farmhouse south of Bowling Green so he could visit an old friend.

Booth relished the hospitality he received the first day at the Garrett farmhouse. At first, he was treated like an honored guest, wined and dined, and allowed to play with the young Garrett children. He was given a bed in the house in which to sleep, and the exhausted fugitive took advantage of the situation to restore himself.

★   ★   🎩   ★   ★

Unbeknownst to Booth, the same day he arrived at the Garrett farmhouse an event occurred that would accidentally set the stage for his capture. On April 24, some detectives working on the case in Washington gained access to a false tip via telegraph: news that two men had been spotting crossing the Potomac into Virginia on April 16.

The men spotted were not, in fact, Booth and Herold, but someone else. Nevertheless, the false report led the detectives, their imaginations fired by dreams of the reward money, to quickly organize a military unit to give chase—the Sixteenth New York Cavalry regiment. Led by two of the detectives, Luther Baker and Everton Conger, and a Lieutenant Edward Doherty, twenty-six soldiers of the unit and their horses boarded a riverboat steamer at Washington's Sixth Street wharf that very day.

The soldiers planned to ride south for Fredericksburg, Virginia, but to get there they had to disembark at Belle Plain, Virginia, and then travel by road to Port Conway, where they would cross the Rappahannock

The Garrett farmhouse in 1865. *Wikimedia Commons*

River. In other words, without knowing it, and quite by accident, the Sixteenth New York was hot on the trail of Lincoln's assassin.

The next day, Tuesday, April 25, was a day of rest for John Wilkes Booth. He slept late, left his guns upstairs in the guest bedroom, and came downstairs for a late breakfast. It was a warm spring day, and the Garrett children had a great time playing hosts to what they believed was their brave Confederate guest. Booth lounged on the grass outside the farmhouse, playing with eleven-year-old Richard Garrett and three-year-old Cora Lee Garrett. Booth liked children and was a gentle and engaging playmate.

At the dinner table that afternoon, the group discussed the exciting news that was sweeping the countryside: the U.S. government was now offering a reward for the capture of Lincoln's assassin in the amount of $140,000! This was a mistake; the actual amount was $100,000 for all three wanted men: John Surratt Jr., David Herold, and John Wilkes Booth.

Booth convincingly feigned ignorance of the events and joined in the discussion with appropriate discretion, only suggesting gently that he didn't think the assassin acted for monetary gain (to be paid by the South) but "did it for notoriety's sake"—a remarkably self-aware admission. No one suspected a thing.

But the illusory idyll did not last. After dinner, Booth sat on the porch, writing in his diary, when he and some of the young Garrett children heard a noise like thunder from the road. An advance guard of the Sixteenth New York Cavalry, fresh off of the ferry across the Rappahannock River, were racing up the main road in front of the Garrett farm. It was only then that Booth's cool head and acting prowess failed him. He yelled at one of the Garrett children to bring him his guns from upstairs. This sudden and violent change of temperament quickly aroused suspicion among the members of the Garrett family, particularly the older boys.

When David Herold showed up a little while later, back from visiting his friend, the older Garrett children were no longer as welcoming. They informed Booth that his "cousin" Herold was not welcome to stay. Shortly after this, two of the Confederate soldiers who had brought Booth to the farm came racing up the lane leading to the Garrett farmhouse. They shouted that a large unit of Yankee cavalry was on its way from the ferry!

Booth and Herold didn't hesitate for a moment. They immediately headed for the woods behind the Garrett farmhouse—another act leading the Garretts to suspect the two men were not who they claimed to be.

Incredibly, the main force of the Sixteenth New York raced right by the Garrett farmhouse and the very men they were so aggressively hunting. When the danger had passed and Booth and Herold had re-emerged from the woods, they could see immediately that the mood among the members of the family had dramatically changed. The older boys, both Confederate veterans, told the two men they had to leave at once and could not stay the night. They were so anxious to be rid of the fugitives that one of the older boys, John Garrett, offered to guide the two men to another location—even though he now suspected that Booth might steal his horses and perhaps even kill him on the road.

After tense and increasingly hostile negotiations, the Garretts agreed to let Booth and Herold sleep in their ramshackle tobacco barn on the property. They led the men there, showed them inside, and closed the barn doors. However, the Garretts were worried that Booth might steal their horses or even rob them in the night. They had young siblings, aging parents, and unmarried women to protect.

As a result, after they settled Booth and Herold into the barn, the Garrett sons did something that changed history: they very slowly and quietly closed the big metal lock on the barn door, locking Booth and Herold inside. The two fugitives didn't suspect a thing and soon fell asleep.

Unbeknownst to the Garrett boys and Booth, the Sixteenth New York regiment that raced by that afternoon now had substantial information about Booth's whereabouts. When the main force of the Sixteenth had reached the ferry crossing at Port Conway around four o'clock that afternoon, the leaders, Detectives Luther Baker and Everton Conger, began questioning the very same fisherman who had initially agreed to take Booth and Herold across the river. The fisherman confirmed that a lame man had indeed crossed the river the day before—and he proceeded to tell the investigators everything they wished to know, including identifying Booth and Herold from their photographs.

And the fisherman and his wife told the detectives even more than that. They described and named the three Confederate soldiers who had befriended Booth. They were known to many locals, and the wife of the fisherman even knew where the three soldiers were likely staying in Bowling Green. It turned out that one of the soldiers, a young man named Willie Jett, was courting the sixteen-year-old daughter of an innkeeper in Bowling Green. The name of the inn was the Star Hotel.

Baker and Conger couldn't believe their good fortune. After nearly twelve days in which the Booth trail had gone cold, they suddenly had picked up the scent again!

When the soldiers of the Sixteenth raced by the Garretts' farm, therefore, they missed Booth but were headed directly to where the three Confederate soldiers who had helped Booth were likely staying. The two detectives knew that Booth was almost certainly still in the immediate area, and they were determined to track him down without a moment's delay. The Union soldiers were also keenly aware that they were still deep in enemy territory. No matter what the politicians might say about the war being effectively over, there were still more than 100,000 heavily armed Confederate troops in the field—and if the twenty-six soldiers of the Sixteenth happened upon a Confederate unit of sufficient strength, they could easily have ended up being the ones pursued and not the other way around. For this reason, the detectives' methods were brutal and quick.

About an hour before midnight, the mounted soldiers of the Sixteenth New York crept as quietly as possible into Bowling Green. They didn't want to alert anyone prematurely to their presence. The soldiers quickly found and surrounded the Star Hotel, but to their dismay they couldn't get anyone to answer the front door. As a result, they marched around the back to the servants' quarters, known as the "Negro House," and entered the house that way.

The soldiers were quickly informed that Willie Jett was upstairs in bed. Despite his reputation as a member of Mosby's Rangers, the young Confederate soldier was compliant. The soldiers dragged him downstairs and began interrogating him. Within minutes, Jett agreed to tell the soldiers everything they wanted to know. He told them that John Wilkes Booth was hiding out in a farmhouse on the road to Port Royal—the very same road the soldiers had just traveled.

Jett even volunteered to take the soldiers directly to the Garrett farmhouse himself, right then. "I will go there with you, and show where they are now, and you can get them," he said.[3]

The detectives Baker and Conger were nervous. It occurred to them that they might have succeeded in frightening Booth off when their cavalry unit had raced by the farmhouse earlier that evening. Nevertheless, the entire unit set off from the hotel about half-past midnight with Jett leading the way. It took about two hours to reach the farmhouse. Just before three in the morning, therefore, the Union soldiers and the detectives dismounted. With their guns drawn, the men crept up the dirt lane from the main road toward the Garrett farmhouse.

After crossing through a second gate, they mounted their horses—and charged! As the horses galloped toward the farmhouse, the farm dogs began barking furiously. Asleep in their house, the Garretts instantly awoke. Inside the tobacco barn, Booth, too, quickly sat up and listened in the darkness. He understood instantly what was happening and woke up Herold.

David Herold jumped to his feet and ran to the barn door. "We went right up to the barn door and tried to get out," Herold later told investigators, prior to his trial, "but we found it was locked."

They were trapped. While the Union soldiers surrounded the Garrett farmhouse, Booth and Herold did everything they could to break out of the tobacco barn, using all of their weight to kick at the heavy boards that made up the barn's walls. Much to their horror, the boards didn't budge an inch. The tobacco barn didn't look like much—the boards had four-inch spaces between them—but it was solidly built. Booth was too lame to kick very hard, and Herold, too, wasn't able to knock loose any of the boards.

In the meantime, the detectives were playing hardball with the Garrett family. When the elder Garrett explained that the two men staying at their farm had left and that he didn't know where they had gone, Conger threatened to hang him on the spot—and even instructed a soldier to go get a rope. When young John Garrett rushed to his father's defense, yelling that he would tell the soldiers where the man they were seeking was located, Army lieutenant Doherty grabbed him roughly by his shirt, put a revolver to his head, and ordered him to reveal that instant where Booth was located or he would be shot.

"In the barn!" young Garrett screamed in reply. Terrified of what could become of his parents and younger siblings, John Garrett quickly marched across the yard in front of the farmhouse and pointed to the tobacco barn. It was still dark, and there was little light. "There," he said.

The Union troops quickly fanned out and surrounded the barn. Inside, Booth and Herold could hear everything that was happening. The soldiers, too, could hear Herold moving about inside, alerting them that the two men had not fled the premises, as the elder Garrett had said.

The detectives decided to order young John Garrett to go inside the barn and inform Booth, whom he had betrayed by locking him inside the tobacco barn, that he had to give up his weapons and come out. Understandably, John Garrett looked upon this order as a suicide mission. However, the Union soldiers were very persuasive. They informed the young man that if he did not comply they would burn the family's entire farm to the ground.

Nervously, John Garrett turned the bolt on the barn door latch and cautiously opened the door. He expected to be shot at any second. Booth stood at the back of the barn, in the darkness, his pistols at the ready. John Garrett nervously informed Booth that the barn was surrounded, resistance was futile, and that he should give up.

"Damn you!" Booth hissed in reply. "You have betrayed me! If you don't get out of here I will shoot you! Get out of this barn at once!"[4] The actor limped forward and Garrett suddenly saw Booth's burning eyes in the dim light. Booth reached behind him for one of his pistols lying in the hay. John Garrett turned on his heel and ran for his life.

Yet Booth didn't fire. And neither did the soldiers. Secretary Stanton likely wanted Booth taken alive. He wanted to interrogate him to discover if Confederate leaders had helped him. Now the detectives decided to try a different approach. Baker yelled through the closed barn door that if Booth didn't surrender, he would burn the barn down in fifteen minutes.

"Who are you?" Booth yelled back. "What do you want? Whom do you want?"

"We want you!" the detective said matter-of-factly. "We know who you are. Give up your arms and come out."

Booth replied that he would think about it. The assassin knew he had no chance. He wanted to die fighting. But he knew he had to let young Herold go. At first, Booth threatened to blow Herold's brains out if he tried to leave, even calling him a "damned coward." But then he relented. "I am alone, there is no one with me," he yelled out to Detective Baker.

Baker knew that was a lie and said so. Booth then changed his tactic. "Captain, there is a man here who wants to surrender awful bad."

Next came a prolonged and bizarre period of bickering over Booth's weapons. The detectives wanted Herold to hand over his weapons and come out—but Herold said he had no weapons.

Nonsense, the detectives shouted back. The Garretts had given the detectives an itemized list of the weapons the men had: two revolvers and a Spencer carbine.

Herold and the soldiers kept bickering over this until finally Booth, frustrated, shouted out that the weapons were his and he wasn't giving any of them to Herold. "I own all the arms and intend to use them on you gentlemen," Booth shouted. He added that Herold was innocent.

More bickering and delays ensued. Finally, the detectives agreed to allow Herold to leave the barn if he came out with his hands in the air. Booth's last request of his comrade was that he not tell the men what weapons he actually did have. The door of the barn opened slowly. Herold stuck out first one empty hand, and then another—and was quickly grabbed and hauled out of the building.

It was now the final act. Booth knew it and so did the soldiers. Booth had prayed in his diary that God might spare him a criminal's execution and "let me die bravely." That was his final intention.

The soldiers debated whether they should set fire to the barn. The detectives had been instructed to capture Booth alive, if possible. Burning the barn might force him out, but it might also kill him. Rushing him through the barn door would likely get at least some of the men killed. Yet at the moment it was still dark, and that gave them an advantage.

The detectives decided it was safer to set the barn on fire. Once again, they forced the Garrett boys to do their dirty work for them. John and William Garrett gathered twigs, straw, and moss from the surrounding area and laid it along the sides of the barn. At one point, as John Garrett was piling up hay against the barn wall, he heard Booth whisper through the four-inch gaps in the boards. "Young man, I advise you for your own good not to come here again," he hissed. "If you do not leave at once, I will shoot you."

Booth tried to negotiate. He told Detective Baker that he could have killed him easily through the slats in the boards but had not done so. Then, incredibly, Booth challenged the soldiers to a kind of duel. "If you'll take your men fifty yards from the door, I'll come out and fight you," the actor declared. "Give me a chance for my life." The detectives declined the offer.

With a wax candle Baker had been foolishly holding in the darkness, making himself a perfect target for Booth, Conger lit the kindling and hay piled up against the barn. Within moments, the fire spread to engulf the walls of the building. Through the slats in the boards, the soldiers could now see Booth inside. He stood in the center, away from the rapidly spreading flames. Witnesses described him standing with a crutch under his arm and fumbling a pistol with one hand and the Spencer carbine with the other.

"One more stain on the old banner!" Booth yelled outside, probably referring to the Confederate flag. As Booth was struggling to find his balance, a Union soldier, Sergeant Thomas H. "Boston" Corbett, had crept up to one side of the barn. Through the four-inch openings between the wall boards, Corbett could easily watch every move Booth made.

A thirty-three-year-old British immigrant and hatter, Corbett was a very unusual man. Devoutly religious, he used to wear his hair shoulder-length in imitation of Jesus. Once, after encountering two prostitutes on the street, Corbett decided to take literally Jesus' admonitions about cutting off the hand that offends and making oneself a eunuch for the kingdom. He went home and, using a pair of sharp scissors, managed to castrate himself before going out for dinner.

Earlier, the sergeant had volunteered to go into the barn and fight Booth one-on-one, but his superiors had turned down the offer.

Now Corbett stood erect, pointing the barrel of his pistol through one of the openings, aiming directly at Booth. He held his fire even when Booth moved directly towards him.

The flames were getting hotter and hotter. According to Corbett, Booth was preparing to fight his way out. Corbett would later insist he saw Booth raise the carbine and begin to take aim. Corbett steadied his pistol on his arm and pulled the trigger. A shot rang out. Booth collapsed in an instant, falling to his knees. The carbine and pistol fell on the floor. Within seconds, the two detectives burst through the barn door and caught the assassin before he fell on his face.

Corbett's bullet had passed through Booth's neck, paralyzing him. At first, the detectives assumed Booth had shot himself; only later would they discover that it was Corbett who had taken matters into his own hands. Despite Stanton's desire that Booth be captured alive, no such orders were actually ever given to the rank-and-file soldiers; Corbett later insisted he acted

Thomas H. "Boston" Corbett (1832–1894), a thirty-three-year-old sergeant who castrated himself after an encounter with prostitutes on the street, shot John Wilkes Booth through the neck with his service revolver. He would later claim that Booth was preparing to open fire on his fellow soldiers. *Wikimedia Commons*

to save the lives of his fellow soldiers. He was never disciplined.

The barn was going to collapse soon. As a result, Baker, Conger, and some soldiers lifted Booth up off the barn floor and carried him outside, laying him on the grass. Booth looked dead. But like Lincoln, Booth fought to stay alive. His eyes flicked open, the detectives splashed water on his face, and the dying actor struggled to speak. His vocal cords, which had earned him several fortunes over his short life, now failed him.

Baker leaned down and put his ear close to the killer's mouth. "Tell mother, I die for my country," Booth whispered hoarsely.

As occurred with Lincoln's final moments, all present were keenly aware that they were witnessing history unfold before their very eyes. As a result, Conger made sure he heard correctly what he thought would be Booth's last words. He repeated what Booth said, and Booth nodded that the detective had the words right. But Booth wouldn't die, much to his own annoyance. He had made his grand exit, pronounced his final words for history, and yet still lived.

With the barn now a veritable conflagration, the soldiers decided to move Booth up to the farmhouse porch where Booth had spent a relaxing afternoon only hours before. He was bleeding from his neck wound, and so some of the Garrett children went to get bedding and pillows to make their former guest more comfortable. Herold was tied to a tree with rope, only a few feet from where Booth lay paralyzed and dying. He saw everything that occurred.

Booth was now in agony, writhing on the wooden floor of the porch. He couldn't swallow or cough, and several times begged Conger to kill him. A local doctor soon arrived on the scene and examined the pitiful prisoner. Booth was delirious, passing in and out of consciousness. The assassin spotted Jett, the Confederate soldier who had betrayed him. He asked Baker if Jett had betrayed him and the detective ignored the question.

As the detectives searched through Booth's pockets, looking for clues, a single woman who stayed at the Garrett farmhouse, Lucinda Holloway, knelt at Booth's head and tried to comfort him. Even at the end, the charismatic actor had his female admirers. Holloway could see Booth was thirsty and used a handkerchief to wet his tongue several times. Again, he repeated the words he wanted as his epitaph, "Tell mother, I die for my country."

But as fate would have it, those were not Booth's final words.

Utterly paralyzed, he tried to move his hands but couldn't. "My hands!" he whispered hoarsely. The tough detective Baker had pity on the dying assassin. He grabbed Booth's hands in his own, cleaned them slightly, and then raised them so Booth could see them. "Useless," Booth said. "Useless."

Right as the sun's light broke over the horizon, Booth began to choke and gasped for air. Holloway massaged his temples, feeling his pulse grow weaker. Baker bent over Booth, watching. Booth struggled to breathe, the blood in his throat now choking him. At the last moment, the sun shone on Booth's face. His body suddenly convulsed. And then he was dead.

The tragic saga that had occupied the last six months of the famous actor's life—and which claimed the life of America's sixteenth president and destroyed the lives of many others in the process—was finally over.

14 | THE AFTERMATH

The assassination of Abraham Lincoln was one of the greatest disasters to occur in the history of the United States. Just as the nation could see an end to a bloody civil war that had claimed 600,000 American lives, Booth's rash act threw the government into confusion and the nation into depression. It seemed that the killing was going to continue after all, and that peace might never come.

Lincoln's plans for broad amnesty and mercy towards the conquered people of the South were quickly short-circuited both by his own party (the so-called Radical Republicans) and by the Democrats. In a gesture of national reconciliation, Lincoln had tapped a Southern Democrat, Andrew Johnson, to be his vice president. Now that Lincoln was dead and he had assumed the presidency, Johnson set about reversing many of Lincoln's lenient policies toward the South. He also did his best to sabotage the dead president's plans for the emancipation and advancement of former slaves. It would take more than half a century, at least, before the work of reconciliation and rebuilding would be completed and the country would become one nation again.

As for the people most involved in the assassination, the family and friends of the victims and perpetrators, the coming days and years did little to ease the trauma.

The Lincoln Family

The night John Wilkes Booth was shot and killed, the early morning of April 26, Abraham Lincoln's body was on its way from New York City to Albany as part of the long funeral-train procession that Stanton had arranged so the country could say a final goodbye to its leader.

The train bearing his body had left Washington, D.C., on April 21 and would make stops at Baltimore, Maryland; Harrisburg and Philadelphia, Pennsylvania; New York City, Albany, and Buffalo, New York; Cleveland and Columbus, Ohio; Indianapolis and Michigan City, Indiana; and Chicago. It would arrive in Lincoln's adopted hometown of Springfield, Illinois, around nine o'clock in the morning on May 3. Illinois politicians wanted to bury Lincoln in a magnificent monument near downtown on land that would later become the site of the Illinois Capitol building. However, Lincoln himself had stated his preference to be buried in the simple Oak Ridge Cemetery a few miles outside of Springfield, and that was where Mary Lincoln finally decided should be the late president's final resting place.

Robert Todd Lincoln (1843–1926) when he was ambassador to Great Britain, circa 1890. *Wikimedia Commons*

The day after the funeral train arrived in Springfield, May 4, following funeral services, Lincoln's body was placed in a temporary vault at Oak Ridge Cemetery. The body of his young son, William Wallace Lincoln, who had died of typhoid fever at age eleven in 1862 shortly after Lincoln's arrival in Washington, was exhumed from its grave in Georgetown and brought along with Lincoln's body for burial in Springfield.

Eventually, a series of elaborate tombs and monuments were

IN THEIR OWN WORDS

"My bereavements have been so intense, the most loving
and devoted of husbands, torn from my side, my hand
within his own...I am living through a very sad time
myself, this season of the year, with its reminiscences,
renders me anything but cheerful. I am leading a life of
retirement and daily send up my supplications to Him, the
ruler over us all, to reconcile and soften the pathway I
have been called upon to tread within the last few years."

—*Mary Todd Lincoln, letter to Edward Lewis Baker Jr., 1877*

built to house the remains of Lincoln and his family members. Today,
Lincoln's tomb in Springfield is a National Historic Site.

Lincoln's family was devastated by the assassination. Following the
deaths of two of her children and her husband, Mary Todd Lincoln never
really recovered. She would receive a modest pension from the U.S. government of three thousand dollars annually (about sixty thousand dollars
today), and she lived with her two sons in Chicago.

However, the mysterious death of her son Thomas "Tad" Lincoln at age
eighteen, perhaps from pneumonia, was the final straw for Mary Lincoln.
Her behavior became increasingly erratic, bordering on insane, and her son
Robert Lincoln, then a successful Chicago lawyer, had her involuntarily
committed to a private asylum in 1875, a decade after the assassination.

However, with the help of friends, Mary Lincoln was able to publi-
cize her plight in the newspapers and she was eventually allowed free.
She left the United States and spent the next four years in Europe, settling
in the small French town of Pau. Mary Lincoln returned to the U.S. in
1880 and spent the last months of her life at her sister's home in Springfield, where she died of a stroke on July 16, 1882.

Robert Todd Lincoln, the sole surviving member of the president's immediate family, remained estranged from his mother until her death. She never forgave him for the committal proceedings against her. He eventually became secretary of war from 1881 to 1885 in the administration of President James Garfield. In a strange twist of fate, Robert Lincoln was present when Garfield was assassinated in a Washington, D.C., train station on July 2, 1881. Robert Lincoln was also nearby when another president, William McKinley, was shot by a Polish American anarchist in 1901. McKinley died eight days later.

Later, Robert Lincoln would serve as ambassador to the Court of St. James from 1889 to 1893. He refused all requests to run for president and settled in a small town in Vermont, where he became a dedicated golfer and amateur astronomer. He died at the age of eighty-two on July 26, 1926. With the death in 1985 of Robert's last surviving grandson, Robert Todd Lincoln Beckwith, the line of Abraham Lincoln's undisputed descendants came to an end.

The Booth Family

Following his death in the early morning of April 26, 1865, John Wilkes Booth's body was placed on top of an old service blanket belonging to Lieutenant Edward Doherty. The soldiers borrowed a thick needle from the Garrett family and sewed Booth's body up in the blanket, leaving an opening only for his feet. They then confiscated a rickety old cart belonging to a freed black man who happened by, loaded Booth's body into it, and took it, the cart, and the free black man back north towards the ferry crossing at Port Conway. Booth's body dripped blood much of the way there.

After crossing the Rappahannock River, the small detachment of soldiers continued to Belle Plain on the Potomac. Baker and some others loaded Booth's body into a rowboat and rowed it out to a steamship just offshore, the *John S. Ide*. The ship sailed up the river to Washington where, at 1:45 in the morning on April 27, it met the *Montauk*, the very same monitor Abraham Lincoln and his wife had toured just two weeks earlier. Stanton had decided to keep Booth's body as well as some of the imprisoned conspirators on the ship offshore to frustrate any attempted lynchings or souvenir hunters.

Booth's body was laid on out a bench on the *Montauk*'s deck, stripped naked, photographed, and examined by doctors. A gruesome and brief autopsy was performed. The photographs and plates have never been found and are presumed destroyed. After Booth's body was positively identified by many people who knew him in life—everyone could see the distinctive tattoo, JWB, he had on his hand—the government decided upon an elaborate ruse. It pretended that Booth's body would be buried at sea, and a rowboat left the *Montauk* to enact this fiction.[1] The government feared that, in death, Booth might become a martyr to the Confederate cause and his grave a rallying point and shrine.

However, Booth's body was not buried at sea. Instead, late on April 27, it was placed back in the old blanket shroud and rowed to a military installation known as the Washington Arsenal Penitentiary (now part of Fort McNair), located where the Potomac and Anacostia Rivers meet. Inside the brick building, soldiers dug up a section of the brick floor and dug a grave in the earth beneath. They placed Booth's body in a wooden box used to ship muskets, sealed it tightly, and wrote Booth's name on the lid of the makeshift coffin. The soldiers then buried the box in the earth and replaced the bricks so that the unmarked grave could only be found by those who knew where it was located.

Booth's body remained hidden there for four years until, in 1869, President Andrew Johnson gave permission for the War Department to turn over Booth's remains to his family for reburial. In a strange twist of fate during the moving process, Booth's body was temporarily housed in the same shed behind Ford's Theatre, off Baptist Alley, where he temporarily kept his horse on the fateful night of the assassination. Booth's exhumed remains were examined by his friends and family members, including his mother and sister, to verify that it was his body.

Decades later and ever since, there were rumors that Booth somehow escaped the Garrett barn, that the soldiers had killed someone else in his place, and that the exhumed body was not really that of Booth. The very haste with which the government buried Booth's remains gave rise, early on, to numerous conspiracy theories. Over the decades, these theories have led to a number of bestselling books (such as the 1977 million-copy bestseller *The Lincoln Conspiracy*) and TV documentaries. In the mid-1990s, distant relatives of Booth mounted multiple court challenges to have Booth's and his brother Edwin's remains exhumed once again to prove that an imposter lies in his grave, but all the court challenges failed.

On Saturday, June 26, 1869, the remains of John Wilkes Booth were buried by his family and friends in the family plot in Baltimore's Green Mount Cemetery along with those of his predeceased siblings, Frederick, Elizabeth, Mary Ann, and Henry Byron. In the decades after the Civil War, the government's prescient fears were realized as many Confederate veterans did leave mounds of flowers on Booth's grave.[2] Today, there is a plain, unmarked white headstone that visitors believe marks Booth's grave but may be that of his sister, Asia. On top of this marker, visitors often leave copper pennies with Lincoln's image facing upwards, a final rebuke and reaffirmation of Lincoln's ultimate victory.

As for the rest of Booth's immediate family, the assassination of course changed their lives forever. It was not exactly a boost to the careers of Booth's actor brothers, Edwin and Junius Jr. Edwin, who was thirty-two when his hotheaded little brother murdered the president, eventually regained his fame and fortune.

As fate would have it, Edwin had actually saved the life of Abraham Lincoln's young son Robert a few months before his famous father's death. Robert had fallen from a train platform onto the tracks when a mysterious stranger, who turned out to be Edwin Booth, snatched him up from the tracks and saved him from certain death.

It was only later that Edwin learned from eyewitnesses that he had saved the life of Abraham Lincoln's son—and this heroic act bought both Edwin, and the Booth family, a modicum of redemption in the public's eyes. He later founded a famous club for actors and theatre patrons, The Players, in New York City. Edwin lived until age fifty-nine, when he died of a stroke on June 7, 1893. His two-bedroom apartment at the Players club has been kept to this day exactly as it was the night he died.

Edwin Booth (1833–1893) became a famous actor and theatrical producer, founding The Players club for actors in New York City. *Wikimedia Commons*

The rest of Booth's close-knit and very loyal family had a harder time. The shame of the Booth family name weighed heavily upon all of them, as their surviving letters attest. Booth's mother, Mary Ann Holmes Booth, would live to bury six of her children and her husband. She spent the rest of her life after the assassination living with her surviving children, Edwin, Junius, and Rosalie. In 1878, Mary Ann sold the family land and home, Tudor Hall, to a Baltimore businessman named Samuel Kyle for $3,500.[3] She lived another twenty years until she slipped on an icy street, in 1883, and died two years later at the age of eighty-three.

Junius Brutus Booth Jr., the eldest son, retired from acting and settled in Manchester-by-the-Sea, Massachusetts, where he built a luxury hotel and prospered in seclusion. He died in 1882 at the age of sixty-one.

Booth's beloved sister, Asia, who became a poet and later wrote a secret memoir of her infamous brother and family, felt so ashamed that she moved to England with her husband and children. Her opportunistic and disloyal husband, John Sleeper Clarke, who joined her in England and became a famous comedian in his own right, treated her with disdain

IN THEIR OWN WORDS

"[John Wilkes Booth] was of a gentle, loving disposition, very boyish and full of fun—his mother's darling—and his deed and death crushed her spirit."

—*Edwin Booth, letter to Nahum Capen, 1881*

Asia Clarke Booth. *Wikimedia Commons*

and lived "a free going bachelor life and does what he likes," as she delicately put it in her memoirs. Asia's assassin brother had warned her about Clarke when she married him. Asia died at age fifty-two in 1888.

Booth's youngest brother, Joseph, became a respected doctor and lived until 1902. His only child died in infancy. Booth's sister Rosalie never married but cared for her mother until her own death in 1889. Most of the Booth children are buried in the family plot in Baltimore, near their parents and infamous brother.

The Co-Conspirators

As for the co-conspirators, their fates were actually mixed.

With the possible exception of Mary Surratt, the government exacted its vengeance primarily upon those who actually aided Booth *during* the assassination—Lewis Powell (who attacked Secretary of State Seward and his children), David Herold (who helped Powell and then Booth after the attacks), George Atzerodt (who chickened out but who was part of the final plotting), and, finally, Mary Surratt (who took Booth's binoculars down to her farm and allegedly told her tenant to get hidden weapons ready for people who would claim them later that night). The government also wanted to arrest Mary's son, John Surratt Jr., who was part of the original kidnapping plot but had backed out when he learned that Booth had changed his plans from kidnapping to murder. Young Surratt may have been in Washington on April 14 but likely was not; either way, he soon escaped to Montreal.

By the time Booth was killed, all of the main conspirators except for John Surratt were in Federal custody. The government ultimately decided to seek lesser charges for those involved in the original kidnapping plot—men such as Booth's childhood friends Michael O'Laughlen and Samuel Arnold. Dr. Mudd was a special case: he came very close to being hanged. His obvious lies and evasions hurt his case, and, unbeknownst to him, the majority of the military tribunal that would try the cases actually voted for the death penalty.

The government was also convinced that the hapless theatre carpenter, Edman "Ned" Spangler, a Confederate sympathizer who publicly denounced Lincoln, was involved in the assassination plot. Witnesses claimed to have overheard Booth, on the night of the assassination, asking Spangler, "You'll help me all you can, won't you, Ned?" It was only the courageous and principled stand of Ford Theatre owner John Ford, who stood up to the military prosecutors and insisted upon Spangler's innocence, that likely saved Spangler's life and had his sentence limited to just prison.

True to its conduct during the Civil War, when it openly arrested recalcitrant judges and others who insisted upon the letter of the Constitution, the Union government had no intention of allowing civilian courts to block its will by imposing the legal niceties. As a result, Secretary of War Stanton pushed to have the conspirators tried not by a civilian court of law but by a military tribunal. After all, the killing of the commander in chief was an act of war, and at least some of the accused were either former Confederate soldiers or, in the case of John Surratt Jr., agents of the Confederate government.

IN THEIR OWN WORDS

"On Monday when I was leaving Canandaigua I bought some New York papers. In looking over them, my eye lit on the following paragraph which I have never forgot, and don't think I ever will. It runs thus: 'The assassin of Secretary Seward is said to be John H. Surratt, a notorious secessionist of Southern Maryland. His name, with that of J. Wilkes Booth, will forever lead the infamous role of assassins.' I could scarcely believe my senses. I gazed upon my name, the letters of which seemed to sometimes to grow as large as mountains and then to dwindle away to nothing. So much for my former connection with him I thought. After fully realizing the state of the case, I concluded to change my course and go direct to Canada."

—*John Surratt Jr.*

Events proceeded quickly. On April 29, eight of the ten people charged with Lincoln's murder were brought to cells in the Washington Arsenal Penitentiary—the very same building where Booth had been secretly buried just two days before. They were Edman Spangler, Samuel Arnold, Michael O'Laughlen, Mary Surratt, and Lewis Powell, all arrested on April 17; George Atzerodt, captured on April 20; Dr. Samuel Mudd, arrested on April 24; and, last but not least, David Herold, captured April 26 when he fled the Garrett family barn. The ninth, Booth, was buried in the same building. Only John Surratt was still at large.

On May 1, President Andrew Johnson issued an executive order that the prisoners be tried before a military tribunal, not a civilian court. The charge was conspiracy. Even though some of the accused were involved solely in the plot to kidnap Lincoln, that did not absolve them in the eyes of the law of complicity in his murder. Just as a getaway driver in a bank robbery can be charged with murder, even if he didn't pull the trigger that killed a bank guard, so, too, the government merely had to prove that those on trial had knowledge of, and participated in, a conspiracy to achieve an illegal goal.

The trial was held on the third floor of the Arsenal building in a large room converted into a courtroom. It lasted fifty days, from May 10 until June 29, 1865. Nine combat officers presided, almost all generals (two were colonels) and none with any judicial or legal experience, selected by Judge Advocate General Joseph Holt and his assistant, John A. Bingham. Over the course of the trial, 366 witnesses gave testimony that was transcribed and is still in print.[4] The prisoners were well represented by capable attorneys, such as a former chief justice of the Kansas Supreme Court and a former United States attorney general. However, the proceedings were initially conducted in secret, behind closed doors, without any members of the press present. Even worse, at that time the tribunal's judgments were final; there would be no appeals to higher courts. The only appeal permitted was to the president of the United States.

On June 30, the military tribunal announced its decision: all eight of the defendants were found guilty. However, the sentences varied. The four considered most involved in the actual assassination—Lewis Powell, David Herold, George Atzerodt, and Mary Surratt—were sentenced to death by hanging. The three involved in the kidnapping plot—Samuel Arnold, Michael O'Laughlen, and Dr. Samuel Mudd—were sentenced to life in prison. Edman Spangler, the rebel carpenter, was the prosecution's weakest case: he was sentenced to six years in prison.

No one had expected that Mary Surratt would be executed. A devout Catholic mother in her forties, she had vehemently protested her innocence. Lewis Powell, too, stated that Surratt knew nothing of Booth's plans. Moreover, while the tribunal voted to sentence her to death, five out of the nine members also signed a second recommendation for clemency. No woman had ever been executed by the U.S. Federal government before. As a result, a furious campaign erupted on her behalf. It later became clear that Surratt's death was likely due to Johnson's intransigence.

Two days before the scheduled execution date, on July 5, the judge advocate general, Joseph Holt, carried the tribunal's recommendation for the death sentences and for clemency for Surratt personally to Johnson. He signed the execution documents but did not sign the recommendation for clemency. Johnson would later claim he never saw the clemency recommendation, a claim that Holt strenuously denied.

Moreover, Surratt's daughter Anna begged to see Johnson to plead for her mother's life, but Johnson refused to see her. The final proof that Surratt's death was Johnson's doing is that he issued an executive order suspending a writ of habeas corpus in Surratt's case—in other words, directly countermanding an order of the Supreme Court of the District of Columbia that Surratt be brought before the Court.

On July 6, two generals in charge of the Washington Arsenal Penitentiary visited the condemned prisoners and informed them all, including Mary Surratt, that they were to be hanged the next day. Work began immediately on the construction of a gallows in the Arsenal courtyard—work that continued all through the night and which was clearly audible to the prisoners. Next to the gallows four graves were dug in the earth, and four musket boxes were stacked up, similar to the one in which Booth was buried.

The general in charge of the execution, Major General Winfield Scott Hancock, delayed. He was hoping he would receive word to spare Surratt. Earlier in the morning, he had appeared in the chambers of Judge Andrew Wylie of the Supreme Court of the District of Columbia with Johnson's executive order suspending the writ of habeas corpus. Now, all that could save Surratt was a stay of execution from Johnson.

A photograph taken immediately before the execution of (left to right) Mary Surratt, Lewis Powell, David Herold, and George Atzerodt at 1:25 p.m. on July 7, 1865. *Wikimedia Commons*

The four prisoners were brought out from their cells into the hot midday sun at exactly 1:02 p.m. and made to mount the steps to the gallows platform. The outside temperature was an estimated 100 degrees Fahrenheit. Surratt, dressed all in black with a black veil, was accompanied by two Catholic priests. Lewis Powell had a Protestant clergyman with him.

Atop the high brick wall encircling the Arsenal courtyard stood a line of soldiers, witnesses to the executions. Also present nearby on the courtyard ground was a small group of reporters and other witnesses. Rare historical photos of the proceedings show that a surprisingly large gathering of officials and clergy was up on the gallows platform itself, as many as eighteen people plus the four condemned. Because of the excessive heat there were four large, black umbrellas on the gallows to shield Mary Surratt and some others from the sun.

The prisoners were allowed to sit in chairs while one of the generals in charge read the order of execution. The prisoners were then told to stand, their arms and legs bound with white cloth, thick rope nooses placed around their necks and white shrouds over their heads. They were then positioned on the two large trapdoors built on the gallows platform.

Surratt, crying inconsolably, could barely stand. She asked those next to her, "Please don't let me fall." The officials and clergy stepped back from the trapdoors. According to eyewitnesses, only George Atzerodt had any last words. "Goodbye, gentlemen," he said calmly. "May we all meet in the other world." At approximately 1:25 p.m., an Army captain clapped his hands four times.[5] This was the signal for soldiers below to swing large hammers and knock down the wooden beams holding the trapdoors up. The doors swung open, and the four prisoners dropped six feet, the ropes snapping their necks. The bodies of the condemned were quickly buried right on the spot. The bodies would remain there until, four years later, they were released to relatives for reburial elsewhere.

Now that justice was seen to have been done, the fate of the other convicted conspirators almost seemed an afterthought. Michael O'Laughlen, Samuel Mudd, Samuel Arnold, and Edman Spangler were all shipped off to the military penitentiary at Fort Jefferson in the Dry Tortugas, seventy-five miles due west of Key West, Florida. Dr. Mudd was allowed to serve as a physician in the facility, and when an epidemic of yellow fever broke out he worked heroically to serve his fellow inmates. One of these was Michael O'Laughlen, who finally succumbed to the disease on September 24, 1867. The rest of the conspirators would remain at Fort Jefferson until 1869.

Upon the prisoners' release, Dr. Mudd returned to his Maryland farm and continued where he had left off, growing tobacco and being a part-time doctor. He allowed Edman Spangler to come stay with him, even giving him a parcel of land on which to build a house. Before he died in 1883, Mudd confessed to numerous witnesses that he had, in fact, known it was Booth all along when he set his broken leg—an admission that would likely have added him to the list of executed prisoners had it been known during the trial. Samuel Arnold returned to Baltimore and was the only one of the conspirators to write a book about his experiences. He died in 1906.

The last person charged was John Surratt Jr., the only one of the ten conspirators who managed to escape. An experienced courier for the Confederate government who traveled often to Montreal, Surratt was well-equipped to make a getaway. As Surratt told the tale, as soon as he learned of the assassination he traveled directly to New York State and then from there to Montreal, finally finding refuge in a small Quebec town where he was hidden by a Catholic priest. He stayed there throughout the trial and his mother's subsequent execution. From Quebec, Surratt traveled first to Liverpool, England, and then to, of all places, Vatican City. At the Vatican, Surratt enlisted in the small papal army known as the Zouaves that would soon be involved in real battles with the Italian nationalist forces under Giuseppe Garibaldi. He used the alias John Watson.

However, an old family acquaintance who was also serving in the Zouaves soon betrayed Surratt to the U.S. consul and received a ten thousand dollar reward for his trouble.[6] Surratt was taken into custody by Vatican police but managed to escape once again before he could be turned over the American authorities. He traveled by ship to Egypt, but U.S. diplomatic channels were once again tipped off and he was greeted by Egyptian police upon disembarking in Alexandria.

Returned to the United States, Surratt was subjected to a replay of the original conspiracy trial, beginning on June 10, 1867, with many of the same witnesses giving similar testimony. However, this time the trial was before a civilian court with a jury—and it ended with the jury unable to reach a verdict. The government tried again, this time charging Surratt with treason.

But surprisingly, Surratt's luck held out. The presiding judge dismissed the case due to a technicality. The statute of limitations for this

John Surratt Jr. (1844–1916) dressed in the uniform of a Papal Zouave, circa 1867. He was tried for being an accomplice in the murder of Lincoln but never convicted. *Wikimedia Commons*

type of treason was two years—and it was then three years since the alleged offense. Surratt got off scot-free, went briefly on the lecture circuit, married a Maryland woman in 1872, and embarked on a long career with an established steamship company, rising to become a top executive. He died at the age of seventy-two in 1916.

As for the others who aided Booth, virtually all escaped punishment—some because they were discreet and never caught, and others because the government simply lost interest. Union detectives eventually tracked down and arrested the two Confederate agents who helped Booth and Herold after they left Dr. Mudd's house, Captain Samuel Cox and Thomas Jones. The detectives tried to get the two men to implicate one another, even threatening to hang them on the spot. But Cox and Jones were both trained, hardened Confederate agents, so they stuck to their stories and said almost nothing. They knew the only witnesses to their "aiding and abetting," Booth and Herold, were both dead.

Both men were eventually released and never charged. Twenty years later, the journalist George Townsend talked Jones into telling his story for sixty dollars, and the nation learned, for the first time, just how Booth managed to evade a nationwide manhunt for so long.[7] Other people who aided Booth and Herold, such as Elizabeth Quesenberry, Thomas Harbin, and John J. Hughes (the acquaintance of David Herold who fed Booth and Herold near Nanjemoy Creek and likely hid them in an abandoned slave cabin[8]), also walked away without ever facing a court charge.

As for the men who captured or helped to capture Booth, most received at least some of the promised reward money. The government had originally offered $100,000 total—$50,000 for Booth and $25,000 each for Herold and Surratt. At the time the original offer was made, the government was unaware of the roles played by Lewis Powell and Atzerodt. There were thousands of claimants who insisted they provided valuable information or somehow aided the manhunt.

Confederate agent Thomas A. Jones (1820–1895), who helped Booth delay his capture, late in life. He was never charged with a crime. *BoothieBarn blog*

Ultimately, Congress decided who got paid and how much, greatly reducing the amounts originally promised. Lafayette Baker, who organized the successful manhunt down the Potomac River, was told he would get $17,500 but was finally paid only $3,750; his cousin Luther Baker, only $3,000; the detective Everton Conger, $15,000; and Lt. Doherty, $5,250. Boston Corbett, who shot Booth in the neck, received $1,653.84, as did all the other twenty-five enlisted men in the Sixteenth New York Cavalry who participated that fateful night.[9]

The Eyewitnesses

The tragedy of the Lincoln assassination goes far beyond the immediate victims and the men and women who perpetrated it or helped the perpetrators after they escaped. It also greatly changed the lives of

---

IN THEIR OWN WORDS

"Had Abraham Lincoln died from any of the numerous
ills to which flesh is heir; had he reached that good old
age of which his vigorous constitution and his temperate
habits gave promise; had he been permitted to see the end
of his great work; had the solemn curtain of death come
down but gradually—we should still have been smitten
with a heavy grief, and treasured his name lovingly. But
dying as he did die, by the red hand of violence, killed,
assassinated, taken off without warning, not because of
personal hate—for no man who knew Abraham Lincoln
could hate him—but because of his fidelity to union and
liberty, he is doubly dear to us, and his memory will be
precious forever."

—*Frederick Douglass, 1876*

dozens, even hundreds of eyewitnesses and workers in the immediate
area. While the U.S. government was ultimately restrained in its
attempts to impose legal justice, its investigative methods were less so.
The nation was still at war. The top leader of the government had just
been assassinated. It looked very possible that the Confederates had
staged an attempted coup of some sort. As a result, the military and
police authorities simply rounded up anyone who might possibly have
information of value to the investigation—and held them for weeks,
sometimes months without charges.

In this category were many of the employees of Ford's Theatre,
including actors and actresses, stagehands, and even the owner, John T.

Ford himself. Ford was arrested and held for more than a month after the assassination along with his two younger brothers. The U.S. government simply seized his theatre outright—although he was eventually compensated for it.

Even those not arrested saw their lives completely disrupted. Secretary of State Seward, of course, suffered near-fatal wounds at the hands of Lewis Powell that left him permanently disfigured. He eventually recovered but was rarely photographed afterwards. Dr. Charles Leale, the doctor who attended Lincoln right after the shooting, went on to have a long and illustrious career as a New York physician. His written account of Lincoln's final hours, penned just hours after the president's death and long thought lost, was only discovered in 2012 in the National Archives in Washington.

Laura Keene, the producer of *Our American Cousin* who held Lincoln's head in her lap on the floor of the presidential box, somehow evaded the mass arrests that picked up many members of the cast for questioning. Yet with her name now forever linked with the death of Lincoln, Keene's career and health suffered greatly in the years after the assassination. The audiences quickly dried up, her manager and second husband died, and she contracted tuberculosis. She eventually suffered a stroke and died, at the age of forty-seven, in November 1873.[10]

The young couple who were with the Lincolns when the president was shot, Clara Harris and Major Henry Rathbone, had a particularly tragic life. They married in 1867, but Rathbone's mental health saw a rapid decline as he descended slowly into madness, alcoholism, and chronic unemployment. After resigning from the military with the rank of colonel, Rathbone was appointed U.S. consul to Germany in 1882 and moved his young family there. A year later, he shot Harris in the head with a pistol, killing her, tried to kill his children, and then attempted suicide. Rathbone was declared criminally insane and spent the rest of his life (nearly thirty years) in a German insane asylum, dying in 1911. The remains of the couple in a Hanover cemetery were eventually moved to an unmarked plot because no one had ever visited their graves.[11]

Lucy Lambert Hale, John Booth's alleged secret fiancée, was able to keep her involvement with the infamous assassin a secret for some time. Government investigators knew who she was (her photo was one of four found on Booth's body) but, as her father was the minister to Spain and a former U.S. senator, she was never called to testify in the trials. However, eventually Hale's story became public. In the late 1870s, a series of newspaper articles revealed there was some truth behind the rumors. The articles even claimed that Lincoln's murder may have been the result of a love triangle among Hale, Booth, and Lincoln's young son Robert.[12]

Ford's Theatre

The theatrical manager and entrepreneur John T. Ford, owner of Ford's Theatre, was one of the few participants in this drama to prosper after the assassination and live a long and relatively happy life. This is more than could be said for his theatre. After being arrested and held without charges for more than a month, Ford discovered that the government intended on seizing his theatre outright—although there was talk of compensation.

Facing massive debts, the young Ford set out to rebuild his empire. He soon succeeded. Ford was able to lease the National Theatre as well as other theatres in Baltimore. Ford also worked for the release of his old employee, Edman Spangler, who he was sure was innocent and who was then being held prisoner at Fort Jefferson in the Caribbean. Ford settled in Baltimore, became very wealthy, and was the father of eleven children. He died in 1894 at the age of sixty-four.

Ford's Theatre did not fare nearly as well as its namesake. Following the assassination, the U.S. government simply seized the theatre outright, with Congress passing a law that prohibited the building's use as a theatre. John Ford was eventually paid $100,000 in compensation for the seizure. The building was taken over by the U.S. military and used as a records storage facility.

However, on June 9, 1893, all three floors in the interior of the building collapsed, knocking out part of an outside wall and killing twenty-two workers inside. The interior was then rebuilt, and the building was used as a warehouse for a few years and then abandoned for many years. In the years after World War II, there was interest in perhaps reconstructing the building and using it as a memorial to Lincoln. In 1964, Congress funded a reconstruction effort that would restore the theatre (more or less) to the condition it was in when Lincoln was shot, albeit with modern materials.

The owner of Ford's Theatre, John T. Ford (1829–1894), continued to produce theatrical productions for another thirty years after Lincoln's death. *Wikimedia Commons*

Today, the theatre is a National Historic Site, run by the National Park Service and a private nonprofit society, which includes the reconstructed theatre and a museum dedicated to the assassination. The Petersen House across Tenth Street, where Lincoln died, was purchased by the U.S. government in 1896 and is now also a museum. Peter Taltavull's Star Saloon, located on the south side of Ford's Theatre where Booth and many members of the theatre company spent much of their time, was closed after the assassination and eventually torn down in 1930 and turned into a parking lot. Today a façade recreates the look of the original building.

Some of the other buildings that played a role in this story still exist, although many are now gone. The White House, Lincoln's New York

Avenue Presbyterian Church, Ford's Theatre, the Petersen House, the National Theatre (formerly Grover's), the Willard Hotel, Soldiers' Home, and the Navy Yard are all still there. The alley behind Ford's Theatre from which Booth escaped, Baptist Alley, still exists and looks eerily similar to old historic photographs, although it is now surrounded by tall modern buildings.

Mary Surratt's boardinghouse, located at 604 H Street NW in Washington, looks almost exactly the same as it did in Booth's time. It is now a popular Chinese restaurant, Wok And Roll. St. Patrick's Catholic Church on F Street, where Mary Surratt sometimes worshiped, still looks much as it did 150 years ago. The Kirkwood House hotel, where Vice President Andrew Johnson was living on the night of the assassination, was destroyed in 1875 and replaced by a seven-story office building. In the 1960s, this too was replaced by the current structure, a towering office building on the corner of Twelfth Street NW and Pennsylvania Avenue. Booth's residence during the assassination plot, the National Hotel, was an elegant five-story structure on the corner of Pennsylvania Avenue and Sixth Street. It was a Washington landmark for nearly a century, from its construction in 1832 until it was razed in 1942. The Herndon House boardinghouse, where Lewis Powell stayed and where Booth met his co-conspirators for a final briefing before the attacks, stood on the corner of Ninth and F Streets across from the Masonic temple. In 1891, it was torn down and replaced by a massive office building, Washington Loan and Trust Company, which still stands today.

For those who follow Booth's flight out of the city, more historical buildings can be found. Mary Surratt's tavern, Dr. Samuel Mudd's house, John Hughes's home on the banks of the Potomac, and Thomas Jones's Huckleberry Farm all still look remarkably like they did when Booth visited them. The major exception is the Garrett family farm, Locust Hill, where Booth met his death. The U.S. government refused to pay Richard Garrett, a supporter of the Confederacy, a penny in compensation for the loss of his property during the raid on his farm.

His farm business soon collapsed, and the original farmhouse was eventually abandoned and left to rot. In the 1960s, the government built a major highway, U.S. Route 301, which cuts through the Garrett property. Today, all that remains of the Garrett farmhouse is a metal sign on the northbound side of the highway, three miles south of Port Royal at mile marker 122. Nearby, there is a narrow path into the woods to a clearing where the actual farmhouse once stood. Nothing remains. Even the foundation is gone.

SELECT BIBLIOGRAPHY

Abel, E. Lawrence. *John Wilkes Booth and the Women Who Loved Him*. Washington, D.C.: Regnery History, 2018.

Alexander, David. *Hangman's Dozen*. New York: Roy Publishers, 1961.

Alford, Terry. *Fortune's Fool: The Life of John Wilkes Booth*. Oxford: Oxford University Press, 2015.

Andrews, Matthew Page. *History of Maryland*. New York: Doubleday, 1929.

Bogar, Thomas A. *Backstage at the Lincoln Assassination*. Washington, D.C.: Regnery History, 2013.

Booth, Asia Clarke. *John Wilkes Booth: A Sister's Memoir*. Jackson, Mississippi: University Press of Mississippi, 1996.

Burlingame, Michael, ed. *Lincoln Observed: Civil War Dispatches of Noah Brooks*. Baltimore and London: The Johns Hopkins University Press, 1998.

Canavan, Kathryn. *Lincoln's Final Hours*. Lexington, Kentucky: University Press of Kentucky, 2015.

Donald, David Herbert. *Lincoln*. New York: Simon & Schuster, 1995.

Ford's Theatre Society. *The Lincoln Assassination at Ford's Theatre*. Nashville, Tennessee: Beckon Books, 2015.

Good, Timothy S., ed. *We Saw Lincoln Shot: One Hundred Eyewitness Accounts*. Jackson, Mississippi: University Press of Mississippi, 1995.

Holzer, Harold, ed. *President Lincoln Assassinated: The Firsthand Story of the Murder, Manhunt, Trial and Mourning*. New York: Library of America, 2014.

Holzer, Harold and Craig L. Symonds, eds. *The New York Times Complete Civil War: 1861–1865*. New York: Black Dog & Leventhal Publishers, 2010.

Kauffman, Michael W. *American Brutus: John Wilkes Booth and the Lincoln Conspiracies*. New York: Random House, 2004.

Kennedy, Frances H. *The Civil War Battlefield Guide*. Boston: Houghton Mifflin Company, 1990.

Lamon, Ward Hill. *Recollections of Abraham Lincoln*. Lincoln, Nebraska: University of Nebraska Press, 1994.

McPherson, James M. *Battle Cry of Freedom: The Civil War Era*. Oxford: Oxford University Press, 1988.

Pitch, Anthony S. *"They Have Killed Papa Dead": The Road to Ford's Theatre, Abraham Lincoln's Murder and the Rage for Vengeance*. Hanover, New Hampshire: Steerforth Press, 2008.

Reck, W. Emerson. *A. Lincoln: His Last 24 Hours*. Jefferson, North Carolina: McFarland & Company, 1987.

Reed, Robert. *Old Washington, D.C. in Early Photographs: 1846–1932*. New York: Dover Publications, 1980.

Rhodehamel, John and Taper, Louise, eds. *Right or Wrong, God Judge Me: The Writings of John Wilkes Booth*. Urbana, Illinois: University of Illinois Press, 1997.

Richstein, William. *The Stranger's Guide-Book to Washington City, and Everybody's Pocket Handy-Book: Containing the Most Complete Guide to Washington and Vicinity*. Washington, D.C.: The National Book Store, 1864.

Steers Jr., Edward. *Blood on the Moon: The Assassination of Abraham Lincoln*. Lexington, Kentucky: University Press of Kentucky, 2001.

_____. *The Lincoln Assassination Encyclopedia*. New York: Harper Perennial, 2010.

Steers Jr., Edward, ed. *The Trial: The Assassination of President Lincoln and the Trial of the Conspirators*. Lexington, Kentucky: University Press of Kentucky, 2003.

Swanson, James L. *Manhunt: The 12-Day Chase for Abraham Lincoln's Killer.* New York: William Morrow, 2006.

Townsend, George Alfred. *The Life, Crime and Capture of John Wilkes Booth.* New York: Dick & Fitzgerald, 1866.

Winik, Jay. *April 1865: The Month That Saved America.* New York: Harper Perennial, 2001.

NOTES

1

Summer Sunshine

1. Michael W. Kauffman, *American Brutus: John Wilkes Booth and the Lincoln Conspiracies* (New York: Random House, 2004), 215.
2. Katie Mettler, "The Symbolism of Trump's Two Inaugural Bible Choices, from Lincoln to His Mother," *Washington Post*, January 18, 2017, www.washingtonpost.com/news/morning-mix/wp/2017/01/18/the-symbolism-of-trumps-two-inaugural-bible-choices-from-lincoln-to-his-mother/?.
3. W. Emerson Reck, *A. Lincoln: His Last 24 Hours* (Jefferson, North Carolina: McFarland & Company, 1987), 9.
4. Frank Klement, "Small-Town Editor Criticizes Lincoln: A Study in Editorial Abuse," Lincoln Herald LIV (Summer 1952), 30, 32.
5. See https://commons.wikimedia.org/wiki/File:Log_Cabin_at_the_Lincoln_Living_Historical_Farm.jpg.
6. David Herbert Donald, *Lincoln* (New York: Simon & Schuster, 1995), 28.
7. Donald, *Lincoln*, 34.
8. Don E. Fehrenbacher, ed., *Lincoln: Speeches and Writings 1832–1858* (Library of America: 1989), 13.
9. Roy P. Basler, ed., *The Collected Works of Abraham Lincoln*, 9 Volumes (New Brunswick, NJ: Rutgers University Press, 1953), Vol. 8, 223. Cited in Edward Steers Jr., *Blood on the Moon:*

The Assassination of Abraham Lincoln (Lexington, Kentucky: University of Kentucky Press, 2001), 93.

10. Ibid., 94.
11. Elizabeth Keckley, *Behind the Scenes* (New York: G.W. Carlton & Co., 1868), 138. Cited in Reck, *A. Lincoln*, 17.
12. Donald, *Lincoln*, 45.
13. Reck, *A. Lincoln*, 39.
14. Newseum, cf. http://www.newseum.org/.
15. Kauffman, *American Brutus*, 169.
16. Terry Alford, *Fortune's Fool: The Life of John Wilkes Booth* (Oxford: Oxford University Press, 2015), 226.

2
"A Name Known in History Forever"

1. George Alfred Townsend, *The Life, Crime and Capture of John Wilkes Booth* (New York: Dick & Fitzgerald, 1866), 32.
2. "On entering, the first one we saw was J. Wilkes Booth. I can see him now, handsome, with piercing black eyes, rather long, wavy hair, as black as night, a fascinating theatrical air of self-conscious-ness, as if he were only to be seen to be admired, and wearing a long, light-colored overcoat which capped the climax of style." M. Helen Palmes Moss, "Lincoln and Wilkes Booth as Seen on the Day of the Assassination," *The Century Magazine*, April 1909, 950–53.
3. Constance Head, "J. W. B.: His Initials in India Ink," *The Virginia Magazine of History and Biography* Vol. 90, No. 3 (July 1982), 359–66.
4. John Rhodehamel and Louise Taper, eds., *Right or Wrong, God Judge Me: The Writings of John Wilkes Booth* (Urbana, IL: University of Illinois Press, 1997), 124.

5. Roy P. Basler, ed., *The Collected Works of Abraham Lincoln,* 9
    vols. (New Brunswick, NK: Rutgers University Press, 1953),
    8:404. Cited by Edward Steers, *Blood on the Moon: The
    Assassination of Abraham Lincoln* (Lexington, Kentucky:
    University Press of Kentucky, 2001), 91.
6. "Evidence for the Unpopular Mr. Lincoln," American Battlefield
    Trust, https://www.battlefields.org/learn/articles/evidence-
    unpopular-mr-lincoln.
7. As recounted by Booth's biographer, Terry Alford, Booth's
    co-conspirator David Herold told his attorney, Frederick Stone,
    that it was this speech on April 11 that convinced Booth that
    he now had no choice but to kill Lincoln. Terry Alford,
    Fortune's Fool: The Life of John Wilkes Booth (Oxford:
    Oxford University Press, 2015), 257.
8. John Harrison Surratt and George Purnell Fisher, eds., *Trial of
    John H. Surratt in the Criminal Court for the District of
    Columbia, Hon. George P. Fisher Presiding,* Vol. 1 (Lawbook
    Exchange Ltd., 2008), 495.
9. The location of Surratt in the city on April 14 is disputed.
    However, this was the testimony of the barber, Charles Wood,
    given in a deposition and part of court records.
10. Edwards Pierrepont, *Argument of Hon. Edwards Pierrepont to
    the Jury: On the Trial of John H. Surratt for the Murder of
    President Lincoln* (Washington, D.C.: U.S. Government Printing
    Office, 1867), 75.
11. Steers, *Blood on the Moon,* 260.
12. Michael Kauffman, *American Brutus: John Wilkes Booth and the
    Lincoln Conspiracies* (New York: Random House, 2004), 213.
13. Reck, *A. Lincoln,* 67.
14. E. Lawrence Abel, *John Wilkes Booth and the Women Who
    Loved Him* (Washington, D.C.: Regnery, 2018), 196. See also, M.
    Helen Palmes Moss, "Lincoln and Wilkes Booth as Seen on the
    Day of the Assassination," *The Century Magazine,* April 1909,

950–53. Available online at: https://www.unz.com/print/Century-1909apr-00950/.

15. The actor's name was William A. Howell. Cf. Alford, *Fortune's Fool*, 109.

16. Edward Steers Jr., *The Lincoln Assassination Encyclopedia* (New York: Harper Perennial, 2010), 63.

17. Alford, *Fortune's Fool*, 11.

18. Ibid., 17.

19. Abel, *John Wilkes Booth and the Women Who Loved Him*, 189.

20. Kauffman, *American Brutus*, 217.

21. Kathryn Canavan, *Lincoln's Final Hours* (Lexington, Kentucky: University Press of Kentucky, 2015), 33. Canavan cites a report in the *New York Weekly Day-Book*, a broadsheet newspaper, April 22, 1865.

22. Rhodehamel and Taper, eds., *Right or Wrong, God Judge Me*, 64.

23. Rhodehamel and Taper, eds., *Right or Wrong, God Judge Me*, 125.

24. *Philadelphia Press*, December 27, 1881, cited in Alford, *Fortune's Fool*, 30.

3
An Ominous Dream

1. Ulysses S. Grant, *Memoirs* Volume 2, chapter 52.

2. Cited by Doris Kearns Goodwin, "The Night Abraham Lincoln Was Assassinated," *Smithsonian Magazine*, April 8, 2015.

3. History.com staff, "Did Abraham Lincoln Predict His Own Death?" History.com, A&E Television Networks, October 31, 2012, www.history.com/news/did-abraham-lincoln-predict-his-own-death.

4. John Eaton, *Grant, Lincoln and the Freedmen: Reminiscences of the Civil War* (New York: Longmans, Green and Co, 1907), 90.

5. Michael Burlingame, *Abraham Lincoln: A Life,* Knox College, unedited manuscript, Vol 2, chapter 36.
6. Harold Holzer, "Abraham Lincoln Takes the Heat," *Civil War Times*, February 2001, https://www.historynet.com/abraham-lincoln-takes-the-heat.htm.

4
"His Mind Was Just Not Right"

1. Testimony of James W. Pumphrey: "He came to my stable about 12 o'clock on the 14th of April last, and engaged a saddlehorse, which he said he wanted about 4 or half-past 4 that day," Edward Steers Jr. ed., *The Trial: The Assassination of President Lincoln and the Trial of the Conspirators* (Lexington, Kentucky: University Press of Kentucky, 2003), 72.
2. Loux says this occurred at 12:30 p.m., but this conflicts with the report that Booth chatted with Hawk around 1:00 p.m.
3. Steers, *The Trial,* 72.
4. Kauffman, *American Brutus,* 259.
5. Thomas A. Bogar, *Backstage at the Lincoln Assassination* (Washington, D.C.: Regnery History, 2013), 76. See also Kauffman, *American Brutus,* 218.
6. Alford, *Fortune's Fool,* 259.
7. Kauffman, *American Brutus,* 218.
8. Alford, *Fortune's Fool,* 259.
9. Kauffman, *American Brutus,* 96.
10. Testimony of Harry Hawk: "I met him the first time a year ago. I saw him today about one o'clock." Timothy S. Good, *We Saw Lincoln Shot: One Hundred Eyewitness Accounts* (Jackson, MS: University Press of Mississippi, 1995), 31.
11. Bogar, *Backstage at the Lincoln Assassination,* 77.

12. Ibid., 78.
13. Kauffman, *American Brutus*, 90.
14. John Rhodehamel and Louise Taper, eds., *Right or Wrong, God Judge Me: The Writings of John Wilkes Booth* (Urbana, IL: University of Illinois Press, 1997), 38.
15. Asia Clarke Booth, *John Wilkes Booth: A Sister's Memoir* (Jackson, MS: University Press of Mississippi, 1996), 81, 88–89; cited in Alford, *Fortune's Fool*, 36.
16. Alford, *Fortune's Fool*, 260.
17. This entire anecdote is found in Alford, *Fortune's Fool*, 260, but not in Kauffman.
18. Steers, *The Trial*, testimony of James Pumphrey, 72.
19. Anthony S. Pitch, *"They Have Killed Papa Dead": The Road to Ford's Theatre, Abraham Lincoln's Murder and the Rage for Vengeance* (Hanover, New Hampshire: Steerforth Press, 2008), 88; Kaufmann, *American Brutus*, 219.
20. Rhodehamel and Taper, eds., *Right or Wrong, God Judge Me,* 60.
21. Alford, *Fortune's Fool*, 85.

5
"We Must Both Be More Cheerful in the Future"

1. Reck, *A. Lincoln,* 43.
2. Ibid., 44.
3. See https://commons.wikimedia.org/wiki/File:Lincoln_Home_1.jpg.
4. Steers Jr., *Blood on the Moon*, 102 (citing other sources).
5. Canavan, *Lincoln's Final Hours*, 38.
6. See https://commons.wikimedia.org/wiki/File:Lincoln_Cottage_Rear_Entrance.jpg.
7. "The President and his family have been living out at the Soldiers' Home, about four miles only this side of the rebel line of

skirmishers; but on Sunday night Secretary Stanton sent out a carriage and a guard and brought in the family, who are again domesticated at the White House. The lonely situation of the President's summer residence would have afforded a tempting chance for a daring squad of rebel cavalry to run some risks for the chance of carrying off the President, whom we could ill afford to spare right now." Michael Burlingame, ed., *Lincoln Observed: Civil War Dispatches of Noah Brooks* (Baltimore and London: Johns Hopkins University Press, 1998), 126.

8. Ward Hill Lamon, *Recollections of Abraham Lincoln* (Lincoln, Nebraska: University of Nebraska Press, 1994), 163–64.
9. Reck, *A. Lincoln*, 54.
10. Ibid., 48.
11. Canavan, *Lincoln's Final Hours*, 45.
12. William Richstein, *The Stranger's Guide-Book to Washington City, and Everybody's Pocket Handy-Book: Containing the Most Complete Guide to Washington and Vicinity* (Washington, D.C.: The National Book Store, 1864), 32.
13. "Arrival of First Japanese Embassy at the Navy Yard (1860)," Ghosts of DC, July 3, 2012, ghostsofdc.org/2012/07/03/japanese-embassy-1860/.
14. Thomas Hopkins in Rufus Wilson, ed., *Intimate Memories of Lincoln* (Elmira, NY: Primavera Press, 1945), 397.

6
"There Is Going to Be Some Splendid Acting Tonight!"
1. Steers Jr., The *Trial*, 75.
2. Pitch, *"They Have Killed Papa Dead,"* 91.
3. Ibid.
4. Reck, *A. Lincoln*, 72.

5. Ibid.
6. Alford, *Fortune's Fool*, 98.
7. Ibid., 115.
8. Bogar, *Backstage at the Lincoln Assassination*, 92.
9. Kauffman, *American Brutus*, 220.
10. Canavan, *Lincoln's Final Hours*, 37.
11. Alford, *Fortune's Fool*, 267.
12. Kauffman, *American Brutus*, 221.
13. Alford, *Fortune's Fool*, 260.
14. Kauffman, *American Brutus*, 220.
15. Matthew Page Andrews, *History of Maryland* (New York: Doubleday, 1929), 505.
16. William Shakespeare, *Julius Caesar*, Act 5, Scene 5.
17. Bogar, *Backstage at the Lincoln Assassination*, 66–67.
18. Alford, *Fortune's Fool*, 261; Kauffman, *American Brutus*, 220.
19. John Rhodehamel and Louise Taper, eds., *Right or Wrong, God Judge Me: The Writings of John Wilkes Booth* (Urbana, Illinois: University of Illinois Press, 1997), 147.
20. Rhodehamel and Taper, *Right or Wrong, God Judge Me*, 148–50.
21. Julia Dent Grant, *The Personal Memoirs of Julia Dent Grant: (Mrs. Ulysses S. Grant)*, ed. John Y. Simon, (Carbondale, Illinois: SIU Press: 1988), 155.
22. Pitch, *"They Have Killed Papa Dead,"* 90.
23. Steers Jr., *Blood on the Moon*, 38.
24. Ibid., 42.
25. Ibid, 43.
26. Rhodehamel and Taper, *"Right or Wrong, God Judge Me,"* 126. Quoted by Alford, *Fortune's Fool*, 169.
27. This entire anecdote is found in Alford, *Fortune's Fool*, 169.
28. Rhodehamel and Taper, *Right or Wrong, God Judge Me*, 130. Quoted by Alford, *Fortune's Fool*, 175.
29. Alford, *Fortune's Fool*, 175.

7

"Mr. Lincoln, Are You Going to the Theatre with Me or Not?"

1. Steers Jr., *Blood on the Moon*, 102.
2. Alford, *Fortune's Fool*, 265.
3. Edward Steers Jr. is one of the historians of the Lincoln assassination skeptical of Crook's account. He says it is "unlikely it ever happened." See *Blood on the Moon*, 103.
4. Reck, *A. Lincoln*, 54.
5. See Stern Collection of Lincolnia copy, Library of Congress, https://www.loc.gov/resource/lprbscsm.scsm1371/?sp=14.
6. Ford's Theatre Society, *The Lincoln Assassination at Ford's Theatre* (Nashville, TN: Beckon Books, 2015), 21.
7. Those invited were Julia and Ulysses Grant, Mr. and Mrs. Edwin Stanton, Thomas Eckert, Schuyler Colfax, George Ashmun, Richard J. Oglesby, Richard Yates, General Isham N. Haynie, William A. Howard, Mr. and Mrs. William H. Wallace, Noah Brooks, and Robert Lincoln.
8. Irish Central Staff, "The Assassination of Abraham Lincoln and How Two Irishmen Might Have Prevented It," IrishCentral, April 15, 2018, www.irishcentral.com/roots/history/assassination-abraham-lincoln.
9. Paul Martin, "Lincoln's Missing Bodyguard," *Smithsonian*, April 7, 2010, www.smithsonianmag.com/history/lincolns-missing-bodyguard-12932069/?no-ist=&page=2.

8

"Preparing for the Performance of a Lifetime"

1. Kauffman, *American Brutus*, 220.
2. Ibid.
3. Rhodehamel and Taper, eds., *"Right or Wrong, God Judge Me,"* 126.

4. Ibid., 222.
5. Pitch, *"They Have Killed Papa Dead,"* 89.
6. Kauffman, *American Brutus*, 223.
7. In Edward Steers Jr.'s book on the assassination, *Blood on the Moon*, he traces the development of the modern theory that Booth was aided by the Confederacy to the controversial 1988 book, *Come Retribution: The Confederate Secret Service and the Assassination of Abraham Lincoln,* by the non-academic historians William A. Tidwell, James O. Hall and David W. Gaddy. While most historians agree Booth had some contact with Confederate secret agents, the issue is whether this contact was informal and preliminary or, as the members of *Come Retribution* argue, part of a carefully considered plot by Confederate leaders to either kidnap or kill Abraham Lincoln in retribution for the Dahlgren Raid.
8. Alford, *Fortune's Fool*, 177.
9. Alford, *Fortune's Fool*, 178.
10. Rhodehamel and Taper, eds., *"Right or Wrong, God Judge Me,"* 154.
11. Ibid.
12. Ibid., 181.
13. Ibid.
14. Ibid., 188.
15. Ibid., 193.
16. Rhodehamel and Taper, eds., *"Right or Wrong, God Judge Me,"* 189.
17. Ibid., 194.
18. Ibid., 197.
19. Ibid, 200.
20. Ibid., 212.
21. Ibid., 211.

22. George Townsend, *The Life, Crime, and Capture of John Wilkes Booth* (Dodo Publishing, 2018), 39. Quoted in Alford, *Fortune's Fool*, 213.
23. John Harrison Surratt and George Purnell Fisher, *Trial of John H. Surratt in the Criminal Court for the District of Columbia*, Vol. 1 (Washington, D.C.: Government Printing Office, 1867), 22. Cited in Canavan, *Lincoln's Final Hours*, 51.
24. Canavan, *Lincoln's Final Hours*, 51.
25. Ibid.
26. Alford, *Fortune's Fool*, 261.
27. Ibid., footnote 91, 414.
28. Steers Jr., *The Trial*, 307.
29. Kauffman, *American Brutus*, 224.

9
A Change in Plans
1. Alford, *Fortune's Fool*, 219.
2. Ibid., 221.
3. Ibid.
4. Alford, *Fortune's Fool*, 225.
5. Ibid., 232.
6. Ibid., 234.
7. Ibid., 233.
8. Ibid., 240.
9. Kauffman, *American Brutus*, 205. Kauffman's sources are Poore, 1:48–51 and LAS 4:155–64.
10. James M. McPherson, *Battle Cry for Freedom: The Civil War Era* (Oxford: Oxford University Press, 1988), 848.
11. Kauffman, *American Brutus*, 207.
12. Ibid.
13. Rhodehamel and Taper, eds., *"Right or Wrong, God Judge Me,"* 144.

10
Hail to the Chief

1. Reck, *A. Lincoln*, 81.
2. Bogar, *Backstage at the Lincoln Assassination*, 105.
3. "Ford's Theatre Layout," https://www.
    assassinationofabrahamlincoln.com/theatre-layout.
4. Timothy S. Good, ed., *We Saw Lincoln Shot: One Hundred
    Eyewitness Accounts* (Jackson, MS: University Press of
    Mississippi, 1995), 40.
5. Reck, *A. Lincoln*, 86.
6. Bogar, *Backstage at the Lincoln Assassination*, 104.

11
Sic Semper Tyrannis

1. "Testimony of John Selecman," The Trial of the Alleged Assassins
    and Conspirators at Washington City, D.C.
2. These details come from Thomas Bogar's remarkable
    reconstruction of the final minutes before Lincoln was shot in his
    essential book, *Backstage at the Lincoln Assassination*, 106–7.
3. Kauffman, *American Brutus*, 225.
4. Bogar, *Backstage at the Lincoln Assassination*, 107.
5. Ibid., 108.
6. James L. Swanson, *Manhunt: The 12-Day Chase for Abraham
    Lincoln's Killer* (New York: William Morrow, 2006), 51.
7. David Alexander, *Hangman's Dozen* (New York: Roy Publishers,
    1961), 11ff.
8. Alexander, *Hangman's Dozen*, 111.
9. See https://commons.wikimedia.org/wiki/File:Lincoln_Box_and_
    door_Booth_used_-_Fords_Theatre_-_2012-05-20.jpg.
10. Alford, *Fortune's Fool*, 263.
11. Good, *We Saw Lincoln Shot*, 30.

12. Bogar, *Backstage at the Lincoln Assassination*, 112.

13. Alford, *Fortune's Fool*, 264.

14. George Townsend, *The Life, Crime and Capture of John Wilkes Booth* (New York: Dick & Fitzgerald, 1866), 6.

15. Good, *We Saw Lincoln Shot*, 17.

16. Alford, *Fortune's Fool*, 264.

17. Prosecutors assumed that Booth or an accomplice had broken the lock earlier to gain easy entrance. But a month earlier, John Merrick, the desk clerk at the National Hotel where Booth stayed, had attended a play at Ford's with his wife and friends. He would later testify that a stagehand had lost the key to box 8 and had therefore forced the door to let them in. Testimony of Henry E. Merrick, John David Lawson, ed., *American State Trials: A Collection of the Important and Interesting Criminal Trials Which Have Taken Place in the United States, from the Beginning of Our Government to the Present Day: With Notes and Annotations*, Volume 8 (St. Louis: F.H. Thomas Law Book Co., 1917), 395.

18. Testimony of Henry Rathbone, Good, *We Saw Lincoln Shot*, 76.

19. "When you look in the literature, a lot of people say that Booth fired from two or three feet away and others say that it was point-blank. We do know from a few accounts that there was a powder burn around the bullet entrance wound in the back of Lincoln's head. If that's the case, it would have had to have been at the most about a foot away and more likely a few inches away." Blaine Houmes, "A Doctor's View of the Lincoln Assassination," http://www.abrahamlincolnonline.org/lincoln/education/medical.htm.

20. Saloon owner James Ferguson testified that he was looking right at Lincoln when he was shot. He said, "At the moment the President was shot, he was leaning his hand on the railing, looking down at a person in the orchestra...." Good, *We Saw Lincoln Shot*, 32.

21. "Conflicting reports exist as to the actual path of the bullet." See "Autopsy, Abraham Lincoln," Edward Steers Jr., *The Lincoln Assassination Encyclopedia* (New York: Harper Perennial, 2010), 21.

22. Alford, *Fortune's Fool*, 265.

23. Ibid..

24. Hawk: "(I) saw him jump from the staff and drop to the stage." (Hawk was closer to him than anyone.) Kent: "…swinging himself down partly by the curtains and partly jumping." Richards: "…let himself down by the aid of the flagstaff to the center of the stage, dropping or leaping some four or five feet before reaching the floor." Taylor: "…neither did he jump from the box full height with arms outspread and upstretched, as we often see him in illustrations. On the contrary, he placed both hands upon the rail of the box and swung himself over in that manner, thereby lessening the fall by the distance of his own height." Maynard: "…slid down from the front of the box onto the stage." Owen: "…clambered down the side of the box." BoothieBarn, "John Wilkes Booth's Movements at Ford's Theatre, July 17, 2014, https://boothiebarn.com/2014/07/17/john-wilkes-booths-movements-at-fords-theatre/.

25. Rhodehamel and Taper, eds., *"Right or Wrong, God Judge Me,"* 154.

26. Some experts question whether Booth broke his leg from his leap on the stage or later, when he fell from his horse. No witnesses reported seeing him limp at all on the stage. In addition, Booth later told Dr. Mudd, who set his break, that he had been injured in a fall from his horse. However, Mudd would later claim that Booth was concealing his true identity, wearing a disguise, and so would naturally have concocted a story to explain his broken leg, not say that he broke his leg while shooting the president.

27. Harold Holzer, ed., *President Lincoln Assassinated: The Firsthand Story of the Murder, Manhunt, Trial and Mourning* (New York: Library of America, 2014), 23.
28. Good, *We Saw Lincoln Shot*, 76.
29. Alford, *Fortune's Fool*, 268.
30. Some accounts say Booth only struck Burroughs in the chest, pushing him away.

12
Belonging to History

1. The commercial lines were down for two hours but the separate, and more secure, military telegraph lines were still functioning throughout the crisis. See Steers Jr., *Blood on the Moon*, 129.
2. Kauffman, *American Brutus*, 226–27.
3. See https://commons.wikimedia.org/wiki/File:SurrattHouse.jpg.
4. See https://commons.wikimedia.org/wiki/File:Dr._Samuel_Mudd_House_%2821592081012%29.jpg.
5. James L. Swanson sides with the angels. See his endnote on the subject, Swanson, *Manhunt*, 430. See also Carl M. Cannon, "Lincoln: Does He Belong to 'the Ages' or 'the Angels'? RealClearPolitics, April 15, 2015, https://www.realclearpolitics.com/articles/2015/04/15/lincoln_does_he_belong_to_the_ages_or_the_angels_126278.html.
6. "A Great National Calamity. Assassination of President Lincoln!" *Baltimore Sun*, April 15, 1865, http://www.baltimoresun.com/news/maryland/bal-150th-anniversary-of-abraham-lincolns-assassination-20150408-photogallery.html.
7. Harold Holzer, "The Assassination of Abraham Lincoln," *Smithsonian*, March 2015, https://www.smithsonianmag.com/history/what-the-newspapers-said-when-lincoln-was-killed-180954325/.

13
"Tell Mother, I Die for My Country"

1. Note: My primary source for the final chapter of Booth's life is James L. Swanson's excellent, detailed and painstakingly researched account, *Manhunt: The 12-Day Chase for Abraham Lincoln's Killer* (New York: William Morrow, 2006). Most of the details in this chapter come from his account, which I have greatly abbreviated for space reasons.
2. Alford, *Fortune's Fool*, 284.
3. Swanson, *Manhunt*, 312.
4. Ibid., 321.

14
The Aftermath

1. Swanson, *Manhunt*, 354.
2. Alford, *Fortune's Fool*, 333.
3. Stephen M. Archer, *Junius Brutus Booth: Theatrical Prometheus* (Carbondale, Illinois: Southern Illinois University Press, 2010), 229.
4. Steers Jr., *Blood on the Moon*, 217.
5. Swanson says 1:26; Steers says 1:21.
6. Steers, *Blood on the Moon*, 231–33.
7. See the fascinating account of Jones's final story in Swanson, *Manhunt*, 242.
8. Cf. "Booth on the Shores of Nanjemoy Creek," *BoothieBarn*, August 6, 2013, boothiebarn.com/tag/hughes/.
9. A complete account of the haggling over the reward money can be found in Swanson, *Manhunt*, particularly from 357 onwards.
10. Bogar, *Backstage at the Lincoln Assassination*, 260.

11. Gene Smith, "The Haunted Major," *American Heritage* 45 (no. 1), February/March 1994, www.americanheritage.com/content/haunted-major?page=2.

12. Abel, *John Wilkes Booth and the Women Who Loved Him*, 246–50.

INDEX

ABOUT THE AUTHOR

Robert J. Hutchinson is an award-winning travel and religion writer and the author of numerous books of popular history, including *What Really Happened: The Death of Hitler* (Regnery History), *The Dawn of Christianity* (Harper Collins), *Searching for Jesus: New Discoveries in the Quest for Jesus of Nazareth* (Harper Collins), *The Politically Incorrect Guide to the Bible* (Regnery), *When in Rome: A Journal of Life in Vatican City* (Doubleday) and, as editor, *The Book of Vices: A Collection of Classic Immoral Tales* (Putnam). He has presented seminars and public lectures for groups in the U.S., Germany, and France.

Raised in the Pacific Northwest, Hutchinson attended a Jesuit high school and university, earned an undergraduate degree in philosophy, moved to Israel in his early twenties to learn Hebrew, and earned a graduate degree in New Testament studies.

For the past thirty years, Hutchinson has worked full-time as a professional writer. He has won numerous writing awards, and contributes essays and columns to such outlets as Fox News, The Blaze, Catholic Vote, MercatorNet, Catholic Exchange, Human Events, Christianity Today, and many more.

An avid traveler, Hutchinson is also the former managing editor of *Hawaii Magazine* and the former Hawaii bureau chief for *The Hollywood Reporter.* He lives with his wife and children in a small seaside village and blogs occasionally at www.RobertHutchinson.com.

STAY IN TOUCH

For more information about Robert Hutchinson and his upcoming books and presentations, visit his website, www.RobertHutchinson.com. You'll find free resources that include these and more:

- Book excerpts
- Exclusive features
- Downloads of audio and video presentations
- Special reports
- Free e-mail updates